1985

THE AMERICAN ROLE
IN VIETNAM
AND
EAST ASIA

THE AMERICAN ROLE
IN VIETNAM
AND
EAST ASIA

Between
Two Revolutions

Henry J. Kenny

With a foreword by
Ambassador Mike Mansfield

PRAEGER SPECIAL STUDIES • PRAEGER SCIENTIFIC

New York • Philadelphia • Eastbourne, UK
Toronto • Hong Kong • Tokyo • Sydney

Library of Congress Cataloging in Publication Data

Kenny, Henry J.
   The American role in Vietnam and East Asia.

   Bibliography: p.
   Includes index.
1. East Asia—Foreign relations—United States.
2. United States—Foreign relations—East Asia. 3.United
States—Foreign relations—Vietnam. 4. Vietnam—Foreign
relations—United States. I. Title.
 DS518.8.K44 1984   327.7305   83-24793
ISBN 0-03-069734-4 (alk. paper)

Published in 1984 by Praeger Publishers
CBS Educational and Professional Publishing
a Division of CBS Inc.
521 Fifth Avenue, New York, NY 10175 USA

© 1984 by Praeger Publishers

456789 052 987654321

Printed in the United States of America
on acid-free paper

To
Mary Frances, Frank,
Susan, John, and Katie

Foreword

Philosophers throughout the ages have pointed out that there is nothing so constant in life as change. The dynamic events of twentieth-century East Asia illustrate this fact well. When I first set foot in Asia over half a century ago, nearly every country in the region was controlled by a colonial power. The appearance of regional stability, however, was deceiving, and the days of colonial rule were numbered. Proud people of ancient heritage could not for long remain subject to foreign domination, and movements for independence soon grew, aided, I might add, by Western ideas of freedom and modernization. Imperial Japanese expansion added to the turmoil, which ultimately drew the United States into World War II.

As the flames of war spread, it became apparent that the political landscape of Asia had changed forever. Japanese advances into Southeast Asia both undermined the authority of colonial regimes and provided a focal point against which resistance forces coalesced. By the time the war ended, the struggle for self-rule had become of paramount importance. In that struggle numerous nationalists turned to revolutionary movements as a vehicle to seize power. Many of these movements were directed not only against the reimposition of colonial rule, but against other rival groups as well.

During more recent years, the winds of change in East Asia have reversed direction, and are today more favorable than in any time in my experience. The dynamic nations of the region are improving the lives of their people in a manner unparalleled in recent history, and they generally appear to be managing the art of peaceful change across a broad spectrum of human endeavor. This trend is due largely to what Henry Kenny labels the second revolution in Asia today—that of free and independent nations developing better lives for themselves and their children, in cooperation with the industrial and post-industrial democracies. Their record is there for all to see—sustained economic growth, rising educational levels, progress in the arts and sciences, independent governments friendly to the United States, a gradually increasing respect for democratic processes, and growing commercial links across the Pacific Basin. Theirs is a revolution not of rising expectations and promises, but of rising social, political, and economic performance. It is a revolution far more attuned to the real needs of Asia today than the violent revolutions of the past. It is, now and for the foreseeable future, of immense consequence to the United States.

I have made no secret of my conviction that the future of our nation is inextricably tied to the dynamic developments in Asia. For better or for worse, the United States is a Pacific nation. While the cultural pull of America has been eastward across the Atlantic, our vibrant push has always been and continues to be westward. The understanding and pursuit of American interests in Asia is thus crucial to the future of our nation. I am very pleased, therefore, that Mr. Kenny has undertaken the ambitious tasks of identifying many of the major changes which have and are taking place in this vast portion of the world, and interpreting their significance for American foreign policy. He has succeeded in both, and in so doing has made a major contribution to the understanding of East Asia and the American role therein. In my opinion, no area of the world is of more importance to the future of the United States than Asia. This book will certainly add to our appreciation of this dynamic region.

Ambassador Mike Mansfield
Tokyo, Japan

Preface

It was late afternoon when I received the order to move my infantry rifle company a distance of some 5 miles to a Vietnamese village which was coming under attack. Like so many towns and hamlets in the area that openly supported Saigon, many of which recently rallied to the government's side, the village had become the target of enemy attacks and reprisals. It was defended only by local militia. Earlier in the day, an American doctor and several medics had entered the village to administer aid and were now trapped therein. Our helicopter support had already been committed to similar engagements across the Dong Nai river, so we had to move as quickly as terrain and security would permit. Crossing alternating jungle and rice paddies characteristic of the area north of Saigon where the Delta yields to the jungle of War Zone D, I wondered whether we would reach the village on time. It was 1968 and the Tet Offensive was in full swing.

Just two years earlier I had built a Special Forces camp deeper in the D Zone, not 10 miles distant, so both the terrain and the village were quite familiar. It was ironic but perhaps not uncharacteristic of the war that the camp subsequently had been abandoned, leaving the village we were moving to assist vulnerable to attack. I had tried to understand the war for many years, and neither the attack nor our response to it were particularly surprising. In 1965 I had directed Vietnamese area studies for the Special Forces at Fort Bragg, North Carolina, where we had emphasized that the political struggle for the "hearts and minds" of the people of Vietnam was being waged just as much by the bullet as by ideas. In declaring their support for Saigon, these villagers sought to exercise freedom of expression, but in so doing were risking their very lives.

It grew dark as we navigated the final stretch of jungle leading to the rice paddies surrounding the village. Rounding a bend in the final wooded area, there suddenly appeared in the darkness the appalling sight of a village entirely engulfed in flames. I halted the company to take a quick assessment of the situation, instructing my radio operator to switch to the frequency of the medical team in the village. As he did so a transmission came in loud and clear. I had studied the Vietnamese language for a full year in 1964, and immediately recognized the Hanoi dialect. A North Vietnamese headquarters was directing a subordinate unit to pull back and leave the village, stating that their trucks were ready to evacuate them from the area. Here we were, not more than 40 miles from Saigon, and there were North Vietnamese troops preparing to board trucks after razing a village.

As we prepared to move on the village itself, several bursts of automatic weapons fire rang out in the night. I felt a sudden bee-sting sensation in both my legs. I was hit and, for a split second, felt the tranquility of approaching death. A brief exchange of fire ensued, and then there was silence. A medic administered mor-phine and tried to slow the rapid loss of blood. Unable to move and rapidly losing consciousness, I told my second platoon leader, a dynamic black lieutenant with outstanding leadership attributes, to take charge of the company. Some time later I was hoisted aboard a rescue helicopter for evacuation to a field hospital. Now an am-putee and, I felt, a cripple for life, I left Vietnam, a land and people I had grown to love, thinking never to return.

Two years later, thanks to some great doctors, nurses, med-ics, and fellow patients, as well as several remarkable professors at American University, I was able to walk into classrooms at the U.S. Military Academy at West Point and teach courses in interna-tional relations and problems of developing nations. I discussed many of those problems with firsthand illustrations from Vietnam, which I felt doubly obligated to cite as many of those cadets, even though the war was winding down, were to serve and some to die in that beleaguered country. It was also my experience during those years to bear the sad news to next-of-kin in nearby areas of New York State, a grim reminder of the price of war. Finally, during the summer of 1972, I joined many fellow officers in trying to make intelligent recommendations to the Secretary of Defense in response to the massive North Vietnamese offensive in South Vietnam.

With the war's end my interests shifted elsewhere. I had de-voted most of my career to Vietnam since graduating from West Point in 1961 and was preparing for a new life as a civilian. Then, in the spring of 1975, the North overran the South. All my personal efforts, not to mention the far greater sacrifice of so many others, seemed to have been in vain. In an emotional reaction I forthwith threw out all my Vietnamese language books.

As irony would have it, that action was regrettable indeed, for just a few months later I was once again en route to Indochina, this time as Deputy Staff Director of the House Select Committee on Miss-ing Persons in Southeast Asia. I stopped in Paris to gain the advice of the former French High Commissioner in Hanoi, Jean Sainteney, and then proceeded to Laos and Vietnam. In Hanoi with Congress-men Montgomery, Gilman, Ottinger, and McCloskey, we initiated the long and difficult postwar process of receiving information on and the remains of American servicemen still unaccounted for in

Indochina. In 1977 I returned to Vientiane and Hanoi, this time
with a Presidential Commission on the same subject. In both visits
it was my strong recommendation, based in part on conversations
with Sainteney, to separate the political and humanitarian issues,
as the former could take many years to resolve. Unfortunately, the
realities of international politics, including Vietnamese links between
war reparations and missing in action (MIA) information, as well as
the Vietnamese invasion of Cambodia, impeded as full an accounting
as might otherwise have been possible.

For the remainder of the 1970s and the first two years of the
present decade I had the good fortune to serve as the special assistant to Ambassador Mike Mansfield in Tokyo. A great American
doing a great job representing the United States, Ambassador Mansfield did everything in his power to direct Washington's attention to
the important changes taking place in Japan and the rest of East
Asia. After cautioning against American overinvolvement for so
many years during the Vietnam era, Mansfield now cautioned
against American underinvolvement in the face of our post-Vietnam
retrenchment in Asia. His vision of Asia and America's role therein greatly influenced my own perceptions. Having helped contend
with the dynamism of revolutionary communism in a nationalist set-
ting in Vietnam, I now supported U.S. interests in light of an even
greater revolution sweeping most of the rest of Asia—that of an entire people building a better life for themselves and their children
through the skill and determination which only freedom can bring.
It is the American response to these two contrasting forces, revolutionary communism in an Asian context and the revolutionary
progress in Japan and the other free countries of the region, about
which this book is written.

Acknowledgments

I am indebted to numerous individuals who, through the years, provided many of the ideas and insights reflected in this book. I wish to thank particularly, for their advice and reviews of various portions of the manuscript, the following persons: Fred Henle, J. Angus MacDonald, Al Seligmann, Jim Auer, Jack O'Connell, Jean Sauvageot, and George McGarrigle. During the past two years considerable assistance in manuscript preparation was also required, for which I am indebted to Phyllis MacDonald and Jeanne Burley. Last, but not least, I thank my wife Mary Frances, without whose help and encouragement this book could never have been written.

Any errors or omissions are, of course, my own responsibility; the views expressed are personal ones and do not necessarily reflect those of the United States government or any agency thereof.

Contents

PART I:
THE HISTORICAL
RECORD

1

Vietnam and East Asia:
Two Centuries of
Escalating American Involvement

The magnification of the importance of Vietnam in American foreign policy was symbolically represented by the huge maps of South Vietnam that came to dominate so many governmental offices and corridors of power during the war. It was also seen in the thousands of publications about Vietnam and Southeast Asia written after the war began—in stark contrast to the handful of books available in English prior to the war, when most Americans could not even locate Vietnam on a map. The significance of the country in American perspective came not so much from events taking place in Vietnam as from its relationship to the rest of Asia, where the United States did and still has long-standing national interests. A brief overview of the background and development of those interests and the perceived challenges to them will help put Vietnam in the perspective of the larger U.S. role in Asia, then and now.

American involvement in the affairs of Asia dates to the earliest days of the republic. When George Washington was inaugurated as President of the United States, there were 13 American clipper ships in the harbor at Canton. In the century that followed, American commercial interests developed slowly but steadily, even though a tremendous share of national energy was channeled into opening the West. During the nineteenth century, missionary activity in China and Southeast Asia developed, and by mid-century America's Asiatic fleet began making periodic port visits throughout the region. It was as part of this activity that Admiral Perry and his famous "black ships" opened the previously insulated Japan to Western trade and influence. The movement west across the Great Plains and the Rockies to the Pacific generated additional pressures for a U.S. presence in the Western Pacific, and soon Yankee traders and

3

investors were importing silk and coolie labor and exporting machinery and textiles.

In 1898 the United States surprised itself and the world by its occupation of the Philippine Islands as a result of the war with Spain. The writer Finley Dunne caught the flavor of popular reaction to this event in the following satire:

> "I know what I'd do if I was Mack," said Mr. Hennesey. "I'd hist a flag over the Ph'lippeenes, an I'd take in the whole lot iv thim."
>
> "An' yet," said Mr. Dooley, "tis not more thin two months since ye larned whether they were islands or canned goods. . . . Suppose ye was standin' at th' corner iv State an' Archery Road, wud ye know what car to take to get to th' Ph'lippeens? If yer son Packy was to ask ye where th' Ph'lippeens is, cud ye give him any good idea whether they was in Rooshia or jus' west iv the thracks? . . ."
>
> "Mebbe I couldn't," said Mr. Hennesey, haughtily, "but I'm f'r takin thim in anyhow. . . ."[1]

Manifest Destiny was alive and well as the westward push continued. Also in 1898 the United States declared an open door policy, designed to maintain growing commercial and cultural links with China by guaranteeing both its territorial integrity and continued American access to that territory amidst the competing claims of the colonial powers. By the time the twentieth century began the main outlines of U.S. policy in Asia had already been established. These were:

1. prevention of hegemony by a single nation or alliance,
2. access to the natural resources and markets of Asia, and
3. the maintenance or development of conditions favoring the transmittal of political and religious ideas.

The history of U.S. participation in Far Eastern affairs during this century is largely the history of efforts to secure these national interests with very limited available means.

The first threat to them emanated from the land Perry had opened to the West less than 50 years before. Japan had defeated Chinese forces in 1894-95 and had taken Formosa (Taiwan), Korea, and the southern tip of Manchuria as the fruits of victory. By the turn of the century she was casting covetous eyes on the rest of China, in emulation of the colonial powers. Then in 1905 the Imperial Navy startled the world with a smashing defeat of the Russian Far Eastern Fleet in the Tsushima Strait off Japan. Subsequently

Japan achieved an understanding with the United States whereby she would be allowed some westward expansion in return for a promise not to threaten American interests in the Philippines. At the same time the United States sought to contain the degree of Japanese expansion through a multipolar balance of power including the European powers. With the advent of World War I, however, the European nations became too embroiled in the struggle for their own survival to pursue secondary interests in Asia. In 1915 Japan presented China its infamous "21 demands" for further economic and political concessions. By the war's end Japan had become the paramount naval power in the Western Pacific and was to remain so until the Battle of Midway in 1942.

During the interwar years, the United States sought to reestablish a balance of power in Asia in order to prevent total control by Japanese Imperial forces. In 1922, for example, the Washington Conference on Disarmament established a capital ship construction ratio of 5:5:3 for the United States, Britain, and Japan respectively. Yet the seeming margin of security offered by this arrangement was illusory. Both British and American navies had higher priority commitments elsewhere and, as is still true today, it was impossible logistically and operationally to sustain much more than one-third of our Pacific fleet thousands of miles from U.S. rear area support bases. Moreover, American potential to influence events became severely limited by pacifist domestic sentiment, which constrained the military budget, and by fears of overextending existing military forces in the face of the rising power of Nazi Germany.

Until World War II it was clear that American interests in Asia were becoming increasingly important, but it was unclear whether the United States could or would support those interests at the risk of war if necessary. Then in 1941, Japan, having already absorbed much of China and northern Vietnam, struck into southern Vietnam in an apparent effort to establish a base for further drives into Malaya and the rest of Southeast Asia. As part of that plan, presaging later American and then Soviet moves, the Japanese built an airfield at Cam Ranh Bay. Despite numerous restraints on the potential use of American power in Asia, this action by Japanese leaders to expand and dominate their Greater East Asian Co-Prosperity Sphere was perceived by American leaders as an unacceptable accretion of power over the people and resources of East Asia. The United States sought to contain this expansion, for it threatened not only choice allied colonies such as the Dutch East Indies, French Indochina, and British Burma and Malaya, but also the American position in the Philippines and vital shipping lanes to and from all these areas. President Franklin Roosevelt therefore reacted to the Japanese move by imposing an oil embargo on Japan, and declaring

American determination to prevent further Japanese expansion into
Southeast Asia. It was this action, more than any other, that con-
vinced Japanese military leaders of the need to strike Pearl Harbor.
Thus it was that U.S. policy in Asia had merely applied a "non-
recognition" doctrine and issued protests concerning Japanese takeovers in Manchuria and China, but called for stern warnings and
economic retaliation with the risk of war in response to Japanese
movement into Vietnam.

The war in the Pacific brought home to Americans the strategic fact that the security of our nation is firmly tied to a balance
of power in Asia, and that no nation can realistically aspire to hegemony in the region without threatening American security. The
technological advances of the twentieth century showed the Pacific
to be a highway rather than a barrier. Pearl Harbor vividly demonstrated that American interest in Asia, as well as the nation's
security, could not be assured by a retreat to fortress America.
Only active involvement, including a military force structure deployed beyond the West Coast, was seen as assuring those interests.
It was in this vein that both Secretary of State Dean Acheson and
General Douglas MacArthur defined a postwar U.S. defensive perim-
eter running from the Philippines through the Ryukyus and Japan to
the Aleutians and Alaska.

In the aftermath of World War II, however, it was to take more
than military power to assure American interests, for the situation
in Asia had been profoundly changed by the war. First, the disrup-
tion of colonial empires and spheres of influence wrought by Japanese
advances into China and Southeast Asia accelerated the mobilization of
nationalist forces throughout the region. Mao Zedong had called for a
people's war for the purpose of land redistribution and other agrarian
reform, but the key factor in his ability to mobilize the masses was
nationalism. He rallied the peasantry with calls for the end of Japanese rule, and when that rule began to weaken in the mid-1940s he
was in an excellent position to inherit the Mandate of Heaven as he
united China under communist rule. Southeast Asian nations faced
a basically similar situation. The occidental colonial powers had
been discredited by their early defeat at the hands of Oriental Japan,
and when the Japanese were themselves defeated and finally withdrew
in 1945, the nationalists were determined to achieve full independence at the earliest possible date.

A second effect of the war militating against a return to the old
order was starvation. Prior to the war most Asians were already
living at a bare subsistence level. The war itself wrought untold
devastation upon the land, the lives, and the transportation network
of the region. Food and material had been expropriated, and carts,
trucks, and boats that could have been used to transport the necessi-

ties of life had instead been directed to support the imperial Japanese war effort. Allied bombing of railroads, bridges, and ports added to the problem. By 1945 China was in massive turmoil, reeling not just from eight years of Japanese rule but from a long period of warlordism and a bloody civil war between Chiang Kai-shek's Kuomintang and Mao's communists. In Southeast Asia the situation was not much better. Nearly 2 million Vietnamese starved to death in 1945 alone, and the people of the Philippines, Burma, and much of the rest of the region were destitute. The European powers themselves were facing deprivation, and were neither able to lend significant aid to starving Asians nor to reassert effective colonial rule. Hesitantly, months after the war, a Dutch contingent found its way into Djakarta, and a French contingent into Hanoi, but the handwriting was on the wall—the days of colonialism in Asia were numbered.

The communist organizations of the region fully exploited the opportunities presented by the turmoil of the war and its aftermath; they sought to fill expeditiously the vacuum of power by capturing the mantle of nationalist leadership. Ho Chi Minh quickly moved to seize the imperial Vietnamese capital at Hue and to declare his Democratic Republic of Vietnam to a cheering crowd in Hanoi, before the arrival of Chinese and British occupation troops. The reintroduction of French troops in 1946 then led to eight years of fighting in the so-called First Indochinese War, between the French and the communist-led nationalists of Vietnam, Laos, and Cambodia.

In nearby Burma, communist groups sought power first by cooperating with the postwar government, and when that failed by moving into active guerrilla war against it. When Burmese independence from Britain finally came in 1948, the security situation was so poor that the government was unable to hold national elections. Minority ethnic groups joined in the antigovernment rebellion, and by 1950 government forces moved outside of Rangoon at their peril. Only divisions within the communist movement itself prevented even further deterioration and, perhaps, a communist Burma.

In neighboring Malaya the situation was also grave. In 1945 the Communist Party, which had enhanced its position through wartime anti-Japanese activities, was in a position to direct the terms of a postwar settlement. Its failure to do so and its subsequent loss of influence in the colonial government drove it underground. With a base of support among ethnic Chinese plantation workers on the jungle fringe, the party soon directed a wide range of terrorist activities and guerrilla warfare. In 1948 the British declared an "emergency," which was not to be lifted for 12 years.

Throughout the rest of Southeast Asia the outlook was anything but reassuring. After the euphoria of victory in 1945 and independence in 1946, the Philippines encountered the severe problems of political and economic development. By the early 1950s, the communist-led Hukbalahap (Huk) rebellion was in full swing, controlling large sections of the countryside, particularly in the depressed Pampanga province, and was drawing scarce government resources from developmental to military programs. Disparities in wealth and inadequate governmental assistance and resource allocation exacerbated the problem, as the Huks sought popular support for massive guerrilla warfare.

Indonesia entered the postwar era facing the even greater problem of immediate demands for independence, which was not immediately granted. At the end of World War II the Dutch were in no position to reassert complete colonial rule in Indonesia, and the nationalist movement had gained considerable momentum. The situation was ideal for the Communist Party of Indonesia (the PKI), which was the oldest Communist Party in Asia. In September of 1948 the PKI led a massive rebellion in East Java, which was put down with massive bloodshed and the loss of 30,000 PKI members and sympathizers. In 1949 Indonesia finally did achieve independence, but the problem of managing a poor country with wide disparities of wealth continued. The PKI capitalized on this situation with promises of reform; by the early 1950s it was the best organized political force in the country, with a phenomenally growing membership. In the 1955 elections the party demonstrated its popular appeal by winning 6.2 million votes, causing many observers to speculate that it could form the first democratically elected communist government in Asia.

The situation of the late 1940s and early 1950s thus presented immense obstacles to the attainment of American interests in Asia. Between 1945 and 1950 nearly every nation in the region had gained independence, and nurtured high expectations of what that independence would bring. New and fragile political institutions were grappling with the massive problems left by the war and years of colonial rule, and instability was rife. The Communist parties of the region, most of which had developed significant popular support as a result of wartime activities, were heavily engaged in either overthrowing existing governments or in gaining a major role in framing postwar policies. As the difficulties of economic and political development became more manifest in the 1950s, it looked as though many of the Communist parties would succeed. The identification of these parties with international communism, coupled with the victory of Mao in 1949, left the clear impression that a monolithic and militant brand of international communism was in the ascendency throughout Asia. The signing of the Sino-Soviet Treaty of Friendship, Alliance, and Mutual Trust in 1950 seemed to solidify the axis of that power for at least another 30 years, and the Chinese occupation of Tibet that year, along with Sino-Soviet support for North Korean aggression, did little to attenuate U.S. concern. Under these circumstances it appeared to many Americans that the situation in Asia was hopeless, and that there was little, if anything, the United States could do about it.

Despite this bleak outlook, the United States realized that it could not abandon the region and its interests therein. A tremendous effort was made in those areas where influence could be exerted with some chance of success, and the American role did make a difference.

Japan was the first and most important area in which the United States could exert a positive role without undue interference. Devastated by the war and with a discredited leadership, the Land of the Rising Sun was a prime target of communist effort. The Soviet Union, which had already occupied former Japanese-controlled territory in Sakhalin and the Kurile islands, as well as four small islands just off Hokkaido, was pressing to influence events in Japan by occupying Hokkaido itself, and by playing an equal role with the United States in the postwar occupation of Japan. General MacArthur, the Supreme Commander of the Allied Powers in Japan, rejected these Soviet demands and launched radical social and economic reforms to lay the basis for the further development of the Japanese state. He abolished the family-dominated conglomerates (the zaibatsu), so as to stimulate competition and initiative, and he redistributed the farmland and established democratic political institutions, including the present constitution. Yet even these Draconian reforms took time to have an impact on society. By 1947 the growing power of the Communist Party in the trade union movement was strong enough for them to call for a general strike. MacArthur banned the strike, but the communists continued to gain strength, polling 9.7 percent of the vote in parliamentary elections in 1949. By the early 1950s, however, it had become apparent that the party was doomed to the periphery of Japanese politics. The MacArthur reforms had taken hold, and a new Japanese government held the reins not only of the process of reconstruction, but of the beginnings of a modern Japanese state with strong ties to the United States, including a mutual security treaty.

Across the Sea of Japan in Korea, the United States played a similarly constructive role, although under wartime conditions. President Harry Truman made the difficult decision to help defend South Korea, stating his reasons in terms of containing Soviet expansionism: "Our men are fighting . . . because they know, as we do, that the aggression in Korea is part of the attempt of the Russian Communist dictatorship to take over the world step-by-step."[2] During the years 1950-53 a total of 33,629 American servicemen lost their lives in Korea. It was the price needed for a free and independent nation. The United States further helped guarantee that independence with a defense treaty in 1953.

In the Philippines, where Americans had fought side by side with Filipinos to defend against Japanese invasion and later to evict the occupying forces, the United States played a similarly constructive role. First, it granted independence in 1946. In part as a demonstration of confidence in the American system, the Philippine leadership developed a political system largely patterned on the American model. The United States then helped with Philippine reconstruction and advised more equitable distribution of land and wealth as a measure to defeat the Huk insurgents and to improve the life of the people. Finally, in August 1952 the United States ratified a mutual security treaty, further linking the future of both countries.

Meanwhile, the U.S. Seventh Fleet had moved into the Taiwan Strait in furtherance of the effort to prevent a Chinese attack on the island of Taiwan. Tensions remained high through the mid-1950s, as the Chinese threatened to attack Taiwan and did bombard the offshore islands of Quemoy and Matsu. The U.S. role throughout the crisis was one of exercising power with restraint, although there was one close call. In 1954 Secretary of State John Foster Dulles asked Senator Mike Mansfield, who was attending the Manila Conference, to join him in a remarkable scheme. "We're going to bomb China," he told Mansfield, for its provocations in the Taiwan Strait. When asked by Mansfield who he meant by "we," the Secretary replied that the Chairman of the Joint Chiefs of Staff (JCS), Admiral Arthur Radford, Secretary of Defense Charles Wilson, and he had determined that China should be bombed and that he was shortly going to so notify the President. Mansfield asked who was against the bombing. Dulles replied, "General Ridgway" (then Army Chief of Staff). Mansfield then told Dulles, "Sign me up with Ridgway." Significantly, it was also General Ridgway who opposed U.S. intervention in Indochina on behalf of the French when Dien Bien Phu was about to fall in 1954. On his return trip to Washington Dulles stopped off in Denver to raise the subject with President Eisenhower, who was then hospitalized. The President, however, rejected the action. (Mansfield said he always felt better about Eisenhower after that.)

Elsewhere in East Asia the U.S. ability to influence events was much less. Nevertheless, the country was instrumental in helping the nations of the region, nearly all of which were newly independent, to overcome some of the worst hardships and difficulties commonly associated with the early phases of modernization. U.S. postwar relief (1946-48) and Marshall Plan assistance (1949-52), in the form of grants and soft loans, totaled $20 billion in present value.[3] This vast amount was allocated by the Congress and spent by President

Truman because they believed strongly in meeting the new international responsibilities of the United States. As Truman saw them, these included the preservation and protection of nations from the dangers of the aggressive and expanding force of international communism. Eisenhower continued this containment policy in Asia and in 1954 joined with the Philippines, Thailand, and the major allies in Europe in the Southeast Asian Collective Security Treaty, designed to deter and defend against the possibility of communist aggression. By the mid-1950s the following alliance systems bound the United States in Asia:

> The Mutual Defense Treaty with the Philippines—1951
> The ANZUS Pact (with Australia and New Zealand)—1951
> The Treaty of Mutual Security and Cooperation (with Japan)—1951
> The Mutual Defense Treaty with the Republic of Korea—1953
> The Mutual Defense Treaty with the Republic of China—1954
> The Southeast Asia Treaty Organization (with Thailand and the Philippines, the United Kingdom, Australia, New Zealand, Pakistan, and France. A protocol to the pact provided an umbrella for South Vietnam plus Laos and Cambodia who rejected that protection.)—1954

By the early 1960s there were a few who questioned the success of American policy in Asia. Nearly every country in the region had not only rebuilt from the devastation of World War II, but had embarked on programs of modernization in an atmosphere of increasing political stability. With the exception of South Vietnam, the threat of communist guerrilla war had receded from Burma to the Philippines. The return of Okinawa to Japan in 1960 had eliminated a major irritant in relations with that country, and the successful defense of South Korea had left a hardworking and friendly ally in relative peace. Finally the Chinese threat against Taiwan had eased considerably.

Vietnam was the anomaly. First, it cannot be overemphasized that 99 percent of American citizens knew next to nothing about Vietnam. Overoptimistic assessments of South Vietnamese political and social cohesion, of its military capabilities, and of American ability to influence events were the order of the day, matched only by gross underestimation of Viet Cong and North Vietnamese determination and will. Moreover, the very success of American programs in helping stem communism in the rest of Asia made the same seem possible in Vietnam.

The United States had deliberately avoided becoming directly engaged in Vietnam despite strong temptations to do so over the preceding 15 years. In 1944 President Roosevelt expressed his feelings quite clearly in a note that stated, "I don't want the French back in Indochina."[4] The first iteration of American postwar intentions in the area was, unfortunately, a policy that died with the president. It was followed by a posture of noninterference, in which the United States neither supported nor opposed the reassertion of French power in Indochina. During the late 1940s the United States was far too preoccupied with the defense of Western Europe to involve itself in what was considered a French sphere of influence. Ironically, it was this very eurocentric orientation that led to American involvement in the first Indochinese war.

While the tragedy of Soviet domination of Eastern Europe was belatedly being recognized, threats to democracy in Western Europe loomed on the horizon. American allies were faced not only with domestic economic and political crises, but also with the fact that the nearby Red Army did not demobilize. In 1949, for example, an estimated 175 Soviet divisions in Eastern Europe faced 12 NATO divisions. Under these circumstances France let it be known that unless U.S. assistance was forthcoming in Indochina its ability to fulfill commitments in Europe would be seriously jeopardized.[5] With West German rearmament still years ahead, and with France bearing the principal manpower burden for the defense of Western Europe, the request was one which could not be and was not taken lightly.

The French argument was made even more compelling by the progress of U.S. economic and security assistance in containing the spread of communism in Europe. Although the architects of containment, such as George Kennan, did not envision its extension to the Asian arena, the very success of both the Truman Doctrine and the Marshall Plan in Europe seemed to some to augur well for attempting similar programs in Asia. Moreover, there were additional incentives to emphasize containment. In February 1948 parliamentary democracy in Czechoslovakia yielded to a Communist Party government subservient to Moscow. In June the Soviet Union attempted its first Berlin blockade, and in August 1949 exploded its first atomic bomb.

All these events shaped the framework within which Vietnam was perceived. They were considered acts of aggression by communist states espousing an aggressive ideology that challenged both the geopolitical sense of the advocates of realpolitik and the moral sense of the advocates of democracy. Moreover, ideological unity reinforced the apparent unity of the aggressor states. In 1948 Andrei Zhdanov, in addressing the Founding Meeting of the Cominform, and Liu Shaochi, in a speech at the Trade Union Conference of Asian and Australian Countries, proffered nearly identical views of the existing international situation. The world, in this view, is divided into two camps—the imperialist Western states and the liberating communist ones. It is the duty of the latter to foment, encourage, and aid national liberation movements whenever possible in the developing nations. The southeast Asian region, and Vietnam in particular, was mentioned in both speeches as an area in which such liberation movements were definitely possible.[6]

At least three interrelated developments in Vietnam itself further prompted American involvement in Vietnam. First was the establishment of a supposedly independent noncommunist Vietnamese regime. According to the Ha Long Bay agreement of June 1948, France recognized the independence of Vietnam within the French Union, and in the "Elysée Agreement" of March 1949 persuaded the Emperor Bao Dai to return from exile as Head of State of the newly formed Associated States of Vietnam. The fact that the emperor was granted no real power, and was opposed by most noncommunist nationalists, including Ngo Dinh Diem, seemed to make no difference to U.S. officials, who viewed the creation of the Associated States as a necessary precondition to American economic assistance.

A second turn of events affecting American policy was the deteriorating French military position in Indochina. Despite considerable support in wide areas of Cochinchina and in the Catholic bishoprics of Tonkin, French forces in 1948 had done little in pursuit of the destruction of either their enemy's armed forces or will to fight. By late 1949, with Chinese allies on their northern border, the Viet Minh boldly seized the initiative. After major offensives in the Black and upper Red River Valleys, regiment and division-sized Viet Minh units systematically attacked major French border posts in Viet Bac, overwhelming several outposts in a demonstration of hitherto unforeseen military capability, which by the end of 1950 culminated in French abandonment of Cao Bang and Lang Son. These events did not go unnoticed in Washington, D.C., where on May 2, 1950, the Joint Chiefs of Staff reported: "It appears obvious from intelligence estimates that the situation in Southeast Asia has deteriorated and, without United States assistance, this deterioration will be accelerated."[7]

The third internal Vietnamese development prompting U.S. support of the French was the increasing perception of the Viet Minh as an expanding aggressive communist enemy. Significant efforts had been made to emphasize the nationalistic rather than communistic character of the organization. The term Viet Minh itself was an abbreviation for the "Vietnamese Independence League," which had been created in 1941 as a united front for all nationalist forces, including, of course, its heavily communist element. In November 1945 Ho Chi-Minh dissolved the Communist Party in an attempt to further disassociate the independence movement which he dominated from the image of communist orientation. In early 1950, however, Ho reversed previous Viet Minh practices emphasizing united front nationalism and swung to overt communist nationalism and internationalism. In January 1950, he appealed for and received Chinese and Soviet diplomatic recognition. In April he described his Democratic Republic of Vietnam as a "People's Democracy," and announced support for the communist liberation movement in Cambodia. The United States, already concerned about communist guerrilla wars elsewhere in Southeast Asia, reacted with the first official enunciation of the "domino theory" for that region, and in May 1950, a full month before the outbreak of hostilities in Korea, decided to provide $10 million in military assistance to the French.

Thus began 25 years of continuous American aid. This aid increased dramatically in the ensuing months and years as a result of the Korean War, which enhanced the believability of French claims that it was necessary because we were fighting the same enemy. In late 1952 Secretary of State Dean Acheson sought to review U.S. policy to determine "what the situation was and what we were doing if, as, and when we were to take any further step," but the Truman Administration was nearing its end—no time for policy reviews. [8]

As the situation in Indochina deteriorated in 1953 and 1954, American aid increased substantially, totaling over $785 million in fiscal year (FY) 1954 alone. By the war's end the United States was paying 78 percent of French war costs. [9]

American involvement, however, was always highly conditional, even when assistance to Diem supplanted that to the French. President Eisenhower refused to sanction the bombing of Viet Minh units surrounding the French at Dien Bien Phu in the absence of allied, notably British, support. In 1954 he also stated, "I cannot conceive of a greater tragedy than to get heavily involved in an all-out war in any of those regions [Indochina], particularly with large units." [10]

With the partition of Vietnam, the administration decided to support the new government of South Vietnam, in the words of Secretary of State John Foster Dulles, "as a plunge," with cognizance of high risk of failure. Dulles justified American aid as worth it, "even if only to buy time to build up strength." In 1956 President Eisenhower wrote President Diem as follows:

> We have been exploring ways and means to permit . . .
> aid to Viet-Nam . . . provided that your Government is
> prepared to give assurances as to the standards of per-
> formance it would be able to maintain in the event such
> aid were supplied. . . . The Government of the United
> States expects that this aid will be met by performance

on the part of the Government of Viet-Nam in undertaking needed reforms. [11]

The President signaled his intent to follow through on the conditional nature of this policy by reducing U.S. military assistance funding and personnel levels during the period 1956 to 1960.

U.S. Aid for South Vietnam [12]
(millions of dollars by fiscal year)

1955	1956	1957	1958	1959	1960
322.4	377.3	392.7	242.3	249.3	252.9

Thus as the United States entered the decade of the 1960s, the nation had a record of continuous involvement in Vietnam dating back to early 1950. The threat of monolithic Sino-Soviet expansion perceived throughout Asia in the early 1950s appeared to underlie many of the decisions committing American aid and combat advisors to South Vietnam ten years later. Whether viewed as due to externally directed or supported Chinese communist expansion, internal communist revolutionary warfare based on indigenous support, or a combination of the two, the fall of South Vietnam was seen as having a dreadful impact on the rest of Southeast Asia. Dominos were seen falling from Cambodia to Burma and from Laos to Indonesia. The strait of Malacca, through which passed the vital shipping of much of free Asia, was seen as threatened from the east.

Nevertheless, the U.S. government had made no irrevokable or open-ended commitments, and the guerrilla war had not yet threatened the viability of the Diem regime. When Eisenhower discussed major world problems with President-elect John F. Kennedy, he did not even see fit to mention Vietnam. [13] The new president was, therefore, rightly shocked when he received a very pessimistic report on Vietnam from a counterinsurgency expert, Ed Lansdale, just three weeks after his inauguration. In addition he was a leading proponent of the view, which has returned to haunt us in the 1980s, of communist inspired and supported revolutionary wars spreading throughout Third World countries. The nations of Latin America, Africa, and Southeast Asia were considered particularly vulnerable to this threat as they navigated the difficult passage from tradition to modernity, with all the socioeconomic and political changes that journey entails. Like scavengers of the wild, the communist states were seen to be exploiting opportunities this phenomenon presented. [14] Perhaps a bit oversimplified at the time, it was a theory of communist expansionism leaping the boundaries of the glacis of Eastern Europe claimed necessary by Moscow to defend Mother Russia.

Instead, Soviet and Chinese power was perceived as expanding on a worldwide basis, with communism providing the ideological and organizational vehicle for revolution and political power in the developing world. From this situation sprang President John Kennedy's emphasis on counterinsurgency and the necessity of stemming a new and bold communist challenge in Vietnam as a test case of "counterinsurgency" versus wars of "national liberation."

Beyond these geopolitical and semi-ideological explanations for U.S. involvement, there grew, along with that involvement, a challenge to U.S. credibility and prestige worldwide. Initial efforts to stem the tide in South Vietnam had not gone well. Instead of attributing this development to internal political and social conditions in South Vietnam, American leaders saw it as a challenge to U.S. credibility and military capability. There was enough evidence of North Vietnamese direction and support of the southern insurgency to make that challenge an affront. Thus in 1965, President Lyndon Johnson announced to the world that America would do everything necessary to achieve the independence of South Vietnam and guarantee its freedom from attack. With no mention of needed South Vietnamese political reforms, or military mobilization, he declared a general goal of stopping communist aggression: "We must say in Southeast Asia—as we did in Europe—the words of the Bible, 'Hitherto shalt thou come, but no farther.'"[15] Having drawn the line in Korea, the United States sought to do the same in a lineless war in Vietnam.

NOTES

1. Finley Peter Dunne, "On the Philippines," in American Diplomacy and the Sense of Destiny, vol. 1, ed. Peter E. Cranakos and Albert Karson (Belmont, Calif.: Wadsworth, 1966), pp. 75-76.

2. Harry S. Truman, "State of the Union Message," January 1950.

3. Actual values were $2 billion and $3 billion respectively. U.S. Agency for International Development, U.S. Overseas Loans and Grants (Washington, D.C.: U.S. Government Printing Office, 1982). Export implicit price deflators were used to calculate the $20 billion current value.

4. President Franklin D. Roosevelt, "Remarks on French Possessions," in Department of State, Foreign Relations of the United States (Washington, D.C.: U.S. Government Printing Office, 1968), p. 514, and conversation with Kenneth Landon, first U.S. consul in Hanoi.

5. General Dwight D. Eisenhower, "Report to NATO Planning Committee," October 10, 1951, cited in Louis J. Halle, The Cold War as History (New York: Harper & Row, 1967), pp. 184-86.

6. Andrei Zhdanov, September 22, 1947, and Liu Shao-Chi, November 16, 1949, in Vietnam Crisis, ed. Allan W. Cameron (Ithaca, N.Y.: Cornell University Press, 1971), pp. 114-15.

7. Department of Defense, The Pentagon Papers, U.S.-Vietnam Relations, 1945-1967 (Washington, D.C.: U.S. Government Printing Office, 1971), vol. 8, p. 310.

8. Dean Acheson, Present at the Creation (New York: W.W. Norton, 1969), pp. 862-63.

9. The Pentagon Papers, op. cit., vol. 2B, pp. 1-10.

10. Dwight D. Eisenhower, news conference, February 10, 1954, Public Papers of the Presidents, 1954, p. 253.

11. Letter to Mr. Diem, October 23, 1954 in Documents on American Foreign Relations, 1954 (New York: Council on Foreign Relations, 1954), pp. 366-67.

12. The Pentagon Papers, op. cit., vol. 2, IVA4, Table 4, p. 37.

13. The Pentagon Papers, op. cit., vol. 2, IVB1, p. 9; and Walt W. Rostow, The Diffusion of Power (New York: Macmillan, 1972), p. 265.

14. This view was later strengthened by a declaration of Chinese Minister of Defense Lin Piao, "Long Live the Victory of People's War," Spring 1965. Lin advocated the isolation of Europe and America, the "cities of the world," by communist revolutions in Latin America, Africa, the Middle East, and Southeast Asia, the "countryside of the world."

15. Lyndon B. Johnson, speech delivered at Johns Hopkins University, April 7, 1965.

2

Vietnam:
A War Won and
A War Lost

On March 8, 1965, riflemen of the Ninth U.S. Marine Expeditionary Brigade waded ashore near Da Nang, South Vietnam. They had come a long way to reach that distant shore, and had an even longer path to travel before returning home. Indeed, some would never return home. They sweated profusely under their heavy load of ammunition, rations, weaponry, and steel helmets as they reached the beach unopposed in what was essentially an administrative landing. Nevertheless, pictures of U.S. Marines hitting the beach were splattered across newspapers and magazines from New York to Bangkok. The world now knew that America meant business, while for many Americans the action recalled that old World War I refrain:

> Over there, send the word,
> we're coming over, and we won't
> be back till it's over, over there.

No one in Southeast Asia doubted that the United States of America, victors over Japan in World War II and the most powerful country in the world, would prevail, would turn the tide of battle and ultimately the war in Vietnam—no one, that is, except the leadership in Hanoi.

THE SETTING FOR CONFLICT: 1930-60

By the time of the Marine landing, Ho Chi Minh and his colleagues had been engaged in efforts to unify Vietnam under their

19

control for over 40 years. Their efforts had taken many forms, but the tide of nationalism, which they helped direct and ride to victory, was by far the cutting edge of their success.

As a boy of 13 years of age, Ho was inspired by the words "liberty, fraternity, equality," but in the Vietnam of his youth and early manhood these were commodities in scarce supply. Ho turned to communism as an ideology and organizational tool, traveling and studying for many years in Paris and Moscow. In 1925 he returned to the Orient and conspired to eliminate from competition the great nationalist leader Phan Boi Chau. Shortly after the turn of the century, Chau had sought Japanese support against the French to restore imperial power in Vietnam. When that failed and while in exile in China in 1912, Chau had ineffectively proclaimed a republican government. His League for the Restoration of Vietnam had long been a source of Vietnamese nationalist sentiments and activities, thus placing him in a competitive position with Ho for the nationalist constituency. As a consequence, for 150,000 piasters, Ho had Chau turned over to the French authorities who tried, sentenced, but subsequently pardoned him.[1]

Ho continued to outwit his noncommunist nationalist opponents in subsequent years. In 1930, for example, nationalist revolutionaries fatally poisoned French officials at a reception they attended, only to be themselves executed after being identified to the French Sureté by their Vietnamese communist friends.[2] That same year the nationalist party Viet-Nam Quoc Dan Dang (VNQDD) was decimated by the French for sponsoring military uprisings at various locations. Ho, however, after sponsoring a protest demonstration in his native Nghe An province, decided not to challenge French authority directly until the time was right. He had formed the Indochinese Communist Party in 1930 but spent the rest of the decade in China and the Soviet Union. Only when Japanese forces defeated the French along the Sino-Vietnamese border did Ho venture to return to his native land.

In 1941, having recently returned to North Vietnam, Ho formed the Viet Minh in an effort to attract and unite revolutionary nationalists of diverse persuasions in the struggle for independence. It was this organization, controlled by Ho, that helped rescue downed American airmen during World War II. At the time it was a very weak organization militarily, but it had nationalist credentials and strong central political direction. All it needed was an opportunity.

The opportunity finally came as Japanese forces left Vietnam in 1945. The communists again outwitted the splintered nationalists by seizing the imperial palace at Hue with a mere squad of men. In the wake of Japanese withdrawal, Ho also rushed his guerrilla colleagues to Hanoi before the Chinese occupation army could arrive or the French could reassert colonial claims. On September 2, 1945, Ho read a Declaration of Independence in Hanoi proclaiming the new Democratic Republic of Vietnam (DRV). Three months later he promulgated a constitution based on that of the United States and appealed to the Western nations for diplomatic recognition.

But diplomatic recognition never came and the French held on to their colonial claims. In late 1945, French contingents returned to Vietnam, courtesy of Chinese Nationalist forces north of the 16th parallel and British to the south. In early 1946 the French and Chinese agreed to the withdrawal of Chiang Kai-shek's forces from the north and their replacement by French troops. Later that year the French seized the custom houses in Haiphong, obviously to gain a financial and political advantage similar to that which they had enjoyed in mainland China under the crumbling rules of extrality. In response to local opposition, Admiral d'Argenlieu ordered a naval bombardment of the Vietnamese quarter of Haiphong, which resulted in about 6,000 civilian deaths. That indiscriminate bombardment contributed as much as any other factor to the immediate origins of the First Indochina War. The long-standing reasons, of course, were French military and economic domination of Indochina, in which the indigenous population had virtually no voice. The Vietnamese sense of national pride and long-smoldering thirst for independence was kindled into flames. The war had effectively begun.

If the bombardment of Haiphong in 1946 started the war, it was the French defeat at Dien Bien Phu in 1954 that ended it. During the intervening eight years, the French Forces of the Extreme Orient had fought a noble but continually losing battle. Their Viet Minh enemy mined the few main roads, ambushed convoys and patrols, attacked when numbers or surprise favored them, initiated numerous night actions (which the French hated), and effectively kept French forces mired down in their "Beau Geste" forts scattered throughout the countryside. Unfortunately, for France, the charismatic and militarily effective French general, Jean de Lattre de Tassigny, who had begun to reverse French fortunes, left Vietnam in 1951 to die of cancer in his homeland. His successors, Generals Raoul Salan and Henri Navarre, were not among the "great captains of history."

The French had all the advantages of weaponry, logistic and air support, communications, and high-level military command experience. Yet, with all these advantages, they were defeated. It took eight years, but, in the end, the fact was that Ho had mobilized the force of Vietnamese nationalism to defeat a militarily superior force.

The concept of a People's Army, espoused by Ho Chi Minh's top commander, Vo Nguyen Giap, emphasized the inextricable bond between the Vietnamese people and its army. The very title of their controlling organization, the Viet Minh, stressed the principle of unity of purpose. It purported a nationalist "just cause" of liberating Vietnam from the colonial yoke, as it struggled eight long years under the banner of national self-determination.

In the final analysis, the French defeat was equally a product of their own inability or unwillingness to recognize Vietnamese independence and to capitalize on the force of Vietnamese nationalism. From the indiscriminate and provocative bombardment of Haiphong to the last-hour enlistment of too few Vietnamese allies before the battle of Dien Bien Phu, the French failed to read the signs of the times. They paid for that failure in frustration and blood. After the loss of Dien Bien Phu, neither the government nor the people of France were prepared to support further warfare. At the Geneva Conference, French authorities agreed to a division of Vietnam at the 17th parallel, with Ho's control to the north and temporary French control to the south.

There were those who criticized the French for ceding the northern half of Vietnam at that time, but in the words of the American delegate to the Geneva Conference, "It will be well to remember that diplomacy has rarely been able to gain at the conference table what cannot be gained on the battlefield."[3] Indeed, Ho's victory was such that he entertained every expectation that all of Vietnam would soon be under his control. The Geneva accords had called for a nationwide election in 1956, when France was planning to turn over administrative control of southern Vietnam to what Ho viewed as a fledgling and disorganized opposition group led by Ngo Dinh Diem. Diem, however, proved a sterner opponent than Ho originally anticipated. In 1954 he was selected by Bao Dai, former Emperor of Vietnam and titular head of state in South Vietnam, to become premier. Diem agreed with the stipulation that he have full authority over the army and civil administration. Rapidly consolidating his power, Diem administered the resettlement of 900,000 northerners, mostly Catholics, in South Vietnam. He outwitted less capable opposition and cracked down on racketeers and corrupt elements, such as the Binh Xuyen pirates. In 1956 he refused to permit the elections called for by the Geneva Accords because, he said, there could be no democratic elections in the North. Moreover, he directed aggressive operations against Southern Vietnamese Communists (Viet Cong). His methods included direct military attacks on Viet Cong strongholds in the countryside, a certain amount of land reform to elicit peasant political support, and the "strategic hamlet" program. The latter involved the mass movement of population from marginally secure rural areas to "strategic hamlets" defended by sharpened bamboo punji stakes, barbed wire, and local militia.

Diem's programs, however, did not take the people's needs sufficiently into account. While the first two programs were relatively successful, the strategic hamlet program involved numerous unwilling participants. The movement of farmers from the land they had hewn from the jungles or the swamps, and worked for many years to provide a livelihood, bred resentment that was fully exploited by Diem's enemies, who labeled the hamlets "concentration camps." Diem made the further mistake, which was to cost him dearly, of failing to integrate into his regime the multitude of diverse elements and interests that constituted South Vietnam. North Vietnam is ethnically and culturally relatively homogeneous. South Vietnam is divided in nearly every way. Ethnically it consists of some 10 percent Montagnards, 10 percent Cambodians (the Mekong Delta was part of Cambodia 200 years ago), 9 percent Chinese, and the remainder mostly Vietnamese. Religiously it was 10-15 percent Catholic, 10-15 percent Theravada Buddhist (prevalent in Southeast Asia), 10 percent Cao Dai (a combination of many religions), 10-15 percent spirit worship, and over 50 percent Mahayana Buddhist (prevalent in Northeast Asia), with many religious beliefs in various combinations. The society was further divided regionally, from the more traditional elements in the vicinity of the former imperial capital of Hue to the cosmopolitan nature of Saigon, to local political-religious organizations such as the Cao Dai of Tay Ninh province and the Hoa Hao of the western Mekong Delta. A mandarin with very conservative views, Diem did not tolerate opposition to his government from these diverse elements. After initially attempting to accommodate some of them, he soon divorced them from real power in the new government of the Republic of Vietnam (RVN), and eventually suppressed elements of the Cao Dai, Hoa Hao, certain Buddhist sects, and local peasant armies such as that of Tring Minh The. In so doing he alienated, and in many cases drove into Viet Cong support the very forces that, if they had been successfully integrated into South Vietnamese political and economic life, could have proven to be a bulwark against the Northern onslaught which was one day certain to come. But in the late 1950s and early 1960s Diem dimly realized this fact. Consequently, he began to encounter increasingly strong and organized resistance that coalesced around a united front typically utilized by communist conspirators to seize national power.

In North Vietnam, meanwhile, Ho Chi Minh had been preoccupied with the problems of an insurrection resulting from disastrously mismanaged collectivization. Liberalizing enough to

recapture peasant support, Ho determined that the time had come
to change tactics in the south, from clandestine political activity to
more direct confrontation. He had at his immediate disposal some
5,000 to 10,000 of Giap's soldiers that had remained in the South in
1954 in violation of the Geneva Agreement. They provided a convenient cadre for building a potent guerrilla force, and in 1957 the
cadres began preparing for action.

About 90,000 politically indoctrinated southern Viet Minh
soldiers had been required by the Geneva Agreement to regroup to
North Vietnam in 1954. When chances for peaceful reunification
of Vietnam (under Ho Chi Minh, of course) evaporated, the regroupees were given additional training and indoctrination and
formed into infiltration units for their return to the South. Prepa-
rations began in 1958 for upgrading the long-unused Ho Chi Minh
Trail, which ran mainly through eastern Laos. Between 1959 and
1964 from 28,000 to 44,000 of the regroupees returned south to
provide leadership to the stay-behind cadres and conducted guerrilla warfare against the southern regime. In December 1960 the
National Liberation Front for South Vietnam (NLF) was created by
Hanoi as an instrument to overthrow Diem and to establish a uni-
fied communist state. Its link with Hanoi, however, was cleverly
concealed so as to maximize its appeal to a wide spectrum of resistance to Diem, including noncommunists. The combination of
Diem's mistakes and Hanoi's determination led to a doubling of
Viet Cong strength between 1960 and 1962.[4] The stage was being
set for a wider American role.

PHASE I: THE ADVISORY EFFORT, 1961-64

Historians have traced American participation in the wars of
Indochina back much farther than 1961. Some point to our Office
of Strategic Services assistance to Ho Chi Minh against Japanese
forces in World War II. Others point to our aid to the French during
the First Indochinese War, which ended with the United States pay-
ing three-fourths of the colonial war costs, while Americans
kicked "door bundles" of supplies by parachute to besieged French
troops at Dien Bien Phu. Still others refer to commitments during
the Eisenhower Administration, despite the nearly constant reductions in men and material sent to Vietnam during those years. But
it was in 1961 that the United States decided to increase assistance
to South Vietnam substantially. To administer this aid and to enhance the effectiveness of the South Vietnamese armed forces,
American military personnel in the country rose from a mere 685
advisors in 1961 to some 23,000 men by 1964. In 1961 armed

American advisors began accompanying the South Vietnamese Army (ARVN) on combat operations on a routine basis. Casualties began to mount and, from 1961 to 1964, 267 Americans were killed in action. Slowly but surely, the American people began to realize they were somehow involved in a war.

In general, the engagements of this period were small-unit actions, hit-and-run battles fought by indigenous South Vietnamese on both sides. It would seem that the government forces should have had the advantage, especially as American support increased, but, as many American advisors pointed out at the time, heroic actions of ARVN units were all too rare as Viet Cong forces seized, retained, and exploited the initiative. Farmers by day and porters or fighters by night, the Viet Cong were difficult to detect and more difficult to engage in the dense foliage and jungles covering most of South Vietnam, even for natives of the area. Making matters worse, the Viet Cong were systematically and ruthlessly eliminating the vestiges of government control in rural areas. Terrorist action against village chiefs, school teachers, and government officials became routine. In 1963, for example, the Viet Cong killed the Phuoc Thanh province chief and impaled his head on a stake where all could see—a lesson in power politics at the local level. As may be seen in the following chart, acts of terrorism increased substantially during these years.

Viet Cong Terrorism Against Civilians[5]

	Assassinated	Kidnapped	Total
1961	1,000	2,000	3,000
1962	1,719	9,688	11,406
1963	2,073	7,262	9,335
1964	1,795	9,554	11,349

Diem's reaction was to continue his policies and to seek American support for them. He appealed to President Kennedy as well as to the American people, dispatching his beautiful and persuasive sister-in-law, Madame Nhu, to the United States to appeal for aid. Numerous efforts were made, most of them justified, to show the communist nature of the National Liberation Front (NLF) and Hanoi's direction and support of their guerrilla war. These efforts not only resulted in a marked increase in the flow of American servicemen to South Vietnam, but in aid levels, which rose from $209 million in 1961 to $409 million in 1964.

Diem's actions, and the American response to them, were unfortunate for the future of both countries. First, they created a situation and a psychology of dependence by the Republic of Vietnam upon the United States. Later in the war this dependency would grow to ridiculous proportions so that RVN responsibility for its own internal security was nearly obliterated. Second, the policy of Diem substituted American political and economic support for Vietnamese self-reliance. In so doing, Diem diminished his nationalist credentials and enhanced those of his adversary. The sects of South Vietnam did not, at this critical juncture of the new nation's history, react favorably to a crackdown on their prerogatives of autonomy, and the Viet Cong widely and somewhat successfully propagandized that the My Diem (American-Diemist clique) was just another colonial master in disguise. Nationalism was still the most potent force in Vietnam, and the NLF was tapping that force better than its opponent.

The growing opposition to Diem reached crisis proportions in 1963. His assassination in November that year was in no small measure the direct result of his reliance upon American rather than indigenous Vietnamese sources of support. Unfortunately Diem's successors were even more unable to consolidate a broad power base. Coups and countercoups were the order of the day, and amidst the confusion the Viet Cong ran wild. Beginning with the battle of Ap Bac in 1963, they no longer retreated from the battlefield at the sight of ARVN battalions and regiments. Instead, they increasingly stood their ground, and fought and won battles in which their local intelligence, tactics, and tenacity in combat overcame inferiority in manpower, ammunition, and weapons.

By 1964 the Viet Cong were everywhere on the offensive. Small units had coalesced into battalions and battalions into regiments. Major guerrilla units were moving out of the Mekong Delta to join even larger units north of Saigon. Others formed in the Central Highlands, where they hoped to cut the county in two. By the spring of 1965 the ARVN was losing the equivalent of a battalion a week to enemy action. American advisors with South Vietnamese units helped prevent complete disintegration of the situation, but by the spring of 1965 the ARVN was clearly on the defensive, imperiled not only by their own military and political disunity in the face of aggressive Viet Cong who could smell blood, but also by the ominous presence of North Vietnamese units in the South—only a few battalions—but a foreboding of what was to come.

PHASE II: AMERICANIZATION: 1965-68

Thus it was that American troops wading ashore at Da Nang and landing at Bien Hoa in the spring of 1965 faced a situation far more difficult than they or their superiors imagined. Ho and his colleagues were as determined to defeat them as they had been to expel the French several years earlier. For them it was a people's war, a nationalistic struggle of the masses against agents of the American government.

The Viet Cong and their Northern supporters enjoyed a further advantage—the United States had not declared war. The U.S. commitment to the struggle was in the form of a limited war with limited objectives in South Vietnam. This was not the case for the Hanoi and the NLF. To them it was total war with control of all Indochina as the objective. The conceptual imbalance between the United States and the Vietnamese thus ensured the relative security of North Vietnam as the great rear base from which to mobilize and dispatch forces to the South. North Vietnamese forces had already begun developing the vital Ho Chi Minh trail, a series of paths and, eventually, roadways and pipelines funneling into base areas along the Laos and Cambodian borders, which American forces were prohibited from crossing. The evolving situation was really one of incredible danger to South Vietnam if it were to defend its villages, towns, and outposts along and behind over 500 miles of jungle-covered borders.

Finally, the bombing of North Vietnam, which had begun in 1964 as retaliation raids in connection with reported DRV PT boat attacks on two Seventh Fleet destroyers, did not reduce the scope of the problem. During the Rolling Thunder bombing campaign (1965-68), North Vietnamese maneuver battalions in South Vietnam increased from 6 to 97. Bombing was limited to military targets of peripheral value to the overall war potential of the North. American pilots were risking their lives bombing bridges over fordable rivers, PT boat facilities of a nation with no ocean-going navy, and easily movable targets. In early 1967 Admiral U. S. Grant Sharp, Commander-in-Chief of U.S. forces in the Pacific, complained that only 1 percent of the "lucrative targets" identified by the Joint Chiefs of Staff had been struck. The bombing that was conducted was generally reduced in effectiveness due to increasing numbers of Soviet-supplied antiaircraft guns and missiles. The material damage inflicted, while great in absolute terms, was also rendered indecisive by its replenishment from abroad. Finally, the bombing strengthened rather than weakened Hanoi's resolve. Under continuing aerial attack that was not truly effective militarily, but that caused enough civilian casualties to stir hatred, the bombing united the people in a way essential to the unlimited war they were waging at tremendous loss of lives in South Vietnam. In 1966, for example, the following letter was written by a North Vietnamese woman to her husband in the South, which reads in part:

Recently the enemy has sent aircraft to bomb in this area. To each attack our army and people respond fiercely, giving them what they deserve, as you used to instruct us. In order to protect the people, it is necessary to follow the orders of our leaders and block warden. I have stressed the need for patriotism in all our children.

Added to these already immense problems were conflicting interpretations of the U.S. role in the conflict. The American soldier entering Vietnam in 1965 was really entering two wars simultaneously—first an offensive counterguerrilla war against the Viet Cong, and secondly, a defensive conventional war against major North Vietnamese units, even though the flow of these units was just beginning. The fact that both wars were fought simultaneously tended to obscure the significance of their difference. The first was directed against South Vietnamese guerrillas who swam in a sea of friendly, tolerant, or terrorized villages and their surrounding jungles and rice paddies. Contrary to myth, there were far more villages in the latter two categories than in the former, lending some credence to the observation that the Viet Cong were not revolutionary to the extent that they created social grievances rather than reacted to them. The first war, despite its severity and unfamiliarity, was one the U.S. and RVN forces were eventually to win. The second war, on the other hand, was, as RVN Premier Nguyen Cao Ky so succinctly pointed out, like a football game in which the American team was compelled never to cross the 50-yard line into enemy territory. It also was a very difficult war, and it may be remembered more so because, unlike the war against the Viet Cong, the United States and its South Vietnamese ally lost.

Both wars were frustrating. The novelty of combat with no front lines, with an enemy whose identity was often unknown, and in terrain masking enemy fire was an added stress to the usual difficulties of war. Much of South Vietnam is covered by triple canopy jungle in which it is fairly dim even at high noon and vegetation is such that one is lucky to see ten feet ahead. With some notable exceptions, neither U.S. air nor ground forces were very successful in "finding and fixing" enemy units in this environment. The movement of American troops, on the other hand, was usually detected, although they did surprise numerous enemy forces when intelligence was good and the reaction swift. On the whole, though, U.S. forces engaged VC and DRV units on enemy terms under circumstances neutralizing much of their advantage in firepower and tactical mobility.

FIGURE 1

Major Border Battles and Referenced Locations

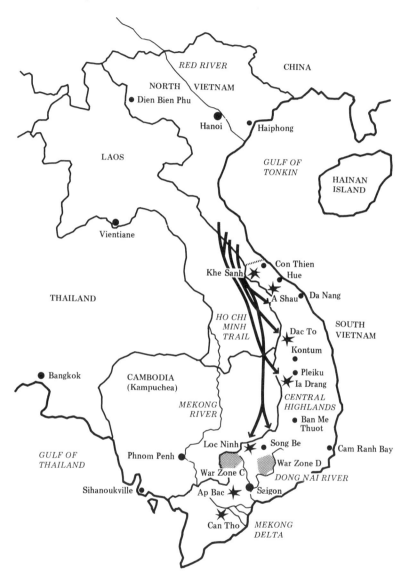

Despite a number of civilian casualties resulting from American aircraft bombing and strafing enemy positions in certain villages, the overwhelming truth of Vietnam was that the tremendous firepower of American forces could not and was not brought to bear on enemy targets for still another reason—the very fear of inflicting civilian casualties. Sniper fire from a village was routinely answered with a very selective small-arms response. The widely reported massacre at My Lai is to be condemned certainly, but the very notoriety of My Lai confirms the exceptional nature of the encounter. On the other hand, terrorism was a routine instrument of enemy tactics. Who, for example, ever heard of Dak Son, when in December 1967 North Vietnamese units entered a Montagnard village just north of Song Be, South Vietnam, and burned to death over 250 Montagnard men, women, and children in an act of barbaric brutality. The violence was reported by the U.S. press, but, because it was not atypical, was soon forgotten. The massacre at Hue a few months later, in which occupying North Vietnamese and Vietcong assassinated some 4,000 civilians, received somewhat more attention, but nothing compared to My Lai.

In the face of these difficulties, American soldiers and their combat leaders brought remarkable skill and determination to their task. Bearing up under heavy loads of ammunition, weapons, helmets, radios, C-rations, canteens of water, and perhaps an entrenching tool and gas mask, they struggled through intense heat and monsoon rains to stem the tide of Viet Cong momentum.

By the end of 1965 they had frustrated the effort of the Viet Cong and their North Vietnamese reinforcements to split South Vietnam in the Central Highlands. A major battle in this campaign, and one of the first full encounters between North Vietnamese and American troops, took place in November 1965, in the dense jungle-covered mountains of the Ia Drang Valley. There American forces inflicted heavy casualties on two North Vietnamese regiments attempting to ambush them. A year later this pattern was repeated near Loc Ninh where an American "truck" column drove into a VC Main Force Unit ambush site. A senior provincial official, known to be a Viet Cong, had been informed of the operation in order to lure the Viet Cong into position. Unknown to the ambushers, American tanks had reinforced the column and fighter aircraft were prepared to attack on a moment's notice, which they did. Still other major battles with North Vietnamese forces took place as a result of enemy attacks on isolated camps, outposts, and even district towns. Some of these were generated by North Vietnamese efforts to draw American forces away from populated areas so as to allow the Viet Cong to regain their momentum and assert control of the people. Thus the border battles of Con Thien, Khe Sanh, A Shau, and Dak To were fought and won by American forces.

The principal American effort of these years, however, was directed against the Viet Cong and took place not in major battles but in a series of small unit engagements usually involving a company or less, wherein individual skill and courage, and small unit teamwork were the decisive factors. Here also the Americans performed very well. Though unfamiliar with the political complexities of Vietnamese society, they placed the Viet Cong increasingly on the defensive, depleted their ranks, and did so generally without alienating the Vietnamese people. The North Vietnamese efforts to ·divert them into border areas is one indicator of their success. Another is the fact that by the end of 1967 most Viet Cong main force units consisted of about half North Vietnamese "fillers," and were largely led by North Vietnamese officers. In a very important way, Hanoi's decision to launch a great offensive in 1968 was precisely to reverse the ill fortunes of the preceding years.

The New Year (Tet) offensive of 1968 was truly the Viet Cong Battle of the Bulge—one last great effort to attain the unattainable. VC cadres who for years had played the relatively passive but important role of intelligence and resource providers to combat units, as well as political cadre at local levels, burst forth under instructions to unleash a mass popular uprising throughout South Vietnam against Saigon authorities and their American allies.

American blood was spilled in a series of bitter battles from Khe Sanh and Hue in the north to My Tho and Saigon in the south. For most of February through May 1968, as the final surge of Viet Cong fury unfolded, nearly 500 American soldiers lost their lives each week. American hospital wards in Vietnam, the Philippines, and Japan were jammed as suffering GIs waited their turn to see a doctor or a nurse. Many of these and other returning veterans were frustrated by the unpopularity of the war in which they had just participated. For them there was no parade, little praise, and frequent jeers on their return home. This also was part of the price of Vietnam.

It is estimated that 45,000 enemy troops perished in the Tet offensive. Thousands more were maimed to the point where they could never fight again. By June a stillness began to settle over the populated areas that had not been equalled in years. The Viet Cong had suffered a catastrophic military defeat from which they never recovered. American forces had proven themselves against great odds in the first of their two wars in Vietnam. The South Vietnamese had also acquitted themselves well, particularly the local Regional and Popular Forces (RF/PF), who defended the villages. By American estimates the South Vietnamese lost 2,800 killed and 8,300 wounded.

The principal results of the Tet offensive were these: the free world media hysterically reported that an American and South Vietnamese disaster of the first magnitude had occurred, resulting in a great psychological victory for the communist Vietnamese, who had lost militarily; (Peter Braestrup, then a <u>Washington Post</u> reporter, noted in his book <u>Big Story</u> in 1977 that "Rarely has contemporary crisis-journalism turned out, in retrospect, to have veered so widely from reality."); U.S. military credibility was seriously questioned, and plans to "Vietnamize" the war gained impetus; there was no general uprising, as the DRV had hoped, RVNAF morale soared, and recruiting improved, a fact that has been much overlooked; the Viet Cong had been rendered impotent, which cleared the way later for North Vietnamese control over the South without their having to neutralize or eliminate the southern communist leaders and forces; truce talks began and the DRV was given an important respite from U.S. bombing when President Johnson gave in to pressure and announced a bombing halt that was to last for four years. Although they had lost the Tet offensive militarily, the North Vietnamese paved the way for their eventual victory.

PHASE II: VIETNAMIZATION, 1968-72

Although American forces had achieved a victory in South Vietnam by late 1968, they had done so at a price. By accepting the role of securing populated areas from hostile forces, the United States had Americanized the war to the disadvantage of its South Vietnamese ally. It is a sad commentary on the American role to note that in reaction to the Tet offensive, 18- and 19-year-olds in South Vietnam finally became eligible for the draft, while Americans of the same age had been fighting for more than two years. What had been an emergency intervention to prevent collapse in 1965 had, by 1969, become a clear case of American "can do" practices taking over from Vietnamese who, in the end, would determine the outcome of the war. What became known as "Vietnamization" under the Nixon Administration was really a reaffirmation of what President Kennedy had come to recognize just before his death, when he told Walter Cronkite: "In the final analysis it is their war. They are the ones who have to win or lose it. We can help them; we can send men out there as advisors; but they must win it—the people of Vietnam—against the Communists."[6] Indeed, President Johnson had also come to support the idea of Vietnamization toward the end of his administration, beginning with his March 1968 shift to a "negotiate and fight" posture, with an increasing share of the "fight" shifting to the South Vietnamese. In April he directed that all ARVN units, popular forces, and local militia, be armed with the M-16 rifle. President Nixon, however, put Vietnamization at center stage in his plan to end the war, stating his strategic concept as follows:

> We have adopted a plan which we have worked out in cooperation with the South Vietnamese for the complete withdrawal of all U.S. combat ground forces, and their replacement by South Vietnamese forces on an orderly scheduled timetable. The withdrawal will be made from strength and not weakness. As South Vietnamese forces become stronger, the rate of American withdrawal can become greater.[7]

While Vietnamization was fine as far as countering remaining Viet Cong forces was concerned, it did not provide the framework within which American or South Vietnamese troops could contend with North Vietnamese attacks on an extended time basis. The United States had always refrained from ground attack against North Vietnam since it could have provoked Soviet, or more likely Chinese, intervention. Except for the relatively ineffectual bombing of the North under the Rolling Thunder campaign, and the occasional reconnaissance missions into Cambodia or Laos by irregular forces, the struggle with North Vietnam was acted out on a stage maximizing the DRV advantage—in the mountains and jungle-covered highlands of South Vietnam. It was a war without end, for just as surely as American forces succeeded in devastating North Vietnamese units in their jungle redoubts, the DRV politburo would order south enough recruits to reconstitute those units across the border in their sanctuaries in nearby Cambodia, Laos, or southern North Vietnam. Six months to a year later the North Vietnamese unit would be back again. Thus the battles of Khe Sanh, the A Shau valley, Loc Ninh, Hamburger Hill, and many others were fought and won by American forces with no decisive effect on the outcome of the war. Hanoi controlled the direction and pace of the war, limited only by the numbers of men and material it chose to introduce at any particular time and place.

To fight a war with no hope of decisive victory reinforced the frustration of the American soldier and citizen alike. Americans were instructed to fight a holding action and to minimize casualties. Beginning in the early 1970s, no major offensive operations were to be initiated. While conserving American lives, the effect of this policy was perceived as abandoning any hope of victory. The war was made even more difficult because, unlike battle lines of previous wars, there was no simple way to measure progress. Khe Sanh and Hamburger Hill, for example, were abandoned shortly after the battles for them ended. A hamlet evaluation system (HES) was developed to show the degree of security or lack thereof in the thousands of villages in South Vietnam. Considerable progress was measured by the system, particularly after Tet, but it was not a meaningful measurement of progress in the war with Hanoi. During the 1972 North Vietnamese all-out attack on South Vietnam, several entire districts reverted from 99 to 0 percent "pacified" on the hamlet evaluation system. It was but a belated reminder that the nature of the war had changed.

The advocates of striking North Vietnam had several chances over the years to press their case. Back in 1961 and again in 1965 the Department of State published a widely disseminated pamphlet, "Aggression from the North," in which it attempted to show documented proof that North Vietnam directed and supported the guerrilla war in the South. America had refrained from a ground offensive against North Vietnam not only because of the perception that decisive results could emanate from counterguerrilla operations, but also from fear of international repercussions, such as the commitment of a Chinese land army as had occurred in Korea. By 1972 President Nixon had enough sense to recognize that neither case still applied. The guerrilla war was won as far as U.S. troops could win it, and discussions with China were already underway in view of the belatedly recognized Sino-Soviet split. The stage was thus set for American strategy to take into account these new dimensions in its war with North Vietnam. The massive 1972 North Vietnamese offensive, coming in the waning days of American ground involvement in South Vietnam, presented the occasion for American policy to incorporate these newly recognized factors into a war strategy. The final phase of American involvement was about to begin.

PHASE IV: U.S. INVOLVEMENT ENDS, 1972-75

In April 1972 North Vietnam unleashed an all-out conventional attack against South Vietnam. Fourteen divisions and 26 supporting regiments participated in an impressive display of combined arms capability.

The Easter Offensive, as it became known, came at a time when American troops were all but gone; the ground fighting was done entirely by Vietnamese forces—North and South. The newly formed Third ARVN division along the DMZ collapsed under the initial onslaught, but the ARVN First Division held the line in heroic fighting north and west of Hue. Elsewhere South Vietnamese forces acquitted themselves well, sustaining heavy casualties to defend their homeland and counterattacking North Vietnamese units that penetrated into populated areas. The South Vietnamese performance in resisting everything the North Vietnamese could throw at them, however, was contingent upon American air support. Both because the South Vietnamese were compelled to defend a vast number of villages and towns while the North Vietnamese could concentrate on particular targets of their choice and because the North Vietnamese were generally more disciplined and united, which was a reflection of their society, American air power was essential to a military balance. Some of this American air supplemented the Vietnamese Air Force (VNAF) in supporting troops in combat, but its really crucial role was farther north.

The U.S. air war against North Vietnam in 1972 was unlike any American air action since World War II. American aircraft systematically attacked the industry, infrastructure, and military "great rear base" of the DRV. They mined rivers and obstructed coastal transport, destroyed roads, railroads, and bridges both from China toward the Red River Delta and from the Delta south to the Republic of Vietnam. The attacks closed Haiphong harbor, destroyed electrical generating plants, and cut DRV supplies moving south to a dribble. Unlike the Rolling Thunder campaign of 1965-68, it was a crushing strangulation of DRV warmaking potential, and, together with strong ARVN resistance, it succeeded.

By the end of 1972 North Vietnamese forces had exhausted their offensive capability and Hanoi was in serious trouble. Nearly all surface-to-air missiles had been fired and U.S. air power was ever more devastating with its new television and radar-guided "smart bombs."

For North Vietnam it was a time for serious negotiations; for the United States it was a taste of near victory in this, the second American war in Vietnam.

But the effort to win in this area had already taken too long. The years of frustration, of not winning, of daily press and television accounts covering not just the normal horror of war, but increasingly as time went on, those rare aspects of the conflict most damaging to American will to win—the atrocity at My Lai, napalm on VC villages, a stray bomb on Bach Mai hospital in Hanoi—all reinforced a perception that America was being dragged down to new lows in its conduct of the war. America was not winning, according to this view, because it was engaged in an immoral war against innocent civilians. The unpopularity of the war, and its inconclusive results over a very long period, ultimately, had become the decisive factor in its outcome.

It is possible to say all this was recognized by North Vietnam. It may well have been. In retrospect it is certainly true that the hearts and minds of Americans, and not the North Vietnamese, were the first to weaken in resolve for their cause in South Vietnam. Much had to do with the fact that for the North it was not a limited war and never had been. It was the chinh nghia, a "just cause," that motivated and permeated DRV cadres who devoted their entire lives to victory. Only for the United States was the war in South Vietnam of a limited nature. If the United States could be severed from its alliance with South Vietnam through frustration, popular disdain for the war, and political inability to draw on a national reservoir of people power, then so much the easier for North Vietnam to attain its goal.

The Paris agreement of 1973 between the United States and North Vietnam formally ended American participation in the war. It committed the United States to stop all military activites against North Vietnam, to end its military involvement in South Vietnam, and to withdraw all its remaining troops, technicians, and advisors. Both parties agreed to a cease fire in-place, which allowed a considerable North Vietnamese presence in the South under the guise of maintaining the territory supposedly controlled by the Viet Cong. The agreement also allowed both sides to maintain existing levels of armaments and munitions, and by 1974 North Vietnam had an estimated 185,000 men, 600 tanks, and 24 regiments of artillery in South Vietnam.[8] The United States, in contrast, withdrew completely and unequivocally in 1973 and thereupon reduced its aid levels to South Vietnam. Perhaps the greatest American link to South Vietnam was the assurance President Nixon had given President Thieu that in the event of flagrant DRV violations of the agreement that the United States would react with force.

The initial goal of the United States, a free, viable, independent Republic of Vietnam, had long since been discarded. Clearly, the goal in late 1972 and early 1973 was to extricate American forces, recover prisoners of war, gain an accounting of the missing in action, and, hopefully, endow the RVN with the capability to defend itself. The DRV's goal was unchanged from its initial expression—reunify Vietnam and dominate the remainder of Indochina.

So it was, having drawn up a peace agreement predicated on a reservoir of popular American support for further action in the event of flagrant North Vietnamese violations, that the United States found itself unable to call on that reservoir when it was most needed. Political difficulties surrounding a besieged president reinforced DRV perceptions that the United States, having withdrawn from South Vietnam, would never again return. Thus in April 1975, ten years and a month from the first landing of U.S. combat troops on the shores of Vietnam, the North Vietnamese launched their final and decisive drive to complete what Ho Chi Minh had initiated 50 years earlier—the control of all Vietnam, "from Lang Son to Ca Mau," under communist leadership. 9

The United States had suffered a monumental defeat in Vietnam, in Asia, in the world, and at home in America.

NOTES

1. David Halberstram, HO (New York: Random House, 1971), p. 45.

2. Conversations with ex-VNQDD party members, 1964. Bernard Fall cites further examples of this type of behavior in The Two Vietnams (New York: Praeger, 1963), p. 93.

3. General Walter Bedell Smith, Undersecretary of State, in Department of Defense, The Pentagon Papers, U.S.-Vietnam Relations, 1945-1967 (Washington, D.C.: U.S. Government Printing Office, 1971), vol. 3, p. 14.

4. The Pentagon Papers, op. cit., vol. 4-A5, Table 4, p. 25; and The BDM Corporation, Study of Strategic Lessons in Vietnam (Washington, D.C.: Department of Defense, Technical Information Center, 1980), vol. 6, pp. 3-31.

5. Roger Hilsman, To Move a Nation (New York: Doubleday, 1967), p. 525.

6. CBS Interview, September 2, 1963, in Background Information Relating to Southeast Asia and Vietnam (Washington, D.C.: U.S. Government Printing Office, July 1967), p. 113.

7. Richard M. Nixon, "The Pursuit of Peace," November 3, 1969, in Department of State Bulletin 8502, November 1969, p. 8.

8. Department of State, "Agreement on Ending the War and Restoring the Peace in Vietnam" (January 1973); the document was signed by Secretary of State William Rogers and Foreign Minister Nguyen duy Trinh. The 1974 figures are from Richard Nixon, The Real War (New York: Warner, 1980), p. 117.

9. Senior General Van Tien Dung, who directed the final North Vietnamese victory, took note of reduced American aid levels when he commented at the time: "The reduction of U.S. aid made it impossible for the puppet (South Vietnamese) troops to carry out their combat plans and build up their forces. . . . Nguyen Van Thieu was then forced to fight a poor man's war. Enemy fire power had decreased nearly 60% because of bomb and ammunition shortages." Van Tien Dung, "Great Spring Victory," in Nhan Dan, April 5, 1975, as reported by the Foreign Broadcast Information Service, Asia and Pacific, April 7, 1975, p. K-5.

3

The Withdrawal Syndrome:
America Washes
Its Hands

Over 57,000 young Americans paid the ultimate sacrifice in
17 years of war in Vietnam. Several hundred thousand others returned to the United States with severe wounds. Some 3 million
service men and women participated in the war, while an even
greater number of families and friends suffered the anguish of a
separation of uncertain end. The war eventually cost the U.S. tax-
payer $300 billion. It was the longest war in American history, and
the most divisive since the Civil War.

Beside this profound impact on the lives of the American people, the war was to generate still another effect—a deep and pervasive desire to disengage not just from Vietnam but from the complex and dangerous world of international politics. This effect was
to be felt first in Vietnam itself, and then in the rest of Asia. It is
still a major influence in American politics today.

As early as 1969 this desire for withdrawal came to be reflected in official U.S. policy, when President Nixon met with news-
men in Guam. After opening remarks he was asked the following
question:

> Mr. President, sir, on the question of U.S. military
> relationships in Asia, if I may ask a hypothetical ques-
> tion: If a leader of one of the countries with which we
> have had close military relationships, either through
> SEATO or in Vietnam, should say, "Well, you are pull-
> ing out of Vietnam with your troops, we can read in the
> newspapers." How can we know that you will remain to
> play a significant role as you say you wish to do in secur-
> ity arrangements in Asia? What kind of an approach can
> you take to that question?

The president had just returned from a tour of Southeast Asia where he had observed firsthand the difficulties attending America's heavy involvement in Vietnam. His response stressed that the threat to the nations of the region was essentially internal, and that under such circumstances only an indigenous solution could effectively counter the threat. He added that while the United States will keep its treaty commitments and provide a nuclear deterrent, the United States is going to encourage and has a right to expect that the nations of Asia will increasingly handle and take responsibility for the problems of their own internal security and military defense.

These informal remarks, not even released for direct quotation at the time, later evolved in White House and Department of State memoranda and brochures as fundamental pillars of U.S. policy in Asia for the 1970s. Succinctly reiterated by the president, they were as follows:

> First, the United States will keep all of its treaty commitments.
>
> Second, we shall provide a shield if a nuclear power threatens the freedom of a nation allied with us or of a nation whose survival we consider vital to our security.
>
> Third, in cases involving other types of aggression, we shall furnish military and economic assistance when requested in accordance with our treaty commitments. But we shall look to the nation directly threatened to assume the primary responsibility for its own defense.[2]

This Guam, or Nixon Doctrine, as it became known, came to symbolize and guide American security policy in Asia for the 1970s. It provided the policy underpinning for our subsequent military withdrawals from Indochina and Thailand, the scaling down of the Seventh Fleet, and force reductions in Korea. The Guam Doctrine presented clear guidelines for U.S. commitments and force structure in the Pacific and provided a rationale for reducing that presence. In so doing, it seemed to bring national policy closer into line with the realities of American politics and commitments elsewhere in the world, for by 1969 domestic opposition to the war was burgeoning, with over 60 percent of Americans viewing the involvement in Vietnam as a mistake. Likewise, American military forces were stretched so thin that the services were questioning American ability to meet commitments in Europe and elsewhere.

The U.S. Seventh Army in Europe had been drawn down, and that was perennially one of the main sources that provided personnel and materiel replacements for Vietnam service, if not directly then by reallocation from the United States. Army morale was low, discipline suffered grievously, and the growing drug problems that sorely affected the troops in Vietnam and the United States were observed in equal measure in Europe.

The first test of the Nixon Doctrine came in Vietnam. American troops and the Republic of Vietnam Armed Forces (RVNAF) had fought for four years against indigenous Viet Cong guerrillas, and it was a tribute to their relative success that America could now declare its intention to let RVNAF handle this situation alone. The progressive buildup of South Vietnamese troops, and their assumption of responsibility through Vietnamization, was expected to assure continued success on that front.

As far as the struggle with North Vietnam was concerned, the doctrine had just the opposite implication. Logically extended, it sanctioned the withdrawal of U.S. forces, despite a continued DRV military presence in South Vietnam. Thus, in May 1971, four years before the fall of Saigon, Henry Kissinger told North Vietnamese negotiators that the United States would leave no residual force in South Vietnam if Hanoi agreed to end its infiltration. In retrospect, it was naive to entertain the notion that Hanoi would cease and desist after a generation of struggle, but as Kissinger knew, American troop withdrawals were inevitable due to public and congressional pressures. He thus sought a quid pro quo while they were still a negotiable instrument. Viewing each incremental troop withdrawal as eliminating another card from his hand, the National Security Advisor sought to implement the Nixon Doctrine by simultaneously opposing a more rapid withdrawal schedule and by supporting accelerated Vietnamization. His strategy further sought to build economic and political links with the Soviet Union and the People's Republic of China that could inhibit their support for Hanoi. In so doing he pursued a viable strategy by which he hoped to reach a settlement that would provide South Vietnam a reasonable chance for survival and the United States "peace with honor."

Historians may never agree on the wisdom of the Nixon-Kissinger strategy, one side saying the South Vietnamese defeat was inevitable and the other blaming it on Congress, Watergate, or Nguyen Van Thieu. What is clear, however, is that by the early 1970s the nation would not tolerate a continued, much less an increased level of involvement without hope of a successful outcome. By the time the Nixon Doctrine was promulgated, public mistrust of American policy in Vietnam was so widespread that any effort to prevent defeat required not just a coherent strategy, which had been previously missing, but a clear and convincing explanation of that strategy to the American people, if necessary by a massive publicity campaign. The penchant for secrecy of President Nixon and his National Security Advisor, however, was diametrically opposed to this end, and seemed to reflect a basic mistrust of the public. The secret bombing of Laos and Cambodia, the secret meetings between Kissinger and Le Duc Tho, and the Christmas bombing of North Vietnam, all naturally raised serious questions deserving public explanation. The administration's failure to rally American public opinion was obvious to the North Vietnamese, who used it as a negotiating tactic against Kissinger.[3] Under the circumstances, they would have been foolish indeed not to delay, and delay again, for an agreement more favorable to them. The name Ho Chi Minh City attests to the success of their strategy, while the names of over 57,000 American servicemen on the dark granite wall of the Vietnam Memorial in Washington, D.C., stands in mute testimony to the failure of American leadership to formulate a coherent strategy early in the war and to communicate that strategy, once formulated, in the Nixon-Kissinger era.

The failure to formulate sound objectives and strategy, and to communicate them to the public, remains a major problem in the conduct of American foreign policy. During the Vietnam era this failure cost the nation in the loss of lives, in defeat, and in the mistrust of American ability to influence events and to play a constructive role globally. The international effects of this mistrust were soon to be felt in the fall of South Vietnam and the nervousness of American friends and allies in the rest of East Asia.

As the United States withdrew from Vietnam the fundamental question, "Is America with us?" came to haunt the leadership of many Asian nations. In South Vietnam, years of reliance on U.S. support had created not just a military dependency but a psychological crutch, which when withdrawn left a feeling of hopelessness. Although the RVNAF had successfully blunted the numerous small-scale attacks by the North Vietnamese Army (NVA) during 1973 and 1974, the reduced military and economic aid from the United States resulted in a rapid depletion of their stores. The 1973 oil crisis quadrupled the cost of fuel needed for generators, commercial vehicles, boats, and small industries in addition to the needs of the military, which had inherited expensive tastes from the departing Americans. Those increased costs further depleted their working capital and inflation soared. The average South Vietnamese soldier earned only one-third enough to support an average-sized family, and he could see the corruption and high living of the senior officers who, being loyal to Thieu, retained their positions and continued to augment their incomes.

By late 1974 the economic position of South Vietnam was fragile. The Paris Agreement permitted a one-for-one replacement of lost or irreparably damaged weapons and equipment, but necessary outlays for fuel, ammunition, and other critical supplies made such replacement impossible.

Strict rationing was imposed: one hand grenade per man per month, 85 rifle bullets per man per month, four rounds of 105mm ammunition per howitzer per day, and two rounds of 155mm artillery ammunition per gun per day. [4] Clearly the South Vietnamese could not expect to hold off a concerted offensive by their enemy without the massive air support promised by President Nixon. And equally clear to all but President Thieu, who continued to believe in that promise, the United States would not or could not respond.

The balance of power in Southeast Asia had changed unalterably against South Vietnam. Laos was under a coalition government, which permitted widespread communist propagandizing. In Cambodia the Khmer Rouge, trained, indoctrinated, and reinforced by the NVA, controlled most rural areas and were threatening urban centers and ingress to them. South Vietnam's neighbors were in dire straits as was South Vietnam itself.

The position of North Vietnam strengthened quickly as soon as the Paris Agreement was concluded. U.S. bombing ceased and efforts to rebuild the damaged infrastructure proceeded unhampered. American teams cleared Haiphong and other harbors of mines, thus permitting the long-interrupted flow of critical imports. Within a year the DRV infiltrated up to 100,000 troops into South Vietnam or nearby border sanctuaries in addition to the 140,000 already in the South. Finally, a major road and petroleum pipeline were established within South Vietnam east of the Truong Son mountains leading directly toward Saigon. Ancillary roads, pipelines, and supply caches were established leading across the mountains from Laos into the highlands and other key areas.

In early January 1975, the opening salvos of the 1975-76 North Vietnamese campaign for total victory came in Phuoc Long province. The airstrip at Song Be, less than 100 miles north of Saigon, was shelled and rendered untenable when communist forces occupied nearby dominating terrain. Land lines of communication to Phuoc Long province had been previously cut off, forcing the garrison to rely on helicopters, light aircraft, and parachutes for resupply. RVNAF's mobile general reserve consisted solely of the Airborne and Marine divisions, and they were already committed in the northern provinces. When the provincial capital fell on January 7, President Thieu reluctantly wrote off the entire province. Similar losses had occurred before, but the significance of the Phuoc Long battle was threefold: the United States did not reintroduce its airpower and made no effort to contest that flagrant violation of the Paris Agreement, indicating that it would not intervene in the future; the

Political Bureau in Hanoi approved plans calling for a two-year campaign to seize South Vietnam; and the people of South Vietnam, who
had loyally supported the government, lost faith in their political
and military leaders and their ability to defend the Republic.

The North Vietnamese leaders next turned their attention to
Ban Me Thuot, an important population center south of the Kontum-
Pleiku plateau in the central highlands. Surmising that the South
Vietnamese defenders would anticipate an attack on Kontum or
Pleiku, North Vietnamese General Van Tien Dung directed elaborate
feints at those two cities while secretly massing his forces for an
overwhelming assault on Ban Me Thuot. After a two-day battle in
which sapper units were the precursor and armored columns the decisive arm, Ban Me Thuot fell.

President Thieu authorized the evacuation of Kontum and
Pleiku presumably to counterattack Ban Me Thuot, but his regional
commander ordered a withdrawal to the coast. That withdrawal
proved to be a debacle. Of the 60,000 troops that set out, only about
one-third reached the coast. The regional commander, General
Pham Van Phu, quickly departed to set up a new headquarters far
to the rear. South Vietnamese aircraft mistakenly attacked friendly
troop units. Downed bridges and other obstacles on the long, restricted road were not repaired or removed in time. Panic spread
among the populace and among the soldiers who saw that no provi-
sions had been made to evacuate their families. The rural and popular forces were not included in the hasty plans for withdrawal, and
they too panicked. The refugee-crowded road eliminated what little
mobility the military units might have possessed and presented lucrative targets for the enemy.

If Phuoc Long had not made it clear that the United States had
abandoned its ally, the tragedies of Ban Me Thuot, Kontum, and
Pleiku now made it obvious. Any vestige of faith that might have remained in Thieu's government and forces disappeared.

Conflicting orders and vacillation on the part of President
Thieu contributed significantly to the loss of Hue and Da Nang shortly after the central highlands fell. Those two cities toppled virtually
without a fight, and once again the roads were clogged with refugees.

Despite some valiant resistance by a few ARVN units, the combined arms forces of the NVA converged on the capital from the
northeast and west. The fall of Saigon was imminent.

In early April President Ford announced the beginning of "Operation Babylift" in which orphan children were flown from Vietnam
to the United States. On April 12, a few days after Cambodian Premier Lon Nol fell, Marine helicopters lifted the last of the official
Americans from Phnom Penh. Eighteen days later the helicopter
evacuation from Saigon was completed for Ambassador Martin's

staff and many select Vietnamese who had worked with or for the Americans. The embassy was already penetrated by looters as the last helicopter took off. Saigon fell. Guenter Lewy expressed the situation quite accurately: "The final defeat of South Vietnam had been brought about by a vast North Vietnamese army, equipped with the most modern heavy weapons, and not by a revolutionary uprising of the people."[5]

Although much of the rest of Asia had expressed approbation regarding American withdrawal and the formal cessation of hostilities in Vietnam, they also developed a feeling of unease regarding the direction of American policy in Asia. The fall of South Vietnam and the humiliating exodus of the remaining American diplomatic community in 1975 projected the image of a nation with neither the will nor the ability to influence events in Asia. The petrification of America in the face of communist challenge in Angola reinforced this perception. So too did the subsequent depletion of U.S. force posture in Asia and the Pacific. The last U.S. military aircraft departed Thailand in late 1975, and the U.S. Military Assistance Command in Thailand was dissolved a few months later. In 1976 a U.S. carrier task force was withdrawn from the Western Pacific and the force level west of Hawaii was reduced to 132,000—the lowest since 1941.[6] In 1976 Admiral Holloway, then Chief of Naval Operations, testified before Congress that the U.S. Seventh Fleet could enter the Sea of Japan only at the sufferance of the Soviets. In 1977 President Carter announced the planned withdrawal of U.S. ground forces from South Korea. A year later the late General George Brown, Chairman of the Joint Chiefs of Staff, shocked concerned Asian leaders with the following statement:

> At current levels of force structure, war in Europe
> would require the great preponderance of US general
> purpose forces. Deployment of a significant portion
> of the Pacific Command's naval resources to the
> Atlantic may be required. If this were to occur, con-
> trol of the seas between the continental United States
> and Hawaii could be maintained, as could the sea lanes
> between Alaska and the Lower Forty-Eight. However,
> broad sea control beyond those lanes would be a diffi-
> cult challenge. Forces of all Services available for
> other contingencies and crises—for example, as in the
> Middle East or on the Korean peninsula—would be
> seriously reduced.[7]

This so-called "swing strategy" was widely interpreted as further evidence of American abandonment of Asia. By the late

1970s the United States had thus given the impression, intended or not, that the withdrawal announced at Guam in 1969, designed to contend with overinvolvement in the internal affairs of one Asian country, had become a withdrawal from Asia across the board, even in the face of external aggression as a result of a growing Soviet buildup in Asia. The actual and perceived U.S. withdrawal from Asia in the wake of Vietnam had created a void, into which the Soviet Union was now prepared to move.

The Soviet Union had begun to entertain hope of seriously ex- tending its influence in Southeast Asia at least as early as 1969, when Brezhnev proposed the creation of a collective security sys- tem to guarantee a zone of peace and security in Southeast Asia. The approach was widely seen in Asia as an attempt to increase Soviet influence at U.S. expense. It would mean, for example, either the removal of U.S. military forces in the region or the in- troduction of a comparable Soviet presence to "guarantee" the peace. Outside of Indochina it was an effort doomed to failure. The mem- bers of the Association of Southeast Asian Nations (ASEAN) were already nervous about American "staying power" in Asia and saw nothing good in the "guarantee" of the patron state of an aggressive North Vietnam.

Undeterred, the Soviets sought and gained the ability to influ- ence regional events through a foothold in Vietnam. The American bombing of North Vietnam had provided the rationale for increased Soviet assistance to Hanoi in the 1960s. The Soviet Union, far better than China, could provide the antiaircraft missiles and guns to coun- ter the Americans. From 1965 on, therefore, Soviet aid and the Soviet presence in North Vietnam increased dramatically. By the time of the U.S. withdrawal from Vietnam the Soviets were well es- tablished. Soviet arms transfers to the North exceeded those of the United States to the South in 1974 and 1975, a fact that not only en- hanced DRV war-making potential, but also helped crystallize the DRV assessment of superpower intentions in reaction to its planned assault on South Vietnam. The message was clear—while the United States was prepared to abandon its ally in Vietnam, the USSR would do no such thing. In April 1975, this assessment proved absolutely correct, for that month witnessed not only the 17-division DRV at- tack to overwhelm South Vietnam, but also the largest peacetime maneuver by any navy in history. With 220 ships and 450 aircraft on worldwide exercises, the Soviets kept the U.S. Navy particularly busy, while Soviet-built tanks rumbled onto the streets of Saigon.[8] Later in 1975, the Soviets began bringing considerable air and in- telligence assets into Laos, while remaining U.S. forces in Thailand departed. As the level of Soviet economic aid to Laos and Vietnam increased, it was commonly recognized that these states were rapidly becoming part of a new Soviet sphere of influence in Southeast Asia.

These developments created a severe problem for Thailand and Cambodia. They left on their very doorstep an aggressive and militarily superior Vietnam, supported by an ambitious and opportunistic Soviet Union, with little or no prospect of outside assistance in case of an emergency. Under these circumstances, and despite their diametrically opposing social, economic, and political systems, both the Thais and Cambodians looked to China. In this manner they hoped to preserve their independent status by deterring aggression from Soviet-supported Vietnam. By seeking accommodation and informal alliance with nearby forces rather than problematic forces 10,000 miles away, both nations were being drawn into the new web of great power competition in Southeast Asia, competition from which the United States was noticeably absent.

Tension in Indochina after the fall of South Vietnam favored the continued growth of Soviet influence in the area. Both the Vietnamese invasion of Cambodia and the Chinese attack on North Vietnam expanded the Soviet role. In November 1978 Vietnam and the Soviet Union signed a Treaty of Friendship and Cooperation, in which each side agreed, in case either party were attacked or threatened with attack, to consult with each other with a view toward eliminating the threat and taking appropriate measures to safeguard their peace and security. Armed with this assurance, Vietnam attacked Cambodia the following month. Even when China retaliated by attacking and temporarily occupying the five northern provinces of Vietnam in 1979, the treaty served notice that there were limits to the Chinese advance. Those limits were reinforced by the presence of at least ten ships of the Soviet Pacific Fleet assisted by reconnaissance flights by TU-95 Bear aircraft over the South China Sea.

This Soviet assistance, as well as that provided earlier, capitalized on the fears of Vietnamese leaders who had experienced a lifetime of war. Their decision to provide fueling stops, then reconnaissance and transport facilities, and finally electronic and logistic air and naval bases was not unusual if taken in this light. The only countervening ideal in the Vietnamese revolutionary movement was that of independence, yet as indicated in 1977 by the name change of "Democratic" to "Socialist" Republic of Vietnam, this factor appears to have had less significance in Vietnamese calculations. And so as the world entered the 1980s, Soviet air and naval forces were permanently ensconced in the former U.S. bases at Da Nang and Cam Ranh Bay, and were making more frequent port calls in neighboring Kampuchea (Cambodia).

Southeast Asia was not the only area where the significance of the American defeat in Vietnam was being digested. In Northeast Asia, where the physical presence and sometimes conflicting interests of China, Japan, the United States, and the USSR intersected, there was grave consternation among growing numbers of Japanese, Koreans, Taiwanese, and Chinese. Since World War II, the United States had been seen as the paramount strategic power not just in Asia but in the world. American military strength in Asia, while not omnipotent in every situation, had always been a factor to be reckoned with, and reckoned with heavily. Now, at the very time U.S. strategic superiority was being questioned, the United States seemed to be abandoning the region. U.S. foreign policy was dominated by concerns over the strategic balance, the weakness of NATO, Mideast oil supplies, and Soviet-Cuban-supported socialist takeovers in Africa and Latin America. East Asia was largely perceived as a backwater of U.S. interest, still seen by Americans largely through the lens of defeat in Vietnam. All Asia watched as America distanced itself from the region, while Soviet power expanded—methodically and ominously.

Ironically, one of the first nations to express concern regarding the diminished U.S. position in Asia had witnessed the strongest anti-Vietnam War protests in the 1960s. Japan had experienced violent demonstrations protesting the war in Vietnam as well as the U.S.-Japanese Mutual Security Treaty. As the decade of the 1970s progressed, however, growing Soviet power was increasingly used in an attempt to coerce Japan into accommodation with Moscow's ambitions in Asia. Soviet naval and air demonstrations increased methodically. Naval ship transits of the Tsushima, Soya, and Tsugaru straits increased from a level of 300 in 1978 to 340 in 1982. Flights of military aircraft approaching Japan increased from 160 in 1975 to nearly 240 in 1982, during which time there were eight violations of Japanese air space. Many of these were so-called "Tokyo Express" flights and were apparently designed to impress the Japanese regarding Soviet capability to reach their capital city. In reaction to these flights, Japanese scrambles rose from under 300 annually in the mid-1970s to over 900 in 1981. Another Soviet military irritant was the closure of sea areas to Japanese navigation and fishing vessels. In the Sea of Okhotsk there were 2 declared closures for missile firings in 1976, 8 in 1977, 16 in 1978, and 39 in 1979. Closures off Japan's Northern Islands (Soviet held) rose from 2 in 1978 to 15 in 1979.[9]

Faced with this activity on its very doorstep, the Japanese naturally looked to the United States for reassurance. Yet in the world of the mid-1970s, that reassurance was not convincing. Public opinion polls in 1976 revealed that 56 percent of the Japanese people believed that the United States would not assist Japan in an emergency. The Japanese government, meanwhile, was treading a very delicate foreign policy line, labeled "equidistance" from the major world powers. In seeking to mollify the expanding Soviets and induce them to a measure of cooperation, Japan appeared to be treating them on a basis no less favorable than that accorded other countries, including China, and, some thought, the United States.

This potential for Japanese accommodation was made all the more cogent by what was happening in Korea. Long considered its first line of defense by Japan, the avowed intention of the United States to withdraw its ground combat troops from Korea was supported by no one in Japan. In fact, most aware Japanese shared increasing South Korean concern about the security of the peninsula.

From a Korean viewpoint, the American defeat in Vietnam and subsequent announced intention to withdraw its Second Division and supporting units was something they felt they had to live with, but did not like a bit. Besides the increasingly belligerent tone of Kim Il-Sung, South Korea had to consider the possibility of that North Korean leader attempting to follow the recent example of North Vietnam in his lifelong bid for total power in Korea. There was also fear that North Korea might choose to attack as soon as the Americans withdrew, just as they had in 1950. This view was reinforced by the very important fact that time was no longer on the North Korean side. South Korea, through determination and hard work, had pulled itself up by its bootstraps and was in the midst of an economic boom paralleled only by the Japanese experience a few years earlier. By the mid-1970s South Korea had twice the population and three times the GNP of North Korea, and the gap was growing. This trend was beginning to affect the considerable North Korean military lead, as can be seen from Figure 2. While the South Korean buildup would not redress the balance on the peninsula for several years, the long-term message was unmistakable—South Korea had the potential, in the long run, to equal if not surpass North Korea in military power. The irony of this conclusion was that rather than reducing anxieties, it raised the specter that North Korea might attack before such a possibility could eventuate.

Across the Yellow Sea, the People's Republic of China (PRC) also appeared nervous about the correlation of forces in the region. Chinese leaders openly declared the inevitability of world war. In addition, they pointed to Soviet encirclement of China highlighted by the Soviet buildup on their northern border and the growing Soviet relationship with Vietnam to their south. They began publicly to castigate the Soviets for seeking hegemony in Asia and at the same time expressed increasing concern over the direction of American policy in Asia, especially with regard to the decreased American military presence.

Elsewhere in Northeast Asia, Taiwan felt the pressure. Long relying on U.S. assurances for its security, Taiwanese joined the rest of Northeast Asia in expressing reservations about the drawdown of U.S. forces in the Western Pacific. The fact that the U.S. Military Assistance Advisory Group in Taiwan was continuously decreasing in size accentuated their wariness of America as an ally, even before the United States terminated diplomatic relations in 1979.

FIGURE 2

Korean Defense Expenditures

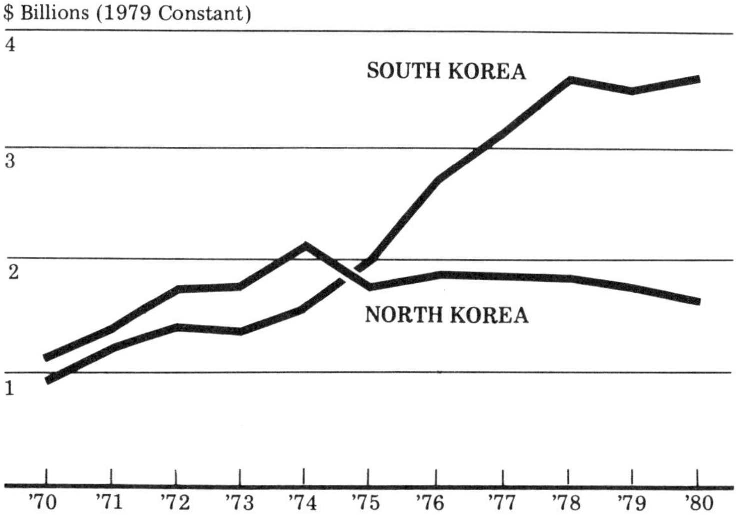

Source: U.S. Arms Control and Disarmament Agency, World Military Expenditures and Arms Transfers, 1982.

Asian concerns regarding American capabilities and intentions were, of course, a reflection of a real withdrawal of substantial military assets from Asia in the wake of Vietnam. They were also related to U.S. economic and military weakness created in large part by its Vietnam involvement. The war in Southeast Asia drained the national treasury in general and the defense establishment in particular at the very time the Soviets were improving their strategic and general purpose forces and their ability to project power worldwide. As can be seen in Figure 3, Soviet annual military expenditures began to surpass those of the United States in 1972, the last full year of U.S. participation in the war. Baseline American expenditures, excluding costs associated with the war in Southeast Asia, were already below those of the Soviet Union in 1968.

FIGURE 3

U.S. and Soviet Military Expenditures

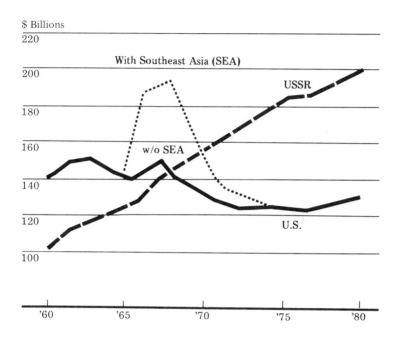

Source: Department of Defense, Annual Report of the Secretary of Defense (Washington, D.C.: U.S. Government Printing Office, 1982).

The cumulative impact of allocating defense dollars, estimated as high as $300 billion, to Southeast Asia rather than to the maintenance and improvement of American forces left the American military seriously weakened and straining to maintain its credibility to meet worldwide commitments as the nation entered the 1970s. The loss of strategic superiority announced by Secretary of Defense Caspar Weinberger and the "window of vulnerability," which became well-recognized in the 1980s, was very much a function of the Vietnam dollar drain. Strategic forces, mobile forces, nuclear forces, and overall U.S. military readiness all suffered. The profligate nature of America's struggle in Vietnam also contributed directly to the adverse trend in the conventional balance of power in Europe and Asia. For example, by the 1980s the Warsaw Pact had twice the combat aircraft in Europe as NATO, three times the tanks, antitank guided missile launchers, and artillery, and over three times the armored vehicles. The resultant military demands on American resources exerted intense pressure to reduce the American presence in Asia. The very fact that Vietnam was identified as a losing cause in Asia further fueled the withdrawal.

A final consequence of America's defeat in Vietnam was the void created in Vietnam itself by our precipitate withdrawal. The United States had developed at Cam Ranh Bay one of the most outstanding naval and air facilities in all of Asia. The airfields at Da Nang were similarly among the very best. It was no wonder, then, when South Vietnam fell in 1975, that the Soviet Union cast covetous eyes on these and other former U.S. military installations in Vietnam.

The Soviet Pacific Fleet was the principal beneficiary. Despite recent modernization and improved ocean-going capabilities, the fleet still faced three serious problems. First, its movements were severely restricted during winter by an immense ice sheet covering Petropavlosk and the Sea of Okhotsk. Second, its routes of entry and egress from the seas of Japan and Okhotsk were subject to possible detection and closure at the various choke points. Finally, the fleet faced immense difficulties in projecting power to distant areas, particularly in Asia where naval facilities and port visits were nearly universally denied. It came as a great boon to Admiral Gorshkov, therefore, when it became possible to use vacated American facilities in Vietnam. And these facilities did become available, gradually at first, but available.

Four days after the Chinese attack on northern Vietnam, Soviet TU-95 Bear aircraft began reconnaissance flights over the South China Sea from bases in Soviet Asia. After the Chinese withdrawal the Bears were permitted to land at Da Nang, where the Soviets had already built a communications station. Soviet transport aircraft began wide use of southern Vietnamese airfields to ferry materials, while Soviet supply ships unloaded at Da Nang and Cam Ranh. By the early 1980s, this presence had grown to a more permanent nature. Several TU-95s, numerous combat and support ships, and submarines were reported in and around Vietnamese ports and waters. These forces served Soviet purposes to constrain Chinese power projection south and eastward, to reconnoiter U.S. deployments in Southeast Asia, to demonstrate a capability for closing the strait of Malacca, and to support Soviet power projection in the Indian Ocean. By the early 1980s, the Soviet Pacific Fleet, owing in part to the use of Vietnamese ports and facilities, was able to maintain simultaneously more than 20 vessels in the Indian Ocean and 10 vessels in the South China Sea.

As Winston Churchill had warned years earlier, the Russian Bear will move with vigor whenever it finds a void, but when it finds resistance, it will desist. In Asia, in the wake of Vietnam, the USSR had found a void, or so it appeared.

NOTES

1. Public Papers of the Presidents of the United States: Richard Nixon, 1969 (Washington, D.C.: U.S. Government Printing Office, 1971), pp. 545–49.

2. Richard M. Nixon, The Pursuit of Peace, November 3, 1969, in Department of State, Pub. #8502.

3. Ibid.

4. William C. Westmoreland, A Soldier Reports (New York: Doubleday, 1976), p. 396.

5. Guenter Lewy, America in Vietnam (New York: Oxford University Press, 1978), p. 215.

6. For a succinct expression of concern regarding this state of affairs, see Admiral Maurice Weisner, Commander-in-Chief Pacific, "The U.S. Military Posture in Asia and the Pacific," Strategic Review, Summer 1978.

7. JCS Statement, "U.S. Military Posture for 1979," 1978.

8. Japanese Defense Agency, Defense of Japan, 1980.

9. Japanese Defense Agency, Defense of Japan, 1976–1982; and Research Institute for Peace and Security, Asian Security 1980.

PART II:
THE PRESENT
SITUATION

4

New Correlations of
Power Emerge

Although in the late 1970s Americans tended to favor withdrawal from East Asia, there were countervailing forces at work impelling America to remain. Three distinct but related changes in the strategic environment of East Asia shook U.S. complacency regarding its policy direction. The first and primary factor in these changes pertained to Soviet capabilities and intentions. The second was the Sino-Soviet split, and the third the increased military importance of the Pacific.

SOVIET EXPANSIONISM

Although U.S. attention to Soviet expansion had focused largely on Europe and certain less-developed countries in Africa and the Mid-East, the record shows that Asia has long been and continues to be an area of prime Soviet strategic interest. Wherever the U.S. withdrawal left a vacuum of power, the Soviets were prepared to fill it. This phenomenon should come as no surprise to students of Russian history, but for some American government officials it came as quite a shock.

Soviet expansion into Asia had its roots in seventeenth-century Tzarist Russia. Russian settlers were encouraged eastward to claim underpopulated regions, and by the end of the century many of them had reached the Pacific. Subsequent expansion brought Russia into direct conflict with a weakened China, with the resultant loss of Chinese suzerainty over huge tracts of territory along the Pacific. Two "unequal" treaties particularly bothersome to the Chinese were the Treaty of Aigun in 1858, whereby China lost

598,000 square kilometers above the Amur River to Russia, and the Treaty of Peking in 1860, by which Russia gained 400,000 square kilometers including the area of its present-day Maritime Provinces. Russia again sought a piece of the Chinese pie when it occupied Manchuria at the beginning of this century, but was forced to withdraw after its defeat by Japan in 1905.

The successors to the Tzars followed a similarly expansionist policy. Although constrained by Japanese power for a generation, they were to seek and exploit opportunities when the time came. In 1941, faced with Nazi Germany on the west and militaristic Japan on the east, the Soviets gladly negotiated a five-year nonaggression treaty with Japan. After benefiting the USSR throughout the war, the treaty was cast aside in 1945 when Japanese and German power no longer constrained Soviet ambitions. On August 9, 1945, just three days after Hiroshima and six days before the end of the Pacific war, the Soviets struck—1.6 million strong. In less than a week they seized Manchuria, southern Sakhalin Island, and the northern half of Korea, pressing their attacks even after Japan had officially surrendered. They occupied the Kuriles in accordance with the Yalta Agreement, and exerted unsuccessful pressure on both Truman and MacArthur to occupy a portion of Hokkaido. Following the war, the Soviets evacuated Manchuria after stripping it of industrial potential. Like a similar Soviet move from Iran in 1946, the evacuation was executed to preclude the possibility of a strong U.S. reaction, which in the case of China was made all the more believable due to close American ties with Chiang Kai-shek, not to mention the presence of American military personnel in China.

At that time the three-century-old Russian expansion again entered a consolidation phase, punctuated by less risky exploitation of opportune targets thought not likely to evoke a U.S. reaction. One such place was Korea. In June 1950, North Korea launched an all-out attack on South Korea with artillery and tanks provided by the USSR and with a senior officer corps trained by the Soviets. Again, it took a countervailing force, this time a strong U.S. contingent under U.N. command, to stem the imperialistic Soviet-supported effort. Undeterred, the Soviets sought to extend influence by military assistance to Indonesia. Exploiting Indonesian government efforts to consolidate authority over its 10,000 islands and capitalizing on the prevalent anti-Chinese sentiment, the USSR poured over a billion dollars of military aid into Indonesia under the Sukarno regime. Again the effort failed. In September 1965, the Communist Party of Indonesia felt strong enough to make a grab for total power in an attempted coup in which six top Indonesian generals were assassinated. The move proved a disaster as the powerful General Suharto survived. With military backing he became president after mass killing of communists and other opposition figures in Indonesia. The new president broke off the military relationship with the distrusted Soviets, and again Russia was frustrated in its ambitions.

Thus by the mid-1970s, the Soviet Union had been frustrated in its attempts to change the face of Asia for a period of over 25 years. The fact that the Soviets did not retain Manchuria, seize Hokkaido, aid and abet successful North Korean aggression, or postulate even further claims on Asian territory or governments was in no small measure the result of countervailing American military power in the region, coupled with a national will to use that force if necessary. But in the wake of Vietnam, both American will and relative military capability were questioned in a way unmatched since 1941.

The current Soviet challenge did not begin with the Vietnam war but is, rather, a result of the overall strengthening of Soviet forces following Nikita Khrushchev's bold attempt to redress the strategic balance in 1962. The humiliation of having his ships en route to Cuba faced down on the high seas not only expedited Khrushchev's exile to the countryside, but also indelibly impressed Leonid Brezhnev never to be placed in the same position. The buildup in Asia proceeded apace with the general militarization of the Brezhnev era, accelerated to a degree by the deterioration of Sino-Soviet relations. By the time the United States appeared to be retreating from Asia in the wake of Vietnam, the Soviet Union had doubled its ground and naval forces, and substantially increased its air arm. The following quantitative trends speak for themselves:

Soviet Strength in Asia[1]

	1965	1970	1975	1980	1982
Number of divisions along Sino-Soviet border		30	43	46	51
Number of ground forces (1,000s) along Sino-Soviet border	180	200	300	450	460
Tons of naval shipping (1,000s)	700	1,000	1,200	1,520	1,600
Number of combat aircraft	1,430	1,870	2,000	2,060	2,120

These indexes of Soviet power are even more impressive when qualitative factors are considered. The U.S. reduction of force in the Western Pacific had long been justified by its considerable technological lead. Yet, as the United States reduced its military presence, the quality of Soviet military forces was dramatically improving. For example, air forces were reinforced with first-line aircraft such as the MIG-23 fighter, the MIG-27 and SU-24 fighter bombers, and the Backfire bomber. By 1980 a large number of Soviet combat aircraft were armed with missiles such as the Kingfish AS-6, with a range of over 100 miles and a speed of Mach 3.0. Over 70 Backfire bombers, with a maximum range (without refueling) of 5,700 km, threatened U.S. forces as far from Soviet Asia as Guam and Hawaii. In their first such action in the Pacific, eight Backfires made simulated missile strikes against American carriers in October 1982.[2] Naval improvements were equally impressive. In 1979 alone, the aircraft carrier <u>Minsk</u>, the assault transport dock <u>Ivan Rogov</u>, and several missile-carrying cruisers and destroyers were added to the fleet. By the early 1980s over one-fourth of Soviet Pacific Fleet combat ships were equipped with missiles capable of carrying nuclear or conventional warheads. The fleet had become the largest unit of the Soviet Navy and boasted some 135 submarines, 65 of which are nuclear powered.[3]

Ground forces were also considerably enhanced, with larger numbers of T-62 tanks, BM-21 multiple rocket launchers, BMP armored infantry fighting vehicles, and 152mm self-propelled artillery pieces. In 1982 the T-72, one of the most modern Soviet tanks, was introduced. More sophisticated surface-to-air missiles, helicopter gunships, and troop-carrying helicopters have further extended ground force capabilities.

It should be noted that many Americans deride Soviet military weapons and equipment as being bulky, unsophisticated, and seriously lacking in built-in creature comforts. These criticisms have some basis in fact, but there are other important considerations. Soviet weapons and equipment are generally rugged and serviceable. First-line troops are well-trained in their employment. The degree of commonality achieved by the Soviet-Warsaw Pact in weapons and equipment is the envy of NATO, where national pride and economic-employment considerations have resulted in numerous weapons systems, which defy international logistic support or cross-servicing. Further, the Soviets have established vast weapons and equipment inventories and the means for continuing their production.

The years after Vietnam also saw the development in Asia of an immense Soviet strategic capability. While Petropavlosk, on the Kamchatka peninsula, and Vladivostok had previously based Yankee, Hotel, and Golf-class strategic submarines, the limited missile range of these submarines necessitated their deployment to waters off the West Coast to be within striking distance of the United States. By 1980, however, the Soviet Union had deployed some ten Delta-class ballistic missile submarines, which, from their Asian home waters, could strike nearly anywhere in the continental

United States. In addition, the Soviet SS-20 mobile intermediate range ballistic missile, which has caused considerable consternation among the NATO allies, made its first appearance in Soviet Asia. By 1983 it was estimated that between one-fourth and one-third of the entire Soviet arsenal of over 300 SS-20s were deployed in the region.[4] Armed with a 5,000 km MIRVed warhead with three reentry vehicles each, the SS-20 put all of Northeast Asia as well as the vital U.S. bases in the Philippines and Guam at risk. Coupled with the even greater range of the nuclear capable Backfire bomber, and the older but increasingly active TU-95 Bear bomber, the strategic coverage of Soviet forces in Asia and the Pacific was a quantum leap forward from that which prevailed during the Vietnam war. An entirely new strategic picture had emerged from that of a decade earlier.

THE SINO-SOVIET SPLIT

The second great strategic alteration in Asia is, of course, Chinese recognition of and reaction to Soviet military power. Had a monolithic Soviet-dominated communist bloc linking the population and resources of China and the USSR emerged at the time of American disengagement from Asia the results would have been catastrophic. Not only Indochina, but all of Southeast Asia, Japan, and South Korea would have had to "accommodate" to the new correlation of forces. Among the ASEAN countries, insurgencies, aided and abetted by China, possibly in collusion with Hanoi and the Kremlin, could have resulted in temporary seizures of power by communist revolutionaries who then could appeal to Moscow for external support in rendering their "revolutions" irreversible. This was the pattern in Mongolia in 1921 and had certain similarities to Afghanistan in 1979. It would be no less a threat if isolated Southeast Asian states were to face the overwhelming combined capabilities of a Sino-Soviet bloc seeking to foster and exploit instability within their borders. In Northeast Asia the results would likely have been equally disastrous. North Korea would have been emboldened, as it was in 1950, by the prospects of both Soviet and Chinese support in its efforts to conquer the South by force. Finally Japan, isolated and threatened by the forces of aggression, would likely have been compelled to choose between nuclear militarization or Finlandization with the added feature of having its industrial might expected to service the needs of the mighty communist empire. None of these outcomes, in no small measure because of the Sino-Soviet split, has eventuated. Instead, the image of a monolithic Sino-Soviet empire dominating the heartland of the Eurasian land mass has been replaced by the reality of independent Asian nations whose interests accord closely with those of the United States, and whose behavior enhances the prospects for peace and stability in Asia and the world as a whole.

The Chinese realignment has also had a profound impact on both Soviet and American strategic calculations. On the Soviet side it has meant the allocation of one-fourth of all combat ground and air power, and nearly one-third of all naval power to Asia, with the vast majority of these assets oriented toward China. Similar to NATO forces in the West, Chinese forces in the East are seen by the USSR as constraining its military power and potential political influence. Soviet planners well know that lack of eastern pressure in 1941 enabled Marshall Greshko to transfer 25 crack Siberian divisions to save Moscow from Wehrmacht attacks less than 25 miles from the city. Transfer of similar forces under circumstances of Sino-Soviet hostility would be extremely risky, and therefore of considerable strategic consequence to the United States and NATO. The Soviets must also be concerned about developing Chinese nuclear programs, which, during the early 1980s saw the launching of the Chinese CSS 4 ICBM and the submarine-launched CSS N3 IRBM, as well as continued nuclear weapons testing.

From an American viewpoint, the Sino-Soviet split, although slow to be recognized and even slower to be integrated into East Asian policy, created conditions under which rapprochement with China, with all its strategic implications, became possible. First were the enormous benefits of the Soviet allocation of military resources in the vicinity of China—forces that could otherwise have reinforced already burgeoning Soviet efforts to control Eastern Europe, threaten NATO, render irreversible communist coups in developing nations, and threaten American strategic forces and lines of communications. Second, the United States moved from a strategy based on an assumed need to be able to fight $2\frac{1}{2}$ wars simultaneously to a $1\frac{1}{2}$ war strategy. This change was in large part due to recognition that it no longer needed to configure forces based on a contingency involving war with China. Third, the related improvement in U.S.-Chinese relations promised a political realignment in Asia unparalleled in a generation. It renewed U.S. interest in Asia, formed the background for improved Chinese relations with Japan, Thailand, and other states in the region, and promised even greater rewards in the form of closer Western participation in the future progress of one-quarter of the human race.

There has been a great deal of talk in recent years which questions the permanence, or even the reality, of these strategic benefits. The thrust of the discussion is that the Sino-Soviet split may be at an end, and that the consequent advantages supposedly accruing to the United States are either nonexistent or in jeopardy. The record of Sino-Soviet diplomatic moves is frequently used to support this conclusion. In March 1982 Soviet President Leonid Brezhnev attempted to break the ice in a speech at Tashkent in which he offered to resume border talks with the Chinese, and intimated Soviet readiness to reestablish economic, scientific, and cultural ties in the context of socialist solidarity. He specifically emphasized Soviet opposition to a two-China policy, stating that the USSR fully recognizes Beijing's sovereignty over Taiwan. Coming at a time of Chinese-American tension over continued U.S. arms sales to Taiwan, the conciliatory tone of Brezhnev's remarks could not be interpreted other than seizing a perceived opportunity to reassert Soviet influence in China at U.S. expense.

Former Chinese Foreign Minister Huang Hua responded by citing Brezhnev's remarks as a crude attempt to exploit Chinese-American differences. He stated that the Chinese wanted deeds, not words, and demanded specifically that the Soviets reduce their forces along China's northern border, cease support for Vietnam's occupation of Kampuchea, and stop its own aggression in Afghanistan. Nevertheless, rumors of possible Sino-Soviet rapprochement continued to spread. Chinese anti-Soviet rhetoric began to decline and on September 1, 1982, at the opening of the Twelfth Chinese Communist Party Congress, General Secretary Hu Yaobang went so far as to mention the "possibility of Sino-Soviet normalization." Brezhnev appeared to respond to this overture in a speech at Baku, stating that he considered normalization with China important for the future of Asia. In October, Soviet Deputy Foreign Minister Leonid Ilyichev visited Beijing for the first round of high-level consultations since before the invasion of Afghanistan nearly three years earlier. Later that month Brezhnev pledged to an assembly of Soviet generals that Moscow would do all that it could to improve relations with China, so as to enable the Soviet military to better position itself to contend with the West. In November China conveyed a message on the occasion of the anniversary of the Bolshevik revolution stating it is "genuinely striving to remove all obstacles which stand in the way of normalizing Sino-Soviet relations." Later that month Huang Hua was in Moscow for the funeral of Brezhnev, whom he described as "an all-around statesman." He took the opportunity to talk with Andrei Gromyko in the first meeting of Chinese and Soviet foreign ministers since 1969. A second round of consultations at the vice foreign ministerial level took place in Moscow in March 1983. Although the agenda was open-ended, discussion reportedly centered on border problems and the possibility of cultural, scientific, educational, and increased economic exchanges, and on a tripling of the very low level of bilateral trade. Later in 1983, additional discussions took place in Beijing.

The wide-ranging nature of the talks has led many American officials to question the basic premise upon which Sino-American relations developed—the antagonism between Moscow and Beijing. There are genuine reasons on both sides for rapprochement, not the least of which is the sheer cost of maintaining huge forces oriented against each other along their 4,000-mile border. Faced with domestic economic malaise and increased costs of projecting power globally, the USSR may well be interested in economizing its military and financial resources for higher priority areas. For its part, China has put economic modernization at the top of its agenda and could initiate a policy of reducing support for some of its 66 divisions along the border in order to allocate more of its scarce financial resources to economic development. In fact, the general drawdown in the People's Liberation Army (PLA) strength, which began in 1982, may indicate implementation of this very policy. Furthermore, by claiming that Soviet strength along its border totals a million men rather than the 460,000 really there, the Chinese leave room for exaggerating the size of any Soviet withdrawals that might take place in the context of rapprochement.

Economic relations also offer some prospect for accommodation. Soviet hints of economic and scientific assistance may appear attractive to certain sectors in China. Most Chinese factories, for example, were built to Soviet specifications, and there are those in China who believe modernization and expansion of this existing plant and equipment in conjunction with Soviet trade and investment would suit China's needs better than any opening to the West. Despite its superiority, Western technology has been difficult for the Chinese to absorb, leading some to the conclusion that modernization in concert with the West is no more likely to succeed than the opposite extreme of backyard furnaces during the Great Leap Forward. This attitude was reinforced by Chinese perception of U.S. discrimination against them in scientific and technological transfers, although that discrimination appeared to be lessening by mid-1983 when many restrictions were relaxed.

Another issue for discussion, though less amenable to immediate solution, is the territorial issue. The million square kilometers occupied by Russia as a result of what the Chinese label "unequal treaties" of the nineteenth century are still a point of contention. While the Chinese have renounced current claims for all but a small portion of this territory, they have demanded Soviet recognition that the land was illegally acquired. In traditional Chinese negotiating practice, such principles are typically established at the outset of talks so that later practical decisions may be related back to them. (This was the case with Taiwan, for example.) Thus the implication is clear that China seeks some major

Soviet concessions. Given the negative mind-set of current Soviet leaders toward territorial compromise with any nation whatsoever, it is likely that this issue will remain a problem in Sino-Soviet relations, though limited progress may be made.

Just as any assessment of Sino-Soviet relations would be remiss if it did not take into account the possibilities for normalization, it is important to reiterate that there are deep and persuasive differences dividing the two communist giants. The roots of their antagonism have been explained in several works.[5] Suffice it to repeat here that the areas for potential progress already cited are by no means assured. Firstly, Soviet forces along China's northern border continue to exceed those necessary for self-defense, and are improving in quality at a rapid rate. The deployment of modern fighter bombers and SS-20 missiles, both of which have immense destructive potential vis-à-vis China, proceeded unabated during the period of recent talks. Moreover, the territorial question could become inflamed at any time. Secondly, Soviet ability to improve the Chinese economy pales in comparison to that of Japan and the United States. It would be most difficult for the USSR, already heavily committed to over $20 billion annually in foreign aid, to compete effectively with the Japanese and Americans. For example, in December 1981 Japan and the PRC signed a $1.38 billion industrial aid package, which alone was greater than Soviet aid to all of East Asia for the entire year. And so, the message is clear with China as it is with the rest of East Asia—let the USSR compete economically; the Soviet worker has nothing to lose but his chains. Thirdly, Soviet foreign policy is still seen in Beijing, with good reason, as serving expansionist ambitions, or "hegemony" as the Chinese call it. China insists that as a precondition for normalization the Soviets withdraw from Afghanistan, cease its support for the Vietnamese occupation of Kampuchea, and withdraw its forces from Mongolia. Perhaps most basic to bilateral problems, however, is Soviet incapacity to tolerate independent and even critical judgment from a nation espousing the same communist ideology that provides the rationale for the sacrifices of so many Soviet citizens. The cry of the Revolution "All power to the Soviets" is widely interpreted within the empire as all power to the Soviet Union, and this the Chinese cannot accept. The ideological affinity once ascribed to Sino-Soviet relations is now recognized as a myth, with divergent interpretations of communist dogma more likely to lead to conflict than cooperation. Thus in April 1980 the PRC terminated its 30-year-old Treaty of Friendship, Alliance, and Mutual Assistance with the USSR, formally ending the era of "unshakable unity of the communist camp."

All this does not mean that the Soviet side will not attempt to play the China card for all that it is worth. The USSR has a clear if not paramount interest in detaching China from a close relationship with the United States. If Moscow can split Washington from Beijing at the same time as it helps splinter the Atlantic Alliance, it will have succeeded in isolating the United States in a way this country has not experienced since 1939. Thus the main outlines of Soviet strategy are clear. The gut question for the United States is how to react. In addressing this issue the United States enjoys the advantage of recognizing the truly independent status of China, something the USSR acknowledges in principle but abhors in practice. The pragmatism of Deng Xioping and other Chinese leaders may be expected to lead to agreements with the Soviet Union in limited areas where such agreements are possible. At the same time, as discussed in Chapter 9, that very pragmatism may be expected to lead China to seek an increasingly close relationship with the West, which has far more to offer in terms of Chinese priority goals. Just as the Sino-Soviet split, by helping redirect the underlying flow of political, economic, and social forces, was the greatest single strategic change in East Asia of the past generation, so too does cooperation between the world's most populous and most advanced nation have the potential to become the greatest strategic change of this generation. In the wake of the strong bipolar configuration of forces emerging from World War II, the emergence of China as a truly independent national civilization in close cooperation with the United States holds the prospects of unbounded potential for peace, stability, and economic progress in Asia.

THE INCREASING STRATEGIC IMPORTANCE
OF THE PACIFIC

The third and final great change affecting Asia and the Pacific and which, like the Soviet challenge and the opportunities with China, beckons America to remain and increase its role in the region, is the vastly increased strategic importance of the Pacific itself. After Pearl Harbor, and in the aftermath of World War II, it was commonly recognized that America's first line of Pacific defense was along the rim of Asia. Then for many years the intercontinental ballistic missile, coupled with the availability of bases on the periphery of European Russia, diverted attention from this previously well-recognized fact. Instead, attention was focused on superpower vulnerability to ICBMs to the point where neither could defend itself against the number, size, and deployment of such weapons.

By the late 1970s, however, military and political conditions had changed to call attention once again to the strategic importance of the Pacific. The fact is that the Pacific is the largest body of water in the world. Its depths and extensive maneuver room provide submarines an ideal environment in which to operate. With the land-based component of America's Triad increasingly vulnerable to more powerful and accurate Soviet strategic missiles, our submarine-launched ballistic missile force has greater responsibility. The new Trident-class ballistic missile submarines, scheduled for deployment in the Pacific in the 1980s, will be crucial to the maintenance of the worldwide strategic balance for at least the rest of the century. The USS <u>Ohio</u>, the first of these submarines, was deployed to Bangor, Washington in October 1982.[6]

Of similar strategic importance is the host of U.S. bases and facilities that dot the Western rim of the Pacific. Japan immediately comes to mind, looming as it does astride the principal lines of entry and egress of the Soviet Pacific Fleet between its Vladivostok base and the blue waters of the Pacific. Over 100 U.S. military facilities are located in Japan, ranging in size from the only foreign homeport for a U.S. carrier battle group, at Yokosuka, to communications stations of less than an acre. These ports, airfields, communications, and other facilities are vital not only to the defense of Japan, but that of South Korea and perhaps other areas as well. During the Korean and Vietnam wars, they provided essential logistic and general support functions for the American efforts. A Marine amphibious force in Okinawa is the largest forward-deployed air-ground unit in Asia, outside of Korea, while the three Okinawa-based squadrons of America's highest performance intercepter, the F-15, stand ready for missions in the Western Pacific.

Just as U.S. bases and facilities in Japan protect U.S. interests in Korea and other areas of the Far East, so, too, do U.S. bases in the Philippines support the security of Japan and U.S. bases in Japan. Clark Air Force Base and Subic Bay lie astride the commercial lifelines of Japan and provide it a degree of security unattainable by other means. These bases contribute significantly to American ability to project power anywhere in the region, and in the Indian Ocean as well. During the crises in Iran and Afghanistan, these bases proved to be indispensable to the support of American forces dispatched to the Arabian Sea. In fact, without them, it is doubtful the navy and marine contingents could have expeditiously deployed to the Indian Ocean in a satisfactory state of readiness. Both the timeliness and sustainability of the Middle Eastern forces depend on them. It is difficult, however, to sustain operations in the Western Indian Ocean from Philippine bases, and the search for alternatives has kept the United States busy.[7]

United States facilities in Guam have long had a strategic role in the Pacific. B-52s from Anderson Air Force Base and ballistic missile submarines from Agana provide a forward-based deterrent crucial to overall American strategy. In addition, Vice President George Bush reportedly discussed the home-porting of an aircraft carrier in Guam when he met with Governor Paul Calvo on June 29, 1981. [8]

Use of facilities in the Mariannas and Australia provide additional flexibility to American forces in the region. After agreement with the government of Australia, in early 1981, American B-52s began to use the Australian airfield at Darwin as a staging point for surveillance flights over the Indian Ocean, while facilitative assistance in both areas has been forthcoming. [9]

In all cases, U.S. bases and facilities in the Western Pacific tend both to reinforce one another and to make possible the forward-deployed force structure necessary to America's global strategy. In addition, the bases provide a deterrent to regional conflict, support U.S. political and economic objectives, and present a visible reminder of American capabilities and intentions in Asia.

It is thus impossible to overemphasize the strategic importance of the vast area extending from Siberia and the Bering Sea on the north, southward through China, Korea, and Japan to Southeast Asia, Australia, and the Indian Ocean. Its dynamic economies, friendly governments, strategic U.S. bases, and vital sea lanes all serve to sustain long-term American interests in Asia as we enter the final decades of this century of war. Consequently, the protection of this vital area from external aggression is as essential to America as it is to Asian peace and security.

Despite the vital significance of these strategic changes in Asia, the American perception of the region did not fundamentally change as a result of them. While some Americans recognized the changes and sought to alter the post-Vietnam withdrawal syndrome as a result, the prevailing American attitude remained one of reluctance with respect to continuous American involvement in Asia. Besides its identification with Vietnam, Asia never did reach the level of importance which Europe always had in American history. The cultural pull of most Americans has always been toward Europe. So are our predominant economic and security ties. During World War II, the Atlantic war took precedence over that in the Pacific, and in its wake European reconstruction received higher priority than assistance to Asia. The post-World War II military withdrawal from Asia was also more pervasive than that in Europe. Like a similar proposal nearly 30 years later, the pull-out of American ground forces from South Korea in 1949 was but a symptom of overall American priorities. So while great strategic changes in

Asia tended to draw America back to the region, they were not by themselves sufficient to reverse the post-Vietnam withdrawal syndrome. That task depended on recognition of the internal changes within East Asia itself, for while Americans fought and died in Vietnam, the winds of change were blowing across that immense region in a way that would challenge the very premise upon which the Marxist concept of history is based.

NOTES.

1. Japanese Defense Agency, Defense of Japan, 1976 and 1980-1982; and the Research Institute for Peace and Security, Asian Security, 1980.

2. The Washington Post, November 9, 1982, p. A16. The number of Backfires is given by the Department of Defense, in Soviet Military Power, 1983, pp. 53-54.

3. Soviet Military Power, 1983, pp. 53-54.

4. Ibid. See also New China News Agency, "Soviet SS-20 Buildup Serious Concern for US," in Foreign Broadcast Information Service, China, May 11, 1983. "Tokyo, Moscow to Hold Talks on Shifting of Soviet Missiles," Chicago Tribune, July 8, 1983, Sec. 1, p. 5; and Department of Defense, Soviet Military Power, 1983, pp. 51-55. It is estimated that between 1977 and 1983 some 110 SS-20s were deployed in Soviet Asia.

5. One of the earliest and most prescient accounts is that of Donald S. Zagoria, The Sino-Soviet Conflict, 1955-1961 (Princeton: Princeton University Press, 1962).

6. Facts on File, "USS Ohio Reaches Home Port at Bangor, Washington," Yearbook 1982 (New York: Facts on File).

7. Committee on Foreign Relations, United States Senate, "United States Objectives and Overseas Military Installations," April 1979, pp. 157 ff. The United States and the Philippines signed a five-year renewal of bases agreement on June 1, 1983. The agreement called for American military and economic assistance of $900 million, roughly the same as the annual support to U.S. Forces in Japan from the government of Japan.

8. Pacific Stars and Stripes, July 2, 1981.

9. Japan Times, January 7, 1981, and The Mainichi Shimbun, May 7, 1981.

5

The Pacific Era:
Free East Asian
Economic Dynamism

The final decades of the twentieth century have already been labeled the "Pacific Decades," and the twenty-first century may well come to be known as the Pacific Century. The dynamic progress so evident in East Asia today, however, did not begin to manifest itself until America had become so engrossed in Vietnam that it was unable to focus on changes taking place elsewhere in the region. Actually, the tremendous transformation of Asia from traditionally oriented, often colonially dominated nation-states with little experience in self-government, to the modernizing states of Asia today, began in a large way immediately after World War II, and was initiated in no small degree directly by contact with the West. The American role in this transformation has been described elsewhere. Suffice it to say here with respect to the two countries under American occupation in the aftermath of the war, that the Philippines was granted independence in 1946 and subsequently received American assistance in areas as diverse as management, mining, agriculture, and counterguerrilla operations; and that Japan benefited both from American-style democracy, which was interwoven into the fabric of its political and social life, and from the knowledge and skills of American technicians and economists who taught methods of increasing productivity to those charged with rebuilding a devastated economy.

But it was the people of Asia themselves who provided the motivation and talent essential to dynamic progress. Nowhere was this progress more visible than in the economic area. While American attention was riveted on Vietnam for a dozen years, the remainder of the free nations of East Asia were experiencing unprecedented economic growth. During those years, and continuing even until today, the output of goods and services produced in East Asia increased more rapidly than in any area of the world.

Japan led the way. In 1960, its gross national product totaled $35.4 billion. By 1970, that figure had reached $201.2 billion, and in 1980 it was $1.1 trillion. Japan today is the third largest economy in the world, and ranks second, ahead of the Soviet Union, in civilian goods and services produced. An island nation smaller than the state of Montana, 85 percent covered by mountains, and devoid of natural resources, Japan has come to be seen as an economic model by numerous industrialists, businessmen, governmental officials, and union leaders throughout the world.

Phenomenal economic success in Asia, however, has not been limited to Japan. Hong Kong, South Korea, Taiwan, and Singapore in particular, have exhibited amazing industrial and commercial growth. Sometimes referred to collectively as the "Gang of Four," they led the world in 1970-80 export growth as they doubled their combined share of global exports.[1] During the past five years the combined gross domestic product of Hong Kong, Korea, Taiwan, Indonesia, Thailand, the Philippines, Malaysia, and Singapore grew over three times the rate of the Organization for Economic Cooperation and Development (OECD) countries as a whole, while Japan more than doubled OECD growth. The actual growth ratios, which occurred despite a period of astronomic oil price rises, speak for themselves:

Real GDP Growth[2]

	1978	1979	1980	1981	1982	5-year average
Hong Kong	10.0	12.0	9.0	8.0	2.4	8.3
South Korea	11.3	7.1	-3.7	7.1	5.3	5.4
Taiwan	12.8	8.1	6.7	7.5	3.8	7.8
Indonesia	7.8	6.3	9.9	7.6	2.5	6.8
Thailand	10.1	6.1	5.8	6.3	4.2	6.5
Philippines	6.2	7.5	4.4	3.8	2.6	4.9
Malaysia	6.7	9.3	7.8	6.7	4.6	7.0
Singapore	8.6	9.4	10.3	10.0	6.0	8.9
Japan	5.1	5.2	4.8	3.8	3.0	4.4
OECD	4.1	3.3	.2	2.1	-0.3	1.9
United States	5.0	2.8	-0.4	+1.9	-1.7	1.5

During the period 1972-82, East Asia led every region of the world, including the oil-rich Middle East, in overall economic growth, and more than doubled the average Gross Domestic Product (GDP) growth of the world as a whole.[3]

The dynamic growth of East Asian economies is expected to continue for the foreseeable future. Chase Econometrics, for example, predicts the following economic growth rates:[4]

Percentage of Growth in Real
Gross Domestic Product

	1984	1985	1986	1987	1988
Australia	4.5	2.8	2.3	2.6	4.5
Hong Kong	7.9	6.5	4.9	5.5	4.9
Indonesia	4.4	5.6	4.7	5.4	5.9
Japan	3.9	3.4	3.7	4.1	4.4
Malaysia	6.4	6.5	6.6	6.3	6.4
Philippines	3.0	3.7	4.1	4.0	4.2
Singapore	10.6	8.4	7.3	7.7	7.2
South Korea	7.4	8.2	7.4	7.4	7.6
Taiwan	5.9	5.3	5.6	6.0	5.4
Thailand	6.1	5.9	6.1	6.0	6.1

Other leading forecasters also see strong growth in the years ahead, as shown by the following average annual real GDP growth rates:[5]

	Business International (1984–87)	Wharton Econometrics (1984–88)	Data Resources (1986–90)
Australia	4.0	3.4	3.2
Hong Kong	6.0	5.6	6.1
Indonesia	4.6	4.8	3.9
Japan	3.5	3.4	5.3
Malaysia	6.8	6.1	5.7
Philippines	3.8	4.1	5.3
Singapore	6.9	6.4	6.7
South Korea	6.6	6.4	6.0
Taiwan	5.3	6.2	6.3
Thailand	6.4	6.1	5.6

The pattern of economic growth reflected in these figures is a tribute to the ingenuity, skill, resources, management, and interdependence of the nations of East Asia. Their success is a vindication of the principles of increased productivity and comparative advantage inherent in international trade. During the past ten years, for example, the value of East Asian trade has grown some 300 percent, while its share of total world trade rose from 12 to 16 percent.[6] The commercial links joining the region are so strong that

observers as diverse as Max Lerner and Henry Kissinger have
expressed the view that the economic dynamism and long-term potential of the region is so great that the Pacific nations may well
lead the world into the twenty-first century.[7] Indeed, the concept
of a Pacific Basin community of nations with extensive interchange
of goods and ideas has already raised the possibility that modern-
day Pacific nations may be in the early stages of a renaissance
comparable to that of the city states of the Mediterranean during
the European renaissance six centuries earlier.

Before considering the significance of these developments for
the United States, it is well to consider the causes of the dynamic,
both from the point of view of its permanence and from its effects
on the future of the region. It is possible to distinguish at least six
persistent underlying reasons for the great progress of East Asia
today.

First is the people. According to United Nations statistics,
the rate of increase in the population growth in Asia has dropped to
a manageable figure of 1.65 percent annually, which is well below
its present economic growth rates. This pattern is expected to continue, and the highest per capita income growth of any region in the
world is forecast for the foreseeable future.[8] Yet the population,
estimated at 1.7 billion, is the world's largest, providing an ample
labor supply in support of its growing economies.[9]

The education and skill levels of East Asia's labor supply
varies considerably in and between countries, but this fact, as well
as a further division of labor among agricultural, industrial, artis-
tic, and service workers, has served to promote rather than inhibit
regional commerce. Furthermore, during the past 10 years, labor
productivity has increased tremendously through the region, led by
an 83 percent increase in labor output per hour in the major manufacturing industries of Japan.[10] Japanese educational levels are
today higher than those of any other nation except the United States,
and there are more Japanese than Americans studying engineering,
a key to future industrial development. The region as a whole is
experiencing a boom in education, with noncommunist East Asia
having more children in either primary or secondary schools than
Africa, Latin America, and Europe combined, and more college
and university students than any region except North America. Only
China has lagged in this regard. According to UN figures, China has
only 104 students in higher education per 100,000 population, compared to over 200 in Indonesia and Malaysia, 890 in Singapore, and
over 1,000 in Hong Kong, South Korea, and Thailand, and 2,000 in
Japan and the Philippines.[11]

High educational and skill levels translate into a second cause
for East Asian economic growth—a willingness and ability to acquire

and utilize advanced technology. Japan, again, has led the way in
this regard. Unfettered by either intellectual arrogance or xeno-
phobic fear of foreign cultural domination, the Japanese have
adapted the science and technology of the West to suit their own
needs. Less than 20 years after the arrival of Perry's "black
ships" the Japanese had built a railroad—from Yokohama to Tokyo.
In subsequent decades the Japanese eagerly learned and adapted
Western ideas and techniques for their own use. As the Romans
borrowed eclectically from the more advanced nations of the Mediterranean, so the Japanese have borrowed and learned from the
nations of the Pacific, and the Atlantic as well, so that today no
one denies Japan is on the cutting edge of future technological development. To cite but two examples, the Japanese have built 14
medium and large modern integrated steel plants since 1962, compared to only two medium plants constructed in the United States
during the same period. As a result, Japan can import coal from
West Virginia and iron ore from Australia, and sell the steel produced cheaper in New York or Los Angeles than can U.S. industry.[12]
Similarly, although the United States pioneered the development and
use of industrial robots, Japan in 1982 had over 14,000 such robots,
compared to 4,100 stateside.[13]

Across the Sea of Japan in South Korea a similar phenomenon
has occurred. Borrowing heavily upon the example of Japan, South
Korea today is in a sustainable economic expansion deriving from
hard work and use of the latest technologies. Anyone visiting South
Korea can attest to the renewed economic boom now occurring in
that peninsula. As a newly industrialized country, Korea faces
difficulties of transition from a centrally controlled to a market
economy, but despite a temporary economic setback associated
with a change in government in 1980, South Korea is again demon-
strating its capacity for growth.

In China, the prospects for the immediate future are less
sanguine. Frustrated by past inability to modernize their economy
rapidly, Chinese leaders today are planning future economic programs with considerably more realism than anytime in this century. Still a wholly backward nation, even by Asian standards,
China today is seeking to attract Western technology and capital, as
well as assistance in filling the tremendous educational gap resulting from the Cultural Revolution. Perhaps most encouraging is the
realistic assessment by Beijing that knowledge of Western technical
and educational processes is an essential prerequisite to modernization.

The members of the Association of Southeast Asian Nations
(ASEAN), meanwhile, continue to improve their educational and
technological levels. According to UN statistics, for example, the

number of Philippine scientists has increased 350 percent in recent years.[14] During the last decade, industrial production of the Philippines nearly doubled, while that of Malaysia has increased threefold.[15] Productivity has increased in the vital export sector and includes a widening range of mid-to-high level technology products.

A third element in East Asia's growth pattern is natural resources. Japan developed in spite of the dearth of natural resources. Much of the rest of East Asia is developing because of them.

Nowhere has this been more apparent than in the field of energy. Although the extent of East Asian energy resources remains unclear, there were dramatic rises in the region's petroleum exploration and production in the 1970s, and there are strong indications of continued growth in this decade (see Figure 4). With the consolidation of a modernizing leadership there is a good possibility that China, now the fourth largest energy producing nation in the world, will continue to develop its resources. Much hinges on coal and oil resource exploitation, which leveled off during the early 1980s as production peaked at just over two million barrels per day. Chinese oil production had risen 650 percent in the 1970s, and hopes were that increasing offshore production would more than offset declining onshore output.[16] During recent years China has purchased several deep-water rigs and began exploratory drillings in portions of the South China Sea off Hainan Island in 1981. In May 1982 Beijing put up for bid some 43 contract areas in the East and South China Seas. A year later the first five contracts were signed, with more later in 1983.[17] Nevertheless, mismanagement and lack of experience have plagued the Chinese, and earlier OECD predictions that oil exports would reach 1.2 million barrels per day by 1985, are clearly off target. Presently China exports only 250-300 thousand barrels per day, less than 15 percent of its total production.[18] Nevertheless, the offshore oil picture is active, with particularly high expectations for blocks in the South China Sea.

Further south, the ASEAN countries have demonstrated considerable potential for expanding energy production. During the past ten years the electrical production of these nations has increased over 270 percent, largely obtained from fossil fueled systems.[19] Indonesia, Malaysia, and Brunei are all expected to increase their oil exports by over 35 percent by the end of this decade.[20] Thailand has signed an agreement with U.S.-based Union Oil, for delivery from the Gulf of Siam of an expected 250 million cubic feet of natural gas per day for a period of 20 years. By mid-1983 it appeared that this field had peaked at some 150 million cubic feet per day. A $3.5 billion gas project with Texas Pacific

FIGURE 4

Major Oil and Gas Fields and Offshore Exploration

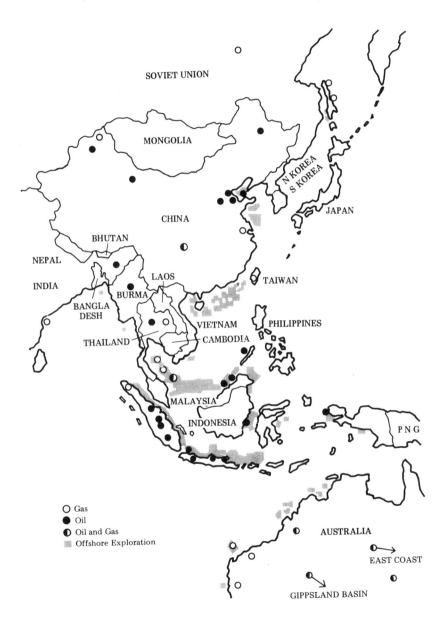

farther south in the Gulf could double that amount if agreement can
be reached on the controlling shares. If successful, this and other
gas projects could give Thailand a degree of energy independence
capable of sustaining limited industrial development for the rest of
this century.[21] Still farther south, Exxon's fields off the Malaysian
coast offer that country a power supplement to its indigenous crude
and thereby enhances its oil export potential. In 1981 Exxon Chairman Clifton Garvin announced his company would double its Malaysian
investments to $1.5 billion due to favorable operating conditions
and substantial discoveries of natural gas. By 1983 Malaysian gas
reserves were estimated at nearly 50 trillion cubic feet, and the
government had announced plans to boost oil production to 360,000
barrels per day from 300,000 barrels per day the previous year.[22]
Another area offering oil and gas prospects is the South China Sea,
but its potential is less assured due to insufficient exploration and
because of continuing territorial disputes involving the People's
Republic of China, Taiwan, Vietnam, and the Philippines. Exploration is planned or underway in the Gulf of Tonkin, off Hainan Island,
near the Spratley and Paracel islands, and in the Philippines' Nido
complex. Indonesia, meanwhile, remains the major oil exporter in
Asia, shipping some 880,000 barrels per day in 1982.[23] Despite
declining oil revenues in the early 1980s, prices and volume are
expected to pick up during the latter half of the decade. A record
285 wells were drilled in 1982 alone, and Indonesian natural gas
production is expanding very rapidly.[24] The president of Pertimina,
the state-owned petroleum company, predicts that Indonesian exports of liquefied natural gas, already nearly a third of the world
total, will increase 75 percent by 1990.[25] Still another important
part of the energy resource picture in East Asia is Australia, considered by some to possess one-fourth of the noncommunist world's
low-cost uranium reserves, a country which already exports substantial amounts of coal, and which is expected to export a substantial volume of natural gas beginning in 1986.[26] Rounding out the
energy scene in New Zealand, where $750 million will be spent be-
tween 1983 and 1986 on offshore oil exploration.[27]

The resource base of East Asia is by no means limited to
energy products. More fish are caught in the Pacific than in any
area of the world, and the commercial catch of Asian nations is
more than twice that of Europe and six times that of North and
Central America combined.[28] The imposition of 200-mile fishing
zones has had minimal effect on the area's net output of fish and
may well be a boon to Australia, New Zealand, and Micronesia.
With the exception of landlocked Laos, the extension of economic
zones has greatly improved Asian access to ocean bed resources
and provides a potentially vast supply of minerals for future

development. This is particularly true for Indonesia, whose territorial control will more than double as a result of the archipelagic
state concept incorporated in the law of the sea convention expected
to come into force in 1985.[29] Asian land resources are likewise
numerous. Its major exports include grain, sugar, textiles (cotton
and wool), lumber, rubber, tin, nickel, coffee, and palm, animal,
and vegetable oils.

A fourth factor underlying the economic dynamism of East
Asia is the increasing modernization of its productive capacity.
Japan has a long-established reputation for savings and investment,
but in Asia today the portion of GNP devoted to capital formation is
even higher in Singapore and Malaysia, while the other nations of
East Asia lead the United States in this category by wide margins.

Gross Fixed Capital Formation as a Percent of GNP[30]

Rank	Country	Percent
1	Singapore	42.3
2	Malaysia	32.7
3	Japan	31.1
4	Korea	28.5
5	Philippines	25.9
6	Australia	25.3
7	Thailand	24.7
8	Indonesia	21.5
9	New Zealand	21.0
10	United States	17.6

These high rates of savings and investment are fundamental to
economic growth and are creating a modern East Asian industrial
base with immense long-term consequences for the future. First,
they have enabled the economies of the region to develop tremendous
dynamism without the risks associated with excessive foreign borrowing found in other parts of the world, particularly Latin America. Debt service ratios are relatively low, with the Philippines
at 19 percent, the highest in East Asia. Recent data indicate that
the combined external debt of the developing nations of East Asia is
only 16 percent of GNP, compared to nearly 40 percent for Latin
America.[31] Second, they have enabled most economies to diversify
in a way reducing the risks of single commodity exporters. Balanced investment in agriculture, mineral and energy resources,
and manufacturing and service industries increasingly characterize
the region. States traditionally known for resource extraction, such
as Indonesia, are making concerted efforts to develop and manufacture a wide range of product lines. Others are moving toward more
sophisticated knowledge—intensive electronics and computer-related

products. The results of this diversification became evident in the East Asian response to the global economic sluggishness of the early 1980s. Despite their reputation for heavy dependence on a healthy international environment, the exports of the region actually increased in 1981 and 1982, as new product lines more than compensated for traditional exports.[32]

A third consequence of high rates of investment is the flexibility it provides East Asian economies in moving across a wide technological spectrum. South Korea, for example, is caught between the twin competitive edges of labor-intensive exports from the less-developed regions of Asia and the capital-intensive higher technological levels of Japan. As a newly industrialized country, South Korea is moving away from the former in a bid to compete realistically in the latter. Although its principal advantage in the past was a disciplined labor force backed by strong government and private industry organization, the country is now beginning to combine more knowledge-intensive skills and technology, often imported from Japan, to develop a more sophisticated industrial base. The other "Gang of Four" nations, Taiwan, Singapore, and Hong Kong, are following a similar pattern, and are increasingly competitive across a broad spectrum of commodities at intermediate technological levels. All are newly modern commercial states whose development and trade in diverse commodities hearkens images of the great transformation wrought in large part by similar economic interchange in Renaissance Europe.

Technological levels in the Philippines, Thailand, and Indonesia are less impressive. Nevertheless, each nation has applied scientific techniques to increase agricultural productivity well beyond that of either past performance or that of communist Asia today. The Philippines is famous for the research and development conducted there for new rice seeds capable of increasing yields per acre some three to four times. "Philippine rice" has now spread to Thailand and Indonesia, as well as many other rice-producing countries. Scientific approaches toward other crops are also noteworthy. Thailand and Malaysian rubber trees, for example, have achieved annual yields five times those attained by Vietnam in the best of times. On the whole, though, these ASEAN nations are on a path of increasing their primary resources and agricultural productivity, while their industry remains limited to lower technological levels. This pattern reinforces intraregional trade, which during the last decade increased fourteenfold.[33] Movement by the lesser developed Asian nations to middle-level technologies should strengthen this trade, as the more developed nations of the region are now advancing into some of the latest technologies.

The emphasis on modern productive capacity, with all its consequences, is also taking root in China. Following the philosophy laid down in the late Premier Zhow Enlai's last speech two years earlier, former Chairman Hua Guofeng in February 1978 announced a plan for rapid modernization in the four areas of agriculture, industry, science and technology, and defense. This so-called "Four Modernizations" plan called for production increases by 1985 of more than double for oil, double for steel and coal, and nearly double for grain. It entailed construction of 120 large-scale projects that depended heavily on Western capital and technology. Simultaneously, China signed a long-term trade agreement with Japan, involving a target of $20 billion in trade during the period 1978-85, later expanded to $60 billion by 1990. China was to increase annually its exports of coal and oil to Japan, while Japan would counter with machinery, plant, and equipment.[34]

In 1980, it became apparent that China would not be able to meet its export goals and, therefore, would lack the foreign exchange necessary to pay for its ambitious modernization program. Cutbacks of $1.5 billion in Japanese contracts were announced in early 1981, and technological and financial problems forced a long delay in the beginning of phase two of the highly vaunted steel-rolling mills at Baoshan near Shanghai. Chinese officials hastened to assure their nervous Japanese counterparts that this did not mean complete abandonment of developmental plans, but merely retrenchment to a more realistic and moderate time schedule. China continued to seek foreign capital, but increasingly restricted to concessional terms from Western governments and international financial institutions.

As of the early 1980s, there was considerable debate about whether China would succeed in its Four Modernizations, with naysayers pointing out enormous problems not just of capital, but of grossly inadequate ports and transportation links, and of Chinese inability to absorb technologically sophisticated industrial systems. National production was still overwhelmingly labor-intensive, with 80 percent of workers in the agricultural sector.[35] To the yeasayers, however, there was hope that resource exploitation would improve, light industry develop, and exports grow. A more balanced view held that, at least for the 1980s, only the more developed regions near the Pacific Coast, with their greater tradition of interchange with the West, would begin to transit the modernization gap separating China from not just the industrialized West but the increasingly modernized trading nations of East Asia.[36]

A fifth factor underlying the growing prosperity in East Asia is the increasing interdependence of Pacific Basin nations.[37] Illustrating this interdependence is the fact that on any given day over

600 merchant ships ply the sea lanes between the Persian Gulf and Japan, bringing to our strongest ally in the Pacific over 70 percent of its total energy needs and most of its industrial raw materials. It is expected that even with accelerated measures to develop alternative energy sources, 50 percent of Japan's energy needs will still be met by this oil in 1990.[38] Each day some 140 ships transit the Strait of Malacca, bringing supplies not only to Japan but also to the United States and other nations of the world.[39] These sea lanes are vital to the continued prosperity and economic progress of Japan, South Korea, Taiwan, Australia, New Zealand, the ASEAN states, as well as the nations of South Asia and the Persian Gulf, and are of potential economic importance to China, the Soviet Union, and Vietnam. Indeed, the sea lanes of the Pacific Basin have become highways of commerce for both Asia and America, making possible the ever greater economic interchange that is the hallmark of efficient production and distribution of goods in the modern era.

The free flow of goods in and between the free nations of Asia has been made possible to a significant extent by the increasing Japanese economic role. As seen in Table 1, U.S. exports to what became the five ASEAN nations as a whole still exceeded Japanese exports to those countries in 1960. The same was true of U.S. trade with Australia, New Zealand, South Korea, and Taiwan. Today Japanese exports exceed those of the United States to every country in East Asia except the Philippines and Australia. Moreover, the balance of trade generally favors Japan's Asian neighbors. During the period of 1979-82, Japan's average deficit with the ASEAN countries as a whole averaged $6.2 billion annually.[40]

Substantial Japanese capital has also begun to flow to the region, with Japan's Export-Import Bank lending rising 254 percent to over $2 billion in 1980. Major projects financed included the Baoshan steel complex near Shanghai, petroleum exploration and development in China, Malaysia, Thailand, and Indonesia, aluminum smelting plants in Australia and Indonesia, and a fertilizer plant in Indonesia. Japanese technology and management play a key role in these and numerous other projects throughout the region. For example, Prime Minister Suzuki, during his January 1981 visit to Southeast Asia, promised a $100 million aid program to support manpower training centers in each of the ASEAN nations.[41] In addition, economists, businessmen, and technical personnel from throughout East Asia flocked to Japan to learn first-hand the lessons of its economic success.

The interchange of goods and services between other East Asian states has also become immensely significant. In 1960 the nations of the region sold $12 billion of goods abroad. By 1980 that figure had increased twenty-fivefold, to nearly $300 billion.[42] In

1967 the Philippines, Indonesia, Thailand, Malaysia, and Singapore formed the Association of Southeast Asian Nations (ASEAN) to promote cooperation in trade and development. Efforts were made to increase trade among the five nations and between them and the rest of Asia. Results were outstanding, as ASEAN both benefited by and contributed to the underlying economic interdependence of the region. During the first ten years of its existence, ASEAN increased its trade with the rest of Asia tenfold, while exports as a percent of ASEAN GNP rose from 15 to 32 percent.[43] While this latter fact highlights the vulnerability of these nations to the vagaries of foreign economic health, it also shows that export development can result in phenomenal economic growth, as witnessed by an average annual real GNP growth of over 7 percent during this period. South Korea and Taiwan, with exports as a percentage of GNP at 36 and 52 percent respectively, are in a similar situation, and have achieved similar high rates of growth.[44]

TABLE 1

East Asian Imports from the United States and Japan
($ millions)

	1960		1980	
	United States	Japan	United States	Japan
Australia	432	137	4,410	3,452
New Zealand	73	20	768	784
Hong Kong	126	165	2,763	5,221
South Korea	118	58	4,890	5,858
Taiwan	113	105	4,600	5,350
ASEAN	501	492	10,013	14,386
Indonesia	89	92	1,613	3,823
Malaysia	29	56	1,632	2,467
Philippines	257	131	2,017	1,705
Singapore	51	97	3,389	4,311
Thailand	75	116	1,362	2,080

Source: IMF, Direction of Trade, except Taiwan, which is AIT.

While the real boom in international trade has been among the market economies of the Pacific, the foreign trade of China has increased dramatically during the 1970s, from less than $4 billion in

1970 to $39.2 billion in 1980. Though starting from a very low export base, the Chinese did succeed in increasing exports during the decade at the same ratio as the great commercial nations of the Western Pacific. Interestingly but not surprisingly, by 1980 93 percent of Chinese trade was with the noncommunist countries. [45]

Finally, the interdependence of Asian nations is highlighted by the growing role of Australia as a supplier of natural resources. Australian trade, too, has grown immensely during the past decade, highlighted by the development and export of fuel, food, and fibers. Its trade, which was once heavily oriented toward Britain, and then the United States, is now principally with Japan and the rest of Asia, with the United States maintaining a share of total Australian trade of about 17 percent. [46]

Thus all the economic ingredients for sustained growth are present in East Asia today—ample and increasingly skilled labor, considerable natural resources, heavy investment in the means of production, technological interchange and innovation, and economic interdependence and cooperation.

The sixth factor favoring economic development, as will be seen in Chapter 6, is the political stability of the free enterprise systems of East Asia. This constitutes a vital, perhaps the most vital, cause of economic success. As a consequence, the nations of East Asia today enjoy a level of progress and relative prosperity that is both deep-rooted and of tremendous consequence to the United States. It is to these benefits that we now turn.

In 1960, as the war in Vietnam was just beginning to register on the American consciousness, U.S. trade with East Asia totaled a mere $5 billion, 14 percent of our total international trade, and less than half our trade with Western Europe. By 1982 that trade had increased to $131 billion, constituted 28 percent of our total trade, and exceeded by 10 percent our trade with all of Western Europe. Japan had become our largest overseas trading partner, our second largest purchaser of American farm products, and a partner and competitor in scientific and technological developments ranging from nuclear power plants to industrial robots and microchips. In the 1970s, our trade with Japan increased fourfold, but despite this impressive growth, declined from 56 to 45 percent as a share of our trade with East Asia. The reason, of course, was that American trade with the rest of East Asia registered even more phenomenal growth. In 1980 two-way trade with the ASEAN states reached $22.1 billion and with Taiwan $11.7 billion, each ten times the 1970 amount. Trade with South Korea totaled $9.1 billion, nine times a decade earlier, while our China trade doubled in 1979 and redoubled in 1980 to $4.9 billion. [47] Indicative of East Asian market potential, as well as competitiveness, is the fact that in the face of a U.S. recession, which reduces imports, and a stronger dollar that inhibits exports, American trade with the region in 1982 declined only 1.2 percent, compared to a decline of 10.3 percent for the rest of the world. [48]

East Asia today accounts for over half of American imports of rubber, tin, titanium, thorium, and zircon, and over 10 percent of our lead, petroleum, nickel, columbium, manganese, and tungsten. [49] Most of these are strategic materials vital to our defense industry, in addition to our civilian economy. Furthermore, we receive from East Asia a wide range of manufactured products. While these sometimes compete with domestically produced products, their price competitiveness tends to dampen American inflation and benefit U.S. consumers directly. Indirectly they also pressure U.S. industry to make the kind of investments necessary to long-term growth and international competitiveness. Japanese steel and autos, Korean chests and pianos, and Taiwanese shoes and shirts are all typical examples. There are parts of the American economy hurting from this foreign competition, but without that competition we would be hurting even more, and could well still be driving very expensive gas guzzlers at a time when the price of gas is out of sight, and wearing leather shoes too costly for use on a moderate walk.

East Asia is also valuable both as a market for U.S. goods and services and as an area of profitable investment. In 1980 America exported over $50 billion in goods to the region, including over $22 billion in machinery and transportation equipment, over $10 billion in agricultural products, $6 billion in chemicals, and several billion dollars in consumer goods. [50] It is estimated that these exports created over a million jobs, directly and indirectly, in the United States. American investment has also proven beneficial. In 1980 cumulative direct investment in East Asia was less than 10 percent of our total overseas investment, yet provided a 27.5 percent rate of return compared to 17.4 percent globally. During the past five years the rate of return on U.S. investment in East Asia was the highest in the world, exceeding the average return from other areas of the world by 27 percent, and was well ahead of returns from Europe, Canada, Latin America, and even the Middle East. [51]

Another measure of progress in the region, which is a direct benefit to the United States, is the fact that East Asia today receives less American aid than any region in the world. This was not always the case. Since World War II the United States has pumped over $27 billion in economic assistance into East Asia. As recently as 1975 that aid constituted 15 percent of all our overseas developmental aid. By 1982, however, American official development assistance had declined to $277 million, just 3.4 percent of our global total.[52]

Because of these and other economic benefits many economists, businessmen, and governmental officials have begun to refer to the United States as a member of the great trading nations of the Pacific Basin. The future orientation of our nation, as well as its continued prosperity, they foresee, depends more on our westward than our eastward direction. Some Americans have undertaken efforts to formalize our Pacific interests by promoting an Organization for Pacific Trade and Development. Whatever their success in this endeavor, the dynamism of East Asia coupled with a strong American participation in its development and progress is bound to generate remarkable rewards and benefits for our nation as we approach the twenty-first century.

But it is not economic remuneration alone that renders East Asia so important to the future of the United States. The very fact that the region is progressing so well enhances its already considerable strategic value. During the 1950s President Eisenhower recognized that the bipolar configuration of power emanating from World War II would result in long-term superpower competition. In his so-called "New Look" the president placed great emphasis on American economic growth so as to compete effectively with the Soviet Union in the long run. This concept is every bit as valid today as it was in the 1950s. American economic strength is inextricably tied to the peace and prosperity of Asia and, for the foreseeable future, we stand to revitalize our economy and maximize our productivity in large part as a direct result of our economic ties with the most dynamic economic region of the world—East Asia.

NOTES

1. International Monetary Fund (IMF), Direction of Trade Yearbook, 1970-76 and 1976-82.

2. IMF, International Financial Statistics, July 1983; "Far Eastern Economic Review," June 30, 1983, for Hong Kong and Taiwan. OECD figures are as reported by that organization.

3. Predicasts, Inc., "World Casts Issue #70," May 20, 1983, pp. A-4 and 5.

4. Chase Econometrics, Far East Forecasts and Analysis, Third Quarter 1983 (Bala Cynwyd, Pa.: Chase Econometrics Associates, 1983), p. 8.

5. Business International Corporation, Asia/Pacific Forecasting Study: 1983-1987 (Hong Kong: Business International Asia/Pacific Ltd., 1983); Pacific Basin Economic Service, Wharton

Econometrics, Pacific Basin Economic Outlook, Fall 1983 (Washington, D.C.: Wharton Econometric Forecasting Associates, 1983), p. 46; and Data Resources, Inc., Asian Review, Third Quarter 1983 and Japan Review, Third Quarter 1983 (Lexington, Mass.: Data Resources, Inc., 1983), pp. 14 and 25 respectively.

6. IMF, op. cit.

7. Max Lerner, "The Pacific Decades," Japan Times, June 5, 1978, and the Los Angeles Times, June 1978. Henry Kissinger, "Gravity Moving Toward East," Asahi Shimbun, June 6-8, 1978. East Asia as used herein includes China, Korea, Japan, Taiwan, the ASEAN states, Indochina, Australia, New Zealand, and Oceania.

8. Predicasts, op. cit., Real per capita income is expected to grow 3 percent annually between 1983 and 1995. See also UNESCO Statistical Yearbook, 1982.

9. Far Eastern Economic Review (FEER) Yearbook, 1981-2 (Hong Kong, FEER, 1982).

10. Bureau of Labor Statistics, "International Comparisons of Manufacturing Productivity and Labor Cost Trends," May 26, 1983.

In 1982, Japan was the only country in which manufacturing output increased.

11. United Nations Statistical Yearbook: 1978 and 1980; and UNESCO, Statistical Yearbook, 1982. Japan has more college and university students than Britain, France, and West Germany combined.

12. The Japan Iron and Steel Federation, July 1977. See also Council on Wage and Price Stability, "Report to the President on Prices and Costs in the U.S. Steel Industry," October 1977.

13. Mike Tharp, "Life with the Robots," in FEER, April 28, 1983, p. 55.

14. UNESCO, op. cit.

15. Predicasts, op. cit., pp. A8-9.

16. British Petroleum, Annual World Energy Survey, July 1, 1978; and Oil and Gas Journal, May 25, 1981.

17. FEER, April 28, 1978; Yomuri Shimbun, July 28, 1978; Mainichi Shimbun, February 12, 1981; and Oil and Gas Journal, May 2, 16, and 30, 1983.

18. OECD Energy Outlook, Paris 1977, and CIA, International Energy Statistical Review, May 1983.

19. Predicasts, op. cit., p. A-11.

20. Petroleum Economist, May 1983, p. 178.

21. FEER, June 30, 1978, and November 12, 1982, p. 56; and Business Week, October 25, 1982, p. 32.

22. Asian Wall Street Journal, June 23, 1981; and Oil and Gas Journal, May 16 and July 11, 1983.

23. See FEER, February 10, 1983.

24. Oil and Gas Journal, May 16, 1983.

25. FBIS, Asia and Pacific, September 3, 1982, p. N2.

26. Mitre Corporation Report, Nuclear Power Issues and Choices (Cambridge, Mass.: Ballinger, 1977), pp. 78-81; and Oil and Gas Journal, April 5, 1982, pp. 93-97.

27. Oil and Gas Journal, July 11, 1983, pp. 32-33.

28. U.S. Department of Commerce, "Fisheries of the United States, 1977," April 1978; and FEER Yearbook, 1983, p. 44.

29. FEER, January 6, 1983, p. 12.

30. IMF, International Financial Statistics, July 3, 1983. The figures cited are for 1981.

31. The Economist, November 13, 1982, pp. 15-22; and Data Resources, op. cit., p. 7.

32. IMF, Direction of Trade Annual, 1983.

33. Ibid.

34. Research Institute for Peace and Security, Asian Security, 1979 and 1980.

35. Asian Wall Street Journal, February 25, 1981; and The Japan Times, June 6, 1981.

36. This thesis was expounded on by Ross Terrill, "China Enters the 1980s," Foreign Affairs, Spring 1980.

37. For an early exposition of the Pacific Basin concept, see the Committee on Foreign Relations, United States Senate (SFRC), An Asian Pacific Regional Economic Organization; An Exploratory Concept Paper (Washington, D.C.: U.S. Government Printing Office, July 1979), pp. 32-35.

38. Japanese Ministry of International Trade and Industry (MITI), Energy in Japan, Facts, and Figures, May 1982; Admiral Weisner, Strategic Review, February 1979. A late 1983 MITI long-term forecast reiterates this point.

39. Asian Wall Street Journal, June 17, 1981.

40. IMF, Direction of Trade Yearbook, 1983.

41. Asian Wall Street Journal, June 25, 1981.

42. Committee on Foreign Relations, United States Senate, An Asian-Pacific Regional Economic Organization: An Exploratory Concept Paper, July 1979; and National Foreign Assessments Center, Handbook of Economic Statistics, September 1982.

43. Committee on Foreign Relations, op. cit.; and the International Monetary Fund, International Financial Statistics, April 1983.

44. Ibid., The Korean figure is an average of 1978-81.

45. PRC trade remained some 6 percent of total East Asian trade during the decade. Total trade in 1980 was $41.0 billion, of which $37.9 billion was with noncommunist nations; National Foreign Assessment Center, op. cit., p. 102.

46. IMF, Direction of Trade Yearbook, 1983.

47. SFRC, op. cit.; and IMF, Direction of Trade, exports f.a.s., imports c.i.f.; and Department of Commerce, FT-990, Highlights of U.S. Export-Import Trade. In the early 1960s, U.S. imports from China continued to rise, but exports fell substantially as Chinese grain imports declined.

48. Department of Commerce, op. cit., December 1982.

49. Economic Handbook, op. cit.; Office of the Chief of Naval Operations, U.S. Lifelines; and U.S. Department of Commerce, FT-135.

50. U.S. Department of Commerce, FT-990, Highlights of U.S. Export-Import Trade, December 1980.

51. U.S. Department of Commerce, Survey of Current Business, October 1977, August 1978, August 1979, and August 1981.

52. U.S. Agency for International Development, U.S. Overseas Loans and Grants, 1983, pp. 4, 65.

6

Contrasting Sociopolitical Performance

The remarkable performance of the free and independent nations of East Asia is a far cry from their dismal outlook in 1945 or 1950. In those years, the fragile governments of the region were still reeling from the devastation wrought by World War II. Their largely agrarian economies were woefully inadequate to the task of providing for their expanding populations. In 1950 the per capita annual income of Indonesia, Malaya, Thailand, South Korea, and Taiwan were each under $100, while no country in Asia, other than Australia and New Zealand, exceeded $200.[1] Moreover, the economic prognosis was pessimistic. Most potential modernizers were bound by their traditional education and interests while the society at large knew little beyond its village horizons. Illiteracy was 90 percent in Indonesia and over 50 percent in most of the rest of Asia. Scientific and technical skills were in very short supply, and political instability was rampant.

It cannot be overemphasized that in the immediate postwar era most national governments throughout East Asia were confronted with challenges to their very existence. In the newly independent states of the Philippines, Burma, Indonesia, and Malaya, communist organizations were seeking to overthrow the fledgling governments by any means possible. They promised to relieve the difficult conditions of the peasantry by ordering a classless society in which all would prosper equally. They engaged in selective terrorism and murder of governmental officials, teachers, and village chiefs, and they armed themselves to overthrow the new governments of these nations by force. In Indochina, where independence had not been granted, the Viet Minh were on the offensive and the French position was rapidly becoming untenable. Northeast Asia

91

faced challenges of equal magnitude. Taiwan had provided refuge for the remnants of Chiang Kai-shek's defeated Kuomintang, but the situation in the Taiwan strait was ominous. Victorious Chinese communist forces, which had driven Chiang from the Mainland, were threatening to storm Taiwan, and were bombarding the Nationalist-held offshore islands of Quemoy and Matsu. Their victory also greatly assisted the Viet Minh, who thereafter used China as a rear base for logistics, intelligence, and operational support. Within months after Mao's victory in China, French positions on the Sino-Vietnamese border fell, and a few years later it was Chinese-provided artillery that sounded the death-knell at Dien Bien Phu. In Korea matters were even worse, as North Korean ground forces violently attacked and nearly overwhelmed South Korea in a premeditated act of open aggression. Nearby Japan was still exhausted from the Pacific war, and faced very powerful leftist domestic political forces, some of which looked to China and the Soviet Union as models for future Japanese development. Naturally, the PRC was tooting its own horn about the tremendous economic accomplishments being achieved under the communist system, and books were being drafted in the United States and elsewhere about China as a new and exciting experiment in socioeconomic growth, as a model for developing nations and as Asia's new giant.

By the early 1950s, it was evident that the ideology and practice of communism was on the ascendency in Asia. The widespread communist guerrilla campaigns seemed to offer good prospects of success, and the recent example of Mao's victory in China added emphasis to that possibility. Moreover, the apparent closeness of the communist powers in Asia made the threat of communist victories even more serious. Sino-Soviet collusion was at an all-time high. Together they appeared to control most of the immense resources in Asia, and gave every evidence of seeking to extend their span of control. They both assisted North Korea in time of war; they both recognized the Ho Chi Minh-led Democratic Republic of Vietnam as the legitimate government of all Vietnam; and they both gave moral support to Communist parties engaged in guerrilla wars in Southeast Asia. The external pressure of a seemingly monolithic communist empire, coupled with serious internal disorders in the free nations of Asia, portended a result clearly inimical to American interests. Everywhere in Asia communism was on the march.

Thirty years later the situation is completely reversed. The communist nations are in disarray, floundering economically, and presenting an uninspiring image of autocracy and privation. Beginning with the Soviet Maritime Provinces on the north to Laos and Vietnam to the south, the working class is dictated to by organs of the state and has virtually no incentive to perform well. A recent visitor to Khabarovsk observed that in this major city of Soviet Asia it is extremely rare to see anyone work. On road gangs, ten stand around while one shovels. The military control nearly everything, from supplies to jobs to government. The population is apathetic, frequently intoxicated, and noticeably unmotivated. In North Korea the situation is better, but bleak by comparison to the South. Prior to the division of Korea in 1945, North Korea had always been more economically advanced than the south. Its mineral reserves were being tapped and an industrial base built. By the early 1970s, however, South Korea had caught up with the North and was surpassing it in nearly every index of industrial production. Seeking to reverse this trend, North Korea, in 1973, opened its economy to "capitalist" credits in the hope of achieving an economic "takeoff." Ill-conceived and based on credits only, rather than any basic change in North Korea's overly centralized economy, the effort failed. After several years of nonpayment, Pyongyang finally made arrangements to pay back a very small portion of the interest on the $1.5 billion borrowed in its frantic effort to catch up.

China faces a similar problem. For years China specialists spoke in glowing terms about Chinese industrial and agricultural productivity, especially in comparison to India and in earlier years Japan.[2] Of course, the references to Japan were dropped by the 1960s. In 1950 the Chinese GNP more than doubled that of Japan, while in 1981 it was less than 30 percent of that of its island neighbor.

In 1955 China produced more goods and services than all of Oriental East Asia combined. Today it produces some one-fourth of that total. In 1955 the Chinese per capita GNP nearly equaled that of Indonesia, South Korea, Malaysia, Taiwan, and Thailand. Today it is less than one-sixth the per capita income of both Taiwan and Hong Kong, a fourth that of Malaysia and South Korea, less than 60 percent of that of Thailand and the Philippines, and some 40 percent less than that of Indonesia. It is estimated that India surpassed China in per capita income in 1983, for the first time in modern history, and an increasing gap is expected. As shown in Figure 5, the People's Republic of China has the lowest per capita income in all of East Asia except Indochina.[3] Indeed, if China had sustained economic progress anywhere near that of the free countries of East Asia, its GNP today would well exceed a trillion dollars. Economic statistics published by China show an average annual growth rate, in real terms, of 9.4 percent between 1950 and 1979.[4] If this were the case China would have today a $1.7 trillion plus economy. Numerous

FIGURE 5

A Comparison of Communist and Non–Communist per Capita GNP

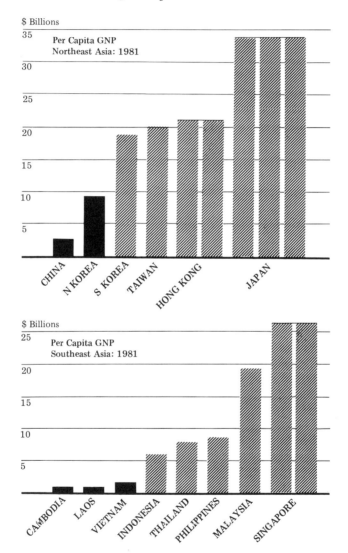

Source: World Bank, 1983 World Bank Atlas, except for North Korea, Cambodia, and Vietnam, whose GNP was estimated based on several governmental and private sources.

American publications, including one produced by the Department of Commerce, have stated that Chinese growth over the past 25-30 years has averaged 6 or more percent annually.[5] If this were true, China today would have a GNP more than twice what it actually has (see Figure 6). Nevertheless, the mythology of the "Great Leap Forward" lives on, despite the evidence revealed in the late 1970s when China opened its doors to foreign scientists, economists, politicians, bankers, businessmen, and others, who were allowed to see not just Beijing and the Great Wall, but much of the infrastructure of that vast country. In 1980 the World Bank revised downward its estimate of Chinese GNP from $425 billion in 1978 to $219 billion, with subsequent adjustment and growth to only $300 billion by 1981.[6]

Of course China has the particular difficulty of filling the educational and technical void left by 13 years of economic disaster associated with the Cultural Revolution. Universities were closed, scientific literature was not produced, and plant and equipment deteriorated. According to official Chinese census figures, one out of every four Chinese was still illiterate in 1982.[7] More important in the long run, however, may be the attitude of the Chinese worker, who has traditionally been described as industrious, but even here, as experienced observers have recently noted, the Chinese suffer from a workforce shockingly lazy in comparison to those of other nations of Asia. It was very well for observers of Chinese society to compare the China of the 1950s with that of the war-torn 1930s, and to say with approbation, "at least they are eating," but when similar comments are heard in the 1980s it strains the imagination to believe great progress characterized the pre-Deng regime.

Farther south in Vietnam, Laos, and Cambodia the story is much the same. The Vietnam war is still being blamed by Hanoi for its difficulties in reconstructing the economy, while Soviet aid is extolled beyond belief for a population basically mistrustful of the Soviets. In late 1975 there were banners and signs all over Hanoi exhorting the population to cooperate in the reconstruction of Vietnam. They called for great victories in the 1976-80 economic plan commensurate with the great victory over South Vietnam. A year later the Communist Party held its Fourth National Congress, the first such gathering in 15 years. The congress laid down the goal of making Vietnam a modernized socialist state by the year 2000. It called for redirecting the energies of the Vietnamese people from warfare to economic development, and the full implementation of the 1976-80 five-year reconstruction plan. At the present time, this goal of the Congress is farther from realization than when announced. Not only did Vietnam scrap the five-year development plan, but by continuing enforced socialization of

FIGURE 6

Gross National Product (1981)

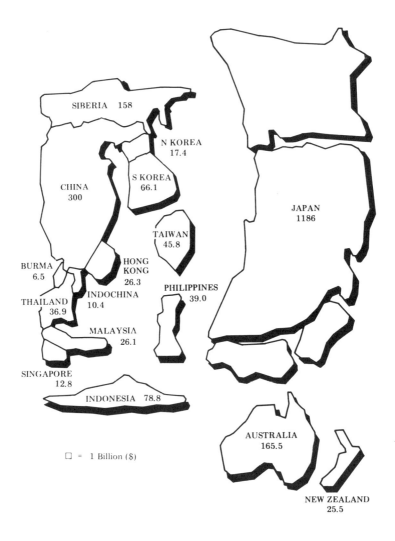

SIBERIA   158

N KOREA
17.4

S KOREA
66.1

CHINA
300

JAPAN
1186

TAIWAN
45.8

BURMA
6.5

HONG
KONG
26.3

PHILIPPINES
39.0

THAILAND
36.9

INDOCHINA
10.4

MALAYSIA
26.1

SINGAPORE
12.8

INDONESIA   78.8

□ = 1 Billion ($)

AUSTRALIA
165.5

NEW ZEALAND
25.5

Source: All figures in $ billions are from the World Bank, 1983 World Bank Atlas, except North Korea, Hong Kong, Siberia, and Indochina, which were developed by the author after consultation with government and private sources.

southern Vietnam and of its northern Chinese population, it drove out many of the very entrepreneurial skills needed for modernization. [8] Having perceived a continuing need to drain the national treasury by deploying troops and resources in Cambodia and along the Chinese border, Vietnam completely failed in realizing the goals set forth by its Fourth Party Congress.

The Fifth Party Congress met in March 1982 to evaluate the problem and recommend solutions. Premier Pham van Dong frankly assessed the situation in his address to the Congress:

> At present, the economic and social situation in our
> country is posing many acute problems. The living
> conditions of our people, of workers and public
> servants in particular, are beset with difficulties;
> the sources of energy, materials supply and trans-
> port facilities are unable to ensure the development
> of existing productive capacities; exports cannot pay
> for imports; markets and prices fluctuate in a com-
> plicated way; the managerial mechanism and planning
> work are still influenced by bureaucratism and a state-
> financing system; negative phenomena in economic and
> social life are still lingering. [9]

Recognizing a problem is one thing—seeking solutions for it is quite another. The Premier continued to blame Western "imperialism" and poor weather for the economy's performance, and to declare reliance on Soviet assistance as the key to the modernization of Vietnam. Proclaiming that Vietnam would advance from a poor country directly to socialism "without passing through the stage of capitalist development," the Vietnamese leader urged popular effort and enthusiasm for economic development commensurate with that demonstrated for the reunification of Vietnam in previous decades.

Alongside the rhetoric inherent in this and other declarations of intent there is an underlying tendency toward practicality in the Vietnamese approach. A system of bonuses and piece-rate wages is under limited trial. The rate of collectivization has been slowed, and some retention of product above quotas is allowed. Vietnam is making some effort to redirect its national energies to the problems of peace. Every national leader who has traveled abroad knows how far behind Vietnam is in the process of economic development, but thus far, their Marxist prism of reality seems to prevent drawing the obvious conclusions. Perhaps as war recedes as the principal determinant of Hanoi's outlook, and as the ASEAN countries continue to improve economically and socially, a new Vietnamese leadership will review their fundamental approach in the light of new conditions. An imaginative and hardworking people, the Vietnamese could, with proper motivation, equal or exceed the economic performance of their ASEAN neighbors, all of whom are doing so much better at the present time.

The winds of change are not restricted to economic matters. Though one clear economic message of modern Asia is that Communism is a recipe for disaster, a clear political message is that the ties of fraternal socialism are very weak indeed. The major areas of conflict in Asia today are no longer centered on the internal stability of the free nations of Asia, but on the difficulties in and between the communist nations. The Chinese and the Soviets have deep and pervasive differences that have resulted in serious political, economic, and military consequences. The Vietnamese are obsessed with fears of a Chinese-Cambodian alliance, to the point of first attacking and then seeking to exterminate Khmer Rouge forces. China sought to teach Vietnam a lesson in 1979, and there have been repeated subsequent manifestations of hostility along their borders. The great friendly rear base that first appeared in 1949 has now become the den of the Larger Dragon. Ironically, the town of Lang Son, which fell to the Viet Minh in 1950, in part as a result of Chinese support, became a prime target of the Chinese in 1979, and was largely destroyed by them. Meanwhile, Laos exists as a haven for Soviet and Vietnamese occupation forces, and resentment builds among what is left of Lao nationalists. In Cambodia the puppet regime depends for its very existence on Vietnam, while communist Pol Pot guerrillas seek to destroy it.

Contrast this with conditions in the free nations of Asia. Although potential for revolution and international conflict still exists, its probability is less now than at any time in this century. The great anticolonial and postcolonial struggles for power are now a thing of the past. So also are most territorial disputes. Throughout the region, modernizing elites have completed the task of wresting power from traditional leaders in what was often violent struggle. The revolutionary movements inspired by nationalist aspirations for independence have also run their course. In Indonesia, and to some extent in Malaysia, the difficult task of unifying diverse peoples with a sense of nationhood has also been marked by great progress. Conflict remains possible over control of oil rights in the South China Sea and over disparities of wealth and ethnic problems in Southeast Asia, but on the whole the political stability of East Asia compares most favorably with both its own recent history and with other regions of the world today. Indeed, much of the increasing unity of the ASEAN states today is a function of a perceived external threat emanating from Vietnam.

In Northeast Asia, Japan stands as a bulwark of political and economic strength. Democratic processes have taken firm root and the resulting political stability has provided the indispensable requisite for economic success. As an island nation all but devoid of natural resources, Japan serves both as an example and a stimulus to development elsewhere in Asia. Most of its aid, which in the early 1980s exceeded $3 billion annually, is directed toward East Asia.[10] This aid is expected to grow substantially in the coming years, and is a definite stimulus to the economies of the region. Japan has offered South Korea $3.5 billion and China $1.3 billion for their current five-year economic plans.[11]

Besides the programs mentioned in Chapter 5, Japan has supported numerous programs in Southeast Asia, including several economically viable major projects. During his May 1983 visits, Prime Minister Nakasone promised the ASEAN states additional credits, assistance in plant renovation and a 50 percent increase in the GSP ceiling on their imports into Japan. He also announced a "friendship program," whereby Japan would annually host 750 potential future leaders of ASEAN.[12] The fact that four consecutive Japanese Prime Ministers—Fukuda, Ohira, Suzuki, and Nakasone—considered it politically advantageous to visit the ASEAN countries early in their administrations speaks well for the prospects of further cooperation. Unlike the violent reception accorded Prime Minister Tanaka in an earlier day, each of the Japanese leaders was received with warmth. Several East Asian nations have emulated Japan by organizing huge industrial-commercial centers, importing Japanese technology and focusing on specialized markets. Perhaps the most overt example of this emulation is in Malaysia, where the government has recently promoted a "Look East" campaign, seeking to pattern future economic development on the Japanese model.

South Korea is already well down the path blazed by Japan. Once an agrarian economy relying on northern Korea for its industrial goods, South Korea today boasts a GNP over three times that of the North, and the gap is growing. Though jolted by the assassination of President Park in 1979, the nation has recovered remarkably well and has resumed the path of economic development and relative political stability. The society has one of the highest educational levels in Asia and the Third World, far surpassing that of North Korea, China, Vietnam, Laos, or Cambodia. Its military forces, though still numerically inferior to those of North Korea, stand ready to defend the nation, and their ability to do so is improving.

Taiwan and Hong Kong have also demonstrated the distinct advantages of a free enterprise system based on political stability

and hard work. Both have achieved a standard of living far beyond
that of the mainland, a fact implicitly recognized in the case of
Taiwan by Chinese Vice-Premier Wang Zhen when he promised no
lowering of Taiwan's standard of living upon its incorporation into
China.[13]

Confronted with such success on their very doorstep, the leadership of the People's Republic of China has been compelled to re-
assess the validity of significant portions of its development theory.

The accession to power of Deng Xiaoping in the late 1970s,
the tremendous emphasis upon the Four Modernizations, the increasing economic interchange with the West, and the growing importance of capitalist incentives all reflect Chinese unhappiness
with their relative economic stagnation. "Economic construction
. . . is the basis for solutions of China's external and domestic
problems," Deng told the Twelfth Party Congress in 1982.[14]

The Chinese leader meant every word. Under his leadership
China instituted several major modernization programs in emulation of the economic boom in East Asia. First is the responsibility
system, by which family farming supplanted collectivization in many
areas of agriculture. Initiated in the late 1970s, the system is
credited with increasing grain production to a record 344 million
tons in 1982.[15] Second is stress on individual business performance
and bottom-line profits. The number of private enterprises has
doubled to 2.6 million since 1979, while state-owned firms have
been allowed to share in some of the profit accruing after payment
of 55 percent of their earnings to the state.[16] Third are the special
economic zones, which have emerged as centers of trade and investment along the coast, particularly in Guangdong and Fujian
provinces. With limited autonomy and considerable potential for
trade and commerce with the rest of East Asia, these zones could
be the cutting edge of China's assimilation into the vibrant economies just off her shores. The fourth area of Chinese adoption of
Western methods is in the area of finance, particularly in its recognition that in the modern era self-sufficiency often leads to ineffi-
ciency. In 1979 China accepted in principle $2 billion in American
Export-Import Bank credits promised by Vice-President Walter
Mondale. In 1981 it concluded a $550 million first loan by the IMF,
and in 1983 announced it had already agreed to $5.8 billion in pledged
foreign credits. That same year Beijing agreed to World Bank
credits of nearly a billion dollars for FY 1984 and $1.5 billion dol-
lars for FY 1985.[17] It is an interesting commentary that I. W.
Clausen, President of the World Bank, who announced these new
credits in Beijing, has for years recognized the impact of East Asia
on Chinese decisions. After one of his visits to China as President
of the Bank of America Corporation, he made the following statement:

"I know at first hand that China admires the economic growth experienced by many Asian countries like Japan, Korea and Hong Kong. China would like to emulate them to some extent, allowing for their history and resources."[18]

The Chinese leadership's decision to modernize, with a goal of quadrupling GNP by the end of this century, is a healthy recognition of where that country stands now in relation to the rest of East Asia, and where they want it to be in the future. If it is results by which theory is to be judged, then successful results on the eastern periphery of the Middle Kingdom undoubtedly already have influenced the decisions for modernization in China, and may be expected to exert a strong influence on continuing reassessments being made in Beijing, and possibly in Pyongyang as well.

The pattern in Southeast Asia could develop in a similar manner. Although not as successful in their economic growth as the free enterprise systems of Northeast Asia, the ASEAN states have continued to register impressive growth rates in GNP, international trade, and standard of living. The livelihood of peasants in the poorest of the lot, Indonesia, compares favorably to that of their Chinese counterparts. The leadership of the ASEAN states has proven far more effective in solving the mundane yet complex problems of economic and social development than their communist neighbors.

The gradual movement of ASEAN political system toward democratic forms is manifest. In 1982 general elections were held in both Malaysia and Indonesia. The former reflected a major shift of support from the Chinese opposition to the National Front coalition, which incorporates the interests of the Malaysian Chinese Association in the government of Prime Minister Mahathir. For a society that has tended to polarize racially, this represents a giant step forward in political integration. The Indonesian election reflected somewhat similar changes, away from the Muslim United Party and smaller minority groups toward a national coalition. In 1983 Thailand held general elections in which popular dissatisfaction with the strong military role in politics was demonstrated, and in 1984 elections are scheduled in the Philippines. Although the actual political power transferred in most of these elections is questionable, the fact that the elections are held, and have reflected increasing national cohesion, speaks well for the ASEAN states. The elections formalize and legitimize these political systems; they are a barometer of public opinion that must be taken into account by national leaders; and they provide a modicum of political participation for large numbers of people, and a focus for popular debate of issues and leaders; finally, they are a necessary precondition for a fuller democratic practices. The economic results of their efforts have already been described. They are as much a result of political leadership as a cause for political change.

The political and economic accomplishments of the ASEAN countries are not, of course, without attendant problems. In Indonesia, for example, the wealth derived from petroleum and other extractive industries has not been evenly distributed, while one negative effect of the Green Revolution is to reduce the labor force required in favor of the more capital-intensive use of pesticides, fertilizer, and irrigation necessary for exploiting the new seeds. Consequently, many farmers are being driven from their small plots of land into either tenancy or urban slums.[19] In Malaysia, the more educated and more affluent Chinese youth of today demand not just the limited economic opportunities that their parents enjoyed yesterday, but also political power in a political system traditionally controlled by ethnic Malay. The Philippines also have faced considerable political problems as a result of socioeconomic change. While President Ferdinand Marcos has reestablished political order through stricter control of violence, his more extreme controls on public expression are not consistent with the long-term stability of that country.[20] The Communist New People's Army is increasing in size and guerrilla activity, and is capitalizing on corruption and governmental neglect in certain areas. In Manila the concentration of power in the hands of President Marcos exacerbates the problem of succession, thereby presenting an even more serious threat to political stability. Thailand, meanwhile, faces less intense internal problems, but must cope with Indochinese refugees and the continued threat of Vietnamese border incursions.

Despite these and other difficulties of stability and modernization, the problems of the free nations of Asia pale in comparison to that of their communist neighbors. While free Asia has moved during the past generation from a condition of relative economic deprivation and political confusion to a position of considerable confidence, stability, and prosperity, the communist states have been beset by chronic problems of underdevelopment. The impressive and sustained growth and trading patterns of the free nations of Asia contrasts sharply with that of China, North Korea, Vietnam, Laos, and Cambodia.

One of the most telling indicators of the dichotomy of the human condition in Southeast Asia is the vast Indochinese refugee flow. While some of the exodus was attributable to the chaos of war, its continuation well into the 1980s highlights the stifling socioeconomic deprivation of communist Indochina. The fear and reality of "reeducation" camps adds to the exodus. Hanoi admits a camp population of 16,000, but Amnesty International and other organizations concerned with human rights put this figure much higher. The

Department of State recently estimated the total at 60,000, which does not include tens of thousands coerced into moving to "New Economic Zones."[21] "The vast majority of political prisoners in Vietnam have not been tried," reports Amnesty International, and most of them have been detained for over eight years. Freedom of speech and the press are virtually nonexistent, and religion is barely tolerated. There is an increasing use of the death penalty, and severe punishment for minor infractions of camp rules are common. Under these circumstances it is not surprising that individuals unhappy with the policies of the present regime should choose to flee the country. Since 1975 some 1.3 million persons have risked their lives in small and overcrowded boats tossed in turbulent seas, and on jungle trails and rivers replete with danger, to escape to freedom. Despite the traditional Vietnamese love of their country, over 4,000 Vietnamese a month still make that dangerous journey—an exodus unprecedented in thousands of years of Vietnamese history. Their flight has placed an additional burden upon the ASEAN nations, but it has also had a sobering effect upon those in Southeast Asia who once looked to communist revolution as a path to freedom and justice.

The gap in political and socioeconomic performance between free and communist Asia, first clearly visible in the 1970s, has now become a chasm. The success of Japan, South Korea, and Taiwan is already exerting a powerful influence on China and North Korea and, if current trends continue, the success of the ASEAN nations could have a similar effect upon the politburo in Hanoi.

The communist states have reacted with a threefold program. First, they are now proclaiming and directing their maximum energy toward modernization. The Chinese embracement of the Four Modernizations, the North Korean effort to catch up, and the Vietnamese plan to move directly from an agrarian to a socialist industrial economy are all a manifestation of the modernization focus. Second, they are seeking to reform their overbearing centrally directed economies by introducing limited production incentives. Thus far, these incentives, such as pay raises or bonuses to more productive enterprises, have been viewed with great skepticism. Although becoming more common in China, they have created a backlash in Vietnam, where they may go the route of the Soviet Lieberman reforms of the mid-1960s, being rejected by ideologues before their effect can truly be judged. Third, they are seeking to import modern technology and procedures by trade with the West. In 1981 Chinese trade reached $10 billion with Japan, $6 billion with the United States, and, interestingly, a half-billion dollars with South Korea. North Korea and Vietnam are also seeking to develop commercial relations with the West.

It is questionable whether these efforts by themselves will overcome the heavy burden of socialism. Nevertheless, they are a step in the right direction and are also manifestations of the independence of these nations. To the degree that North Korea, China, and Vietnam choose to emulate the successful experience of their more advanced free enterprise neighbors, they are choosing pragmatism over doctrinaire ideology. The very fact that they are able to make such choices speaks well of their independence from Moscow and offers marked contrast with the European communist states. Although a similar socioeconomic gap exists between the free and communist nations of Europe, the potential political impact of that gap is constrained by the colonial status of Eastern Europe, which occurred at the very time Asian colonial regimes disintegrated. Thus, any attraction Eastern European states feel toward the economic or political systems of Western Europe is constrained by the dominance of the colonial power, Russia. This is not the case in Asia, where political effects are already apparent in an outward looking China, and where continued ASEAN growth could exert considerable pull on a Vietnam seeking to redirect its energies from the problems of 40 years of warfare to the problems of peace.

The remarkable progress of the free East Asian nations is a reflection of an ability to manage complex issues of development. It is a result of relative stability and political maturity, as well as of economic expertise and entrepreneurial incentives. It derives from powerful internal forces such as those described in Chapter 5, especially the productivity growth associated with free enterprise and trade. The interchange of ideas, technology, capital, goods, and services among the free nations of East Asia has helped generate progress far beyond that of the autarchic policies of communist Asia, and the gap is growing.

Despite their success in revolutionary war, no nation in peacetime runs a comparable risk of failure than does a China or Vietnam isolated from the prosperity and progress of free Asia. With the resolution of the question of political succession to former colonial and traditional governments, as well as the settlement of most territorial disputes, economic growth has become the top priority of Asia today. Free Asia excels in ability to attain this objective, and provides a compelling reason for Communist Asia to follow suit. Unlike Poland or Czechoslovakia, China, North Korea, and Vietnam are independent nations. They can exercise choice free of the heavy-handedness of the Brezhnev Doctrine of limited sovereignty. Their future is theirs to choose, and their choices will in no small manner be determined by their perception of the prospects for continued East Asian peaceful progress, which in many ways still depends on a constructive American role in the region.

The East Asian winds of change have dramatically and force-fully shifted direction since Americans first landed on the shores of Vietnam. They are now favorable winds, to Asians and Americans alike, and with skill the American ship of state can sail with them to the benefit of all.

NOTES

1. World Bank, "World Tables"; Indonesian per capita income in 1950 was $42 per year.

2. For a comparison of Indian and Chinese economic develop-ment, see Wilfred Malenbaum, "Modern Economic Growth in India and China: The Comparison Revisited, 1950-1980," in Economic Development and Cultural Change (Chicago: University of Chicago Press, October 1982), pp. 45-84.

3. 1950 data are from Foreign Area Studies, The American University, Asia Handbook for China (1981), p. 66, with data con-verted by implicit price deflators from The Economic Report of the President, February 1982; doublechecked with UN and World Bank statistics. 1981 data are from the 1982 Far Eastern Economic Review Yearbook, doublechecked with the 1981 World Bank Atlas and with Predicasts, Inc., op. cit., May 20, 1983, p. A-7. The World Bank Annual Report, 1982 paints an even bleaker picture for China. The per capita comparison with India is based on economic analysis by Data Resources, op. cit.

4. The Economic Research Centre, The State Council of the People's Republic of China and the State Statistical Bureau, Almanac of China's Economy, 1981 (Beijing, 1982), p. 961.

5. The United States Department of Commerce, Doing Busi-ness with China, 1981. The other publications are too numerous to mention.

6. World Bank, World Bank Atlas, 1979-1983.

7. The Washington Post, October 28, 1982, pp. A1 and A30.

8. Another reason for Hanoi's driving out the Chinese popu-lation of the North was, of course, the Chinese attack of early 1979, and the Chinese support for Pol Pot. Ethnic Chinese in Vietnam were viewed as a potential or real fifth column. While there is probably some validity in this view, it is also true that the Chinese were unpure racially and ideologically. They were the entrepre-neurs of Hanoi and many, from the very northern provinces, had opposed the Viet Minh. Some of these later constituted the crack Nung forces with the United States Special Forces in South Vietnam.

9. Pham van Dong, "Main Orientations, Tasks, and Targets in the Economic and Social Fields for the 1981-1985 Period and the

Eighties as a Whole," in FBIS, Asia and Pacific, March 30, 1982, p. K-1.

10. Japanese Ministry of International Trade and Industry, White Paper on Economic Cooperation, 1982.

11. "Report of Government Estimates," Nihon Keizai Shimbun, in FBIS, February 9 and 12, 1982; and Kyodo News, "Loan Agreement with PRC signed in Beijing," July 19, 1983.

12. Far Eastern Economic Review, "The Nice Man Cometh," May 19, 1983, pp. 14-15.

13. FBIS, September 16, 1979.

14. Deng Xiaoping, as quoted in Lowell Dittmer, "The 12th Congress of the Communist Party of China," in The China Quarterly, March 1983, pp. 115-16.

15. Far Eastern Economic Review, April 28, 1983.

16. Wall Street Journal, June 3, 1983.

17. The Asian Wall Street Journal, May 5 and June 26, 1981, and July 1983; and the China Daily, June 2, 1983, as quoted by FBIS, China, June 2, 1983.

18. Asian Wall Street Journal, June 19, 1979. It is, perhaps, speculative to infer that the structural changes in the Chinese political hierarchy are also a result of this phenomenon. But to the extent the goals of China and noncommunist East Asia are similar, it is not unreasonable to expect the development of similarities in the political institutions establishing and directing implementation of those goals. The elimination of the Party chairmanship, the division of Central Committee responsibilities, and the reduction of PLA influence, and the reported purge of 3 million left-wing Party members, may all be straws in the wind.

19. The average Indonesian farmer owns only a hectare of land.

20. President Marcos lifted martial law in January 1981 and held elections the following June. However controlled the elections, the fact that they were held is encouraging.

21. Department of State, Country Reports on Human Rights Practices for 1982 (Washington, D.C.: U.S. Government Printing Office, 1983), pp. 823-31; Amnesty International, News Release, April 20, 1983; and the Aurora Foundation, Violations of Human Rights in the Socialist Republic of Vietnam, May 1983.

PART III:
POLICY FOR
TOMORROW

7

Strategies for
Peaceful Progress

In 1973 the United States terminated its military involvement in the longest war in the nation's history. Over 3 million American troops had struggled amidst great adversity in the jungles and rice paddies of that war. Every week busloads of wounded were brought to already congested hospitals, while hundreds of American families received word that their husband or son had just been killed in action. Still other families worried anxiously because they did not receive word regarding their loved ones who had become missing in action or a prisoner of war. Each evening battle scenes flashed across television screens throughout the nation, and each morning newspapers recorded the horrors of the battlefield. Each hour some $3 million was being expended on the war while in front of the White House and on Capitol Hill thousands demonstrated in visible protest of a profligate crusade with ill-defined objectives. [1] It was our third war in Asia within a generation.

A decade and more later, all's quiet on the Far Eastern front. Concern about American overinvolvement in Asia during the Vietnam era has shifted to concern about underinvolvement today, yet that concern is limited in the United States to the few who follow such affairs. For the most part there is silence—silence in American newspapers, television, and radio, and silence in Congress and the White House. Indeed, a sort of silence appears to have fallen across the land itself—from the relative quietude of Korean campuses, to the orderliness of Japanese demonstrations, to the calm of Tienanmen square, to the Vietnamese Gulag without a Solzhenitsyn, to the hallowed ground at the bottom of the South China Sea—there is silence. Meanwhile, the crack of submachine guns is heard on television sets across America, as millions of people stare in questioning concern

at the blood in El Salvador, the sweat in Israel, and the tears in
Lebanon. Compared to the Middle East, Africa, or Central America
today, East Asia is a sea of tranquility. There is no arc of crisis,
no dictator of international terrorism, and, with the exception of the
Philippines, no serious guerrilla warfare.

The big question regarding Asia then becomes, "How does one
react to tranquility?" Obviously one answer is to leave well enough
alone. "If it ain't broke, don't fix it" was a phrase once used to
postulate norms for post-Vietnam American involvement in Asia.
This attitude has strongly influenced American policy toward the
region in recent years and, to a large extent, it is difficult to argue
with success. East Asia is the one region in the world where American interests have been advanced, and advanced rapidly. The realignment of China, the growing solidarity of the ASEAN states, the
economic and social progress and the relative peacefulness of the
region are all very positive factors. Yet to an equal extent there is
a danger in the historic tendency of Washington, so often reflecting
the crisis management approach, to ignore or at best tolerate what
is essentially a tranquil situation.

The problem with this approach is that things never do stay
the same, particularly in Asia. If the dynamic economic, social,
and political change of the past generation is any barometer, then
the Asia that greets the twenty-first century will be even more different from that of today than today's is from the Asia of the Vietnam era. Every indicator points to significant change. On the negative side, the Soviet Union continues to improve its immense Far
Eastern forces, which already number 51 divisions, over 2,100
combat aircraft, and a 1.6 million ton fleet, as well as some 30 percent of Soviet long-range ICBMs, intermediate range SS-20s, and
Backfire bombers.[2] In a region where the Kremlin's political and
economic instruments of policy are weak, the tendency to use the
highest card in the Soviet deck—military power—is always present.
In addition, the Soviet Union could and has attempted to play its
China card in an attempt to at least neutralize further development
of Sino-Japanese-American ties. For its part, China could again
swerve dramatically in its domestic and international policies.
While presently staying the course in pursuing the pragmatic modernization policies of Deng Xiaoping, the Middle Kingdom is extremely
sensitive to its military, economic, and political vulnerabilities in
trying to manage a billion people. Chinese failure to progress could
lead to a desperate embrace of the Russian bear, or a militant lash-
ing out against Taiwan as a unifying cause célèbre. Beijing may also
feel compelled to "teach Vietnam a lesson" once again as a result
of border difficulties, intolerable "insults," Vietnamese incursions
into Thailand, or incidents involving oil or fishing claims in the

South China Sea. Elsewhere in East Asia North Korea may one day seek to exploit perceived political or military confusion in South Korea, resulting in a major war. Vietnam could seek to break the burden of its suzerainty in Kampuchea and Laos by striking perceived support areas in Thailand. The ASEAN states could confront renewed urban or rural guerrilla warfare. Japan could accommodate to Soviet power by restricting American use of bases and by loosening its restrictions on trade, investment, and technological flow to the USSR. Any of these or other possible ill winds could seriously erode the strategically favorable climate we currently enjoy in East Asia. To neglect the region because of favorable trends at this time is to invite disaster at a later date.

Of all the challenges to American interests in Asia none is more dangerous than the growing and overbearing weight of Soviet military power. It is a massive force, whose time has neither come nor is likely to come. It is a force in search of a mission, an instrument of gunboat diplomacy during an era of heightened nationalism and rejection of bullying tactics. Nevertheless, its very presence threatens the stability and peaceful development now proceeding apace throughout the region, and therefore requires close U.S. attention and appropriate policy response.

In the hierarchy of Soviet military objectives the defense of Mother Russia is, of course, of primary importance. The fact that Soviet power in Asia exceeds legitimate self-defense needs by such a wide margin, however, points to other objectives. In view of the history of Soviet activity in Asia in recent years, these appear to include protection and expansion of friendly socialist regimes, neutralization of American friends and allies, and friendship and alliance-building with neutral regimes.

The first objective is well illustrated in Indochina, where some 10,000 Russian military advisers oversee the training and administration of military aid valued at $3 million per day and designed to sustain Vietnamese capabilities in Kampuchea, Laos, and along the Chinese border. Vietnamese dependency on Soviet arms is heightened by both the cut-off of its Chinese arms flow and the fact that captured American equipment is becoming difficult to maintain and in many cases obsolete. The Russian military assistance has not been limited to internal Vietnamese use. Soviet transport aircraft ferry essential military supplies and equipment to Kampuchea, where over 150,000 PAVN troops, armed with Soviet-supplied artillery, armor, and small arms continue to prop up the puppet Heng Samrin regime. In the summer of 1982, for example, the Soviet Union supplied more than 100 T-54 and T-58 medium tanks, as well as large numbers of 155mm artillery pieces and AK-47 rifles. In neighboring Laos, Soviet transport aircraft and technicians help enable a 40,000-man Vietnamese occupation force to preclude concentration of scattered Lao resistance elements into a powerful revolutionary front. The Kremlin pumps some half million dollars a day into Laos. In addition, there is a growing body of evidence that Soviet chemical weapons are being used to suppress "enemies of the state" in both Laos and Kampuchea. Vietnamese forces, under direct Soviet supervision, have been widely reported using trichothecene toxins and nerve agents produced in the Soviet Union, to kill or severely injure thousands of Khmer and Lao people who resist government control.[3] In exchange for all this "assistance," Russian military use of Vietnamese ports and airfields has risen to a level of a dozen or more warships along with several bomber and reconnaissance aircraft. All these actions, together with Soviet provision of intelligence and diplomatic support, are designed to buttress the doctrine of limited sovereignty that Leonid Brezhnev first proclaimed to justify Red Army interference in Czechoslovakia in 1968, and which he extended to Asia in 1979 with the proclamation that "the situation in Kampuchea is irreversible." Unfortunately, the doctrine also appears relevant to Laos.

As the Vietnamese military occupation of Kampuchea drags on into years, efforts to overcome the Brezhnev Doctrine through diplomatic means appear less and less likely to succeed. In March 1981 the Soviet president called for a regional conference to discuss the situation, but only in the context of Southeast Asian recognition of the Vietnamese-installed Heng Samrin regime. The ASEAN states, with U.S. support, opposed the scheme in favor of continued efforts to bring international pressure to bear on Vietnam for its interference in Kampuchea. In September 1981, the UN General Assembly voted 77-37 in favor of maintaining the UN seat of the Khmer Rouge regime. In October the Assembly voted 100-25 for the pull-out of all foreign forces (i.e., Vietnamese) from Kampuchea, a resolution repeated for the fourth successive year in 1982 by an even larger margin, reflecting the role of Norodom Sihanouk as president of the loose coalition of Son Sann, Khieu Samphan, and himself. More recently, Hanoi and Moscow, aware of growing UN disagreement with the legitimacy of the Vietnamese-installed regime, have stopped calling for a credentials vote.

Despite these UN victories, the ASEAN nations in the early 1980s were faced with a relentless Soviet-supported military campaign to exterminate all opposition to the puppet Samrin regime. Provided with excellent communications and intelligence, Vietnamese forces in 1982 drove repeatedly into Khmer Rouge bastions of resistance near the Thai and Lao borders, pounding them with long-range artillery, helicopter gunships, and bomb-laden aircraft. As a result, the Khmer Rouge forces were depleted to less than

20,000 men from the 1980 estimates of double that strength. During the following monsoon season Khmer Rouge and Khmer Serai reestablished their guerrilla bases in Kampuchea, but the Vietnamese pressed them hard the following dry season. The annual seesaw still continues. The fact is that political power in Indochina still grows out of the barrel of a gun, no matter what ASEAN-sponsored resolutions pass at the UN. And the guns for Indochina are now being made in Russia.

A major problem with the occupation of Kampuchea is the perpetuation of Vietnam's conflict with China, which in turn guarantees continued and probably growing Soviet influence in Indochina. There are, of course, other sources of the Sino-Vietnamese antagonism, with its long history of animosity in which Vietnam learned to treasure the word independence. Nevertheless, the Chinese perception of a Vietnamese empire to their south in league with their arch-rival and nemesis to the north is largely based on Vietnamese insistence on denying the Khmer people the very independence they cherish for themselves. The Chinese perceive Vietnam as an aggressive upstart, whose ambitions for expansion threaten to neutralize remaining Chinese influence in the region. Moreover, the Vietnamese have invited the hated Soviets into the area, including Kampuchea, where the Russians have made use of the splendid port at Kompong Som, and began construction of a deep-sea naval base at Ream, thereby further encircling and threatening China.

From the Vietnamese point of view, the fear is just the opposite. Long regarding China as a potential if not actual threat, Vietnam had managed to maintain Chinese support along with that of the USSR during the war. In the mid-1970s, however, China signaled its displeasure with continued Soviet assistance to and presence in Vietnam. Forced to choose between erstwhile allies, Hanoi sided with the more distant (and therefore, it felt, less threatening) power, and one which it perceived as a source of greater technical aid. Vietnamese dependence on the Soviets was also a function of active Khmer Rouge harassment along their border, including forays against Vietnamese border towns and villages, and the fact that China was providing arms, ammunition, and supplies to Pol Pot. In Vietnamese eyes it was they who were being encircled. It was at this time that Vietnam transformed its eschatological vision of an Indochinese federation under the control of Hanoi into a pragmatic policy of occupying Cambodia with tanks and guns. This rationale of self-defense does not accord well with the historical record of Vietnamese intervention in Cambodia, or with the recent movement of tens of thousands of Vietnamese settlers into Cambodia, but it does reflect genuine Vietnamese fears of Chinese encirclement, thereby driving Hanoi into closer alliance with Moscow.

The American dilemma is how to break the vicious cycle of Vietnamese dependence on the Soviets for security and economic development, which dependence is cited by Vietnam as essential to defend against Chinese hegemonism in Southeast Asia, but which leads to increased Chinese antagonism toward Vietnam and thereby perpetuates the very Vietnamese-Soviet collusion that worries the Chinese in the first place. Perhaps an intermediate solution could derive from either Sino-Soviet rapprochement or Chinese recognition of Vietnamese suzerainty in Indochina. Neither alternative is likely, and neither accords well with American goals in Asia. A third alternative could be the Sihanouk-Son Sann "Third Force," but thus far neither the Paris-based Son Sann nor the Beijing-based Sihanouk appears to offer the hapless Khmer the inspirational and organizational wherewithal to conduct a successful protracted resistance. Most Khmer nationalists want the Vietnamese out, but not at the price of restoring the Pol Pot regime. Thus a reduction in Chinese support for Pol Pot's cutthroat Khmer Rouge guerrillas might be the best development. It would create a condition for improvement of Sino-Vietnamese relations and thereby undercut a principal Vietnamese rationale for hosting the Soviet military. It might also provide the Khmer an opportunity for alignment with an opposition force, however latent, to the Vietnamese puppet regime of Heng Samrin, other than that of the murderous Pol Pot.

Still, there is no guarantee that Chinese, ASEAN, or American recognition of Vietnamese suzerainty in Kampuchea would result in repaired Sino-Vietnamese relations to the point of diminishing Soviet influence and access in Vietnam. Soviet military aid has been valuable to Vietnamese conquests in Kampuchea, and Soviet economic assistance has enabled Vietnam to avoid some of the worst hardships and dislocations of a wartime economy. In return the Soviets are given access to Vietnam's ports, airfields, and other facilities, which greatly extend Soviet ability to project military power, not only in Southeast Asia but also into the South Pacific and Indian Ocean areas. On the other hand, certain factors could favor a diminished Soviet role, including Vietnamese resentment of Soviet heavy-handedness and possibly reduced aid levels, Vietnamese recognition that real economic growth depends on substantial links with the nations of free Asia, and improved Vietnamese relations with the United States. The Soviet security blanket is a Vietnamese insurance policy for a nation that has known over 40 years of war and is mistrustful of its neighbors. That policy will be nullified only when Soviet demands make it too expensive, or when the perceived threat to Vietnam is reduced to the point that the insurance policy is no longer deemed necessary.

The second Soviet objective, neutralizing American friends and allies in East Asia, goes back at least as far as Brezhnev's 1969 proposal for a zone of peace and neutrality in Southeast Asia. The failure of this effort to achieve nonalignment among the ASEAN states at a time of relative military inferiority to the United States, however, in no way inhibits Soviet planners today. The 1981 Kremlin requests to make military port calls in Southeast Asia exemplifies the persistent Soviet effort to attain parity of treatment because of parity in military power. The ASEAN states refused to bend, and not only refused warship port calls but flatly rejected Brezhnev's proposal to resolve the problem in Kampuchea through a regional conference in which the neutralization of Southeast Asia was a prime Soviet objective. The Soviet goal, however, continued to be pursued through the efforts of Vietnam. In July 1982 Vietnam proposed a limited international conference, not to resolve the situation in Kampuchea but to neutralize Southeast Asia. The proposal sought to legitimize the Vietnamese presence in Kampuchea while blaming any problem therein on Chinese and ASEAN's support of guerrilla ("reactionary") forces, and called for a demilitarized zone along the Thai border. Foreign Minister Nguyen Co Thach followed through with threats of hot pursuit into Thailand, and statements that Vietnam could repatriate its troops from Kampuchea only when China ceased to threaten Vietnam. He further called for American pull-out from the Philippines, stating that Vietnam can give bases to the Soviet Union just as the Philippines have given the United States bases. To show his "good faith" in the neutralization scheme he announced a "partial withdrawal" of Vietnamese troops from Kampuchea. Again, both China and the ASEAN states rejected the idea. They pointed out that it is Vietnamese aggression and interference in Kampuchea that is at the root of the problem, and called for total withdrawal of Vietnamese forces and self-determination of the Khmer people. Undeterred, Vietnam continues to press its demands for recognition of its suzerainty over Kampuchea. Despite promises of a partial pull-out, Vietnam never did execute a significant net reduction of its occupation forces. Instead, it declared that it would consider repatriating its forces only in the context of the neutralization of Southeast Asia.[4]

In Northeast Asia the Soviets also sought to further their objective by operating under the assumption that military power must inevitably result in political gain. The bold but ill-fated effort to prevent Japan from entering into its 1978 Treaty of Friendship and Cooperation with China is a case in point. Soviet forces moved onto three of the four Russian-occupied northern islands of Japan during the period immediately preceding and after the treaty. Nevertheless, the Japanese signed the treaty with China, which contained an antihegemony clause. Whatever Tokyo's view of the term "hegemony," Moscow's reaction of verbally blasting Japan, coupled with its landing of troops on the Northern Islands, demonstrated clearly that the shoe fit particularly well, albeit uncomfortably. In 1983 the Soviets again sought to control Japanese rights to pursue an independent foreign policy. The issue centered on the Japanese decision to permit U.S. Air Force deployment of two squadrons of F-16 aircraft to Misawa air base in northern Honshu. Japanese and American planners had agreed to the deployment as a partial offset to growing Soviet capabilities to threaten Japan, but Moscow seized the occasion of Prime Minister Nakasone's U.S. visit to condemn the F-16 deployment in threatening terms, saying that Japan could be annihilated by Soviet power—a threat reminiscent of Khruschev's 1956 attempt to intimidate Britain. The Soviet bluster met with the same negative popular and governmental reaction in both cases.

The final Soviet objective, acquiring new friends and allies in East Asia, has met with little success. There has been a concerted effort to obtain port access in the South Pacific, particularly among the newly independent island states of the region, but even here Soviet moves are looked upon with suspicion and a measure of hostility. Efforts to increase Soviet presence in Indonesia by exploiting fears of China have been largely nullified by memories of past Soviet demands for repayment of the billion-dollar Soviet aid program of the Sukarno era, combined with revelations of brash Soviet spy activities.

Elsewhere in East Asia the Kremlin also faces stiff opposition. Distrust of communism and its so-called socialist stepping-stone is widespread. This distrust has been reinforced by Vietnam's attack on Kampuchea and its expulsion of Pol Pot, even though Pol Pot is a doctrinaire communist guilty of the slaughter of millions of his countrymen. Soviet collusion with Vietnam strengthens the ASEAN and South Pacific island nations' suspicion of Soviet motives. Under such circumstances there is little incentive for these nations to cooperate with Moscow.

Meeting frustration at every turn, the Soviets have redirected some of their efforts to economic matters in order to acquire regional influence. The most significant Soviet asset for this purpose is its expanding merchant fleet. Today in Singapore, Sydney, Hong Kong, or Manila, Soviet ships are docked as far as the eye can see. Their presence is a function of the fact that they have dropped freight rates to such an extent that they now undersell traditional flag carriers by an average 15 percent, and in some cases as much as 50 percent. The objective is hard currency, but if successful in squeezing conference shippers out of traditional markets, the Russians will have gained the lion's share of East Asian international commerce, and a powerful economic lever by which to bring pressure in support of their other goals in the region, not to mention the enhanced capability to support the Soviet Pacific Fleet as auxiliaries and part-time intelligence gatherers. Other Soviet economic moves, however, are quite limited. Aid programs have been reduced to the point where they are now the lowest to any region in the world, and are generally restricted to high-visibility projects. In 1982, for example, Moscow offered to construct a cement plant in the Philippines and to cooperate in development of copper smelting and the pharmaceutical industry as well. Coming at a time of Philippine economic malaise, such projects serve as a visible reminder of a socialist alternative to the Marcos brand of capitalism. Thus Soviet economic prowess, while nowhere near a match for that of the United States or Japan, is designed for high political as well as economic impact.

An effective American response to the Soviet challenge in Asia requires the integration of national assets across a wide spectrum of activities. Militarily, it means the maintenance and improvement of both strategic and tactical force structures. First and foremost is the requirement to maintain a nuclear umbrella, so that no nation in free Asia need feel compelled either to develop its own nuclear capability or to accommodate to nuclear blackmail as a result of political intimidation associated with the growing Soviet military capabilities. The United States maintains a strategic presence in the Western Pacific, including submarine and bomber forces in Guam, both to provide a more flexible deterrent and to underpin the viability of commitments in Asia. Although little is said of the theater nuclear balance in Asia, it is very much a part of the overall strategic balance and is a matter of great concern to the governments of East Asia. This was made quite clear to Secretary of State George Schultz during his visits to Japan and China in 1983. There are now over 100 SS-20 IRBMs in Soviet Asia, and the leadership in both Beijing and Tokyo are seeking assurances that any agreement to limit or reduce SS-20 deployment in European Russia or Eastern Europe would not result in additions to that number in Asia. American interest in relieving some of the tension deriving from the sizable Soviet strategic arsenal is best served by both maintaining and improving our own deterrent, including that in Asia, and by taking measures to assure Asian leaders of our overall commitment to the region.

The present conventional force posture, including ground combat troops in South Korea and Okinawa, logistical and air support on the Japanese main islands, mobile forces in Okinawa, key naval bases in Subic Bay and Yokosuka, and air bases at Clark, Okinawa, Suwan, and Misawa, provides the minimum forward-basing structure essential to American credibility in the region. Any withdrawal of troops or major air and naval units would do nothing to reassure friends and allies or caution potential enemies in the region.

Modernization of these forces, such as the replacement of F-4 aircraft in Okinawa with F-15 aircraft in 1979 and 1980 and the addition of two F-16 squadrons at Misawa AFB, Japan, helps to offset some increases in Soviet power, and is a constant requirement. Other initiatives encouraging friends and allies are frequent "show the flag" visits by American ships, joint military exercises such as the annual Rim of the Pacific (RIMPAC) maneuvers with Canada, Japan, Australia, and New Zealand, and the Team Spirit exercises involving U.S. force deployments from the United States to Korea for joint maneuvers. Finally, security assistance to East Asia strengthens the ability of American friends and allies to resist the coercive techniques of the Soviet Union and its proxies. Prudent arms and technology transfers to these states, including China, both reinforce their confidence in American reliability and their own capacity for self-defense.

Much has been said and written about an anti-Soviet military front in Asia, and especially a Chinese-Japanese-American axis, as a sort of "NATO of Asia." References are also made to turning ASEAN into a military alliance and striking a strategic relationship with South Korea. While there are certain advantages to some of these schemes, none of them appears necessary at this time to defend against Soviet conventional attack or political coercion connected thereto. Japan is separated from the Soviet land mass by the 300-mile-wide Sea of Japan and deeply resents Soviet bullying tactics such as the recent militarization of three of the four Northern Isles that the Soviets occupied after World War II. It regards its own defense forces, its diplomacy, and its defense treaty with the United States as the fundamental pillars of its own defense, and it regards any trilateral arrangement incorporating China into an anti-Soviet front as a needless provocation of the USSR. China is in a different position, but the conclusion is the same. Its conventional war strategy is one of protracted guerrilla conflict, with a force structure dedicated not to power projection but to exacting a high toll on any invading Soviet force. A Chinese military alliance with the United States and Japan would do little to raise the Soviet cost and would heighten Soviet hypersensitivity regarding China. Under existing conditions, therefore, a tripartite axis is neither practical nor particularly advantageous. A strategic relationship with Korea also risks unnecessary regional destabilization for questionable gains. Static American strategic forces located close to centers of Soviet power would be vulnerable to rapid and concentrated attacks, and could serve to weld the often cool relationship between Moscow and

Pyongyang into a united front threatening peace on the peninsula. The present bilateral defense relationship with South Korea is more attuned to maintaining that peace. The ASEAN states form an even more unlikely military front against direct Soviet encroachments. Joint cooperation does enhance their ability to resist any Vietnamese expansionism, but it appears at present that only a heightened threat from Vietnam would forge an ASEAN military alliance.

The difficulties of striking a multilateral strategic alliance in Asia comparable to NATO does not mean, however, that bilateral security and cooperation cannot result in a degree of security comparable to that in Europe. The United States is now joined in separate mutual security treaties with Japan, South Korea, the Philippines, Australia, and New Zealand and is committed to the security of Thailand under the Manila Pact. Each of these defense arrangements helps assure the security of the Asian nation concerned, just as they enhance the global security of the United States. Despite their bilateral nature they are mutually reinforcing. For example, the United States maintains a mutual defense treaty with the Philippines. While this and our other Asian treaties have been criticized as being one-way security guarantees, no one questions the value of American military bases in the Philippines—bases that serve not only Philippine but American interests. The air base at Clark and the naval base at Subic are absolutely vital to our entire forward-basing structure in the Western Pacific. They protect vital sea and air lanes linking our most important allies in the region; they directly confront growing Soviet military power in Vietnam; and they provide a link to the Indian Ocean. During the crises in Iran and Afghanistan, the United States deployed carrier battle groups and strategic air assets to the Arabian Sea that could neither have been deployed nor expeditiously sustained without Clark and Subic. Much the same could be said in different ways about the rest of our force structure in the Western Pacific.

Besides balancing Soviet military power with U.S. and allied military strength, support for continued Asian socioeconomic progress is essential in order to preclude the erosion of freedom and the ascendancy of the Russian Bear in Asia. In this regard it is of the utmost importance to recognize that the political, economic, and military interests of the United States coincide nicely with the continued progress of the region. Nations that have achieved economic growth characteristic of free East Asia over the last 15 years are not easily attracted by the magical lure of Marxian prescription, particularly when they see how neighboring states that follow that prescription fare by way of comparison. Nor are nations that jealously guard their independence likely to kowtow to Soviet gunboat diplomacy or appreciate illegal maneuverings such as the spy activi-

ties recently exposed in Japan and Indonesia. The starting point
for any American reaction to Soviet activity in the Far East is
recognition that the political maturity and economic and social
progress of the region render Soviet political penetration extremely difficult. Thus American policy, while countering the military
threat of Soviet power in Asia, can best assure both U.S. and Asian
objectives by promoting interest in and contributions to continued
improvement of Asia's economic and social quality of life. American trade, investment, and technical and economic assistance have
stimulated and benefited from such improvement in the past, and
are likely to continue in this vein provided our political commitment to the region appears firm.

While political commitment is certainly conveyed by the presence of American military forces in Asia, it is equally conveyed by
understanding and able diplomats. Efforts to explain American positions and take into account host-country concerns are the basis of
the favorable position the United States now enjoys in Asia. Bonds
of personal friendship and understanding between Asian leaders and
U.S. officials form the essential underpinning of good relations.
The few but well-publicized cases when prompt consultation did not
occur before the announcement of major policy decisions evoked a
strong negative reaction from concerned friends and allies. The
imposition or lifting of trade sanctions against the Soviet Union and
negotiations to reduce Soviet SS-20 IRBM deployment in Europe are
but two recent examples of political actions originally considered
important only in a European context, but which are also of immense
concern in Asia. Our diplomats in East Asia contend not only with
such Eurocentric aspects of our global policy, but also with the os-
cillations in governmental policy commonly associated with changes
of administrations and with the crisis mentality of some policy makers. They seek to understand Asian security concerns and convey
to sometimes nervous friends and allies the strength of the U.S.
commitment to the region.

Public diplomacy is also vital to the success of American policy in Asia, especially as it concerns Soviet behavior. Publication
of Soviet excesses, such as its "yellow rain" of chemical warfare
against Lao and Cambodian "enemies," can be an effective tool to
reduce or eliminate those excesses. More positively, the tone of
American information flow can and should reflect American confidence, both in itself and in Asia. The United States Information
Agency programs speakers, events, and publications that help explain America and American policies. These and other reports,
speeches, and media interviews can go a long way to spread the
truth of the growing gap in quality of life between free and Communist Asia. Combined with other efforts they can help redirect super-

power competition from military to political and economic matters.
Of course it takes two to do so and the Soviets may shy from the
challenge. Nevertheless, with its imperial economy facing stagnation, Soviet interest in the great economic transformation off its
eastern shores is bound to heighten.[5] It is the job of public diplomacy to complement our diplomatic, economic, and military instruments of policy in order to ensure that the Asian people better understand the democratic values on which our peace and prosperity
rest.

Over the years the tendency to neglect overseas interests when
there has been no problem requiring immediate attention has plagued
American foreign policy. If we are to avoid this pitfall we must
recognize that American attention to and interest in the affairs of
East Asia will determine, more than any other factor, whether the
fundamentally favorable trend throughout the region will continue or
revert to an irreversible situation of the "gospel according to St.
Brezhnev." Tension in the region, such as that between China and
Taiwan, or Vietnam and her neighbors is the precondition for Soviet
participation in the international politics of Asia, and will continue
to challenge American policy makers in the foreseeable future.
Challenges abound, and there is no inevitability to any trend.
America fought three bloody wars to reverse unfavorable developments in Asia, and it would be most foolish now to revert to splendid isolationism in smug satisfaction that all is going pretty well.

Though it is not intended here to address all of the specific
issues of U.S. policy and programs over such a broad and diverse
area as East Asia, it is important to recognize that there is sufficient commonality of interests and challenge to those interests to
make the following observations. First, the United States must
maintain its military strength and forward-basing posture in the
Western Pacific. Second, it must seek to improve and update existing alliance systems and encourage improvement of the self-
defense capability of allies and friends throughout the region. Third,
opportunities must be sought to shift the forces of American-Soviet
competition, insofar as possible, from military to political and economic matters. Fourth, the United States should facilitate and support further trade, investment, and economic and technical assistance in order to reinforce the fantastic socioeconomic progress
that so well serves American and Asian interests alike. Fifth, it
should treat North Korea, China, and Vietnam as independent states,
not as Soviet vassals, so as to minimize the opportunity for Soviet
exploitation of their needs. Sixth, it should strive for consistency
and reliability in its approach, avoiding the vacillation and oscilla-
tions of policy that unnecessarily undermine confidence in America
as a friend or ally. With these observations in mind and an appro-

priate level of political support for the diplomats, the military, and the businessmen working in Asia, the United States will have a much better chance of avoiding further wars and the famous Kipling epitaph "A fool lies here who tried to hustle the East."[6]

NOTES

1. Lyndon B. Johnson, Vantage Point (New York: Holt, Rinehart and Winston, 1971), pp. 406-9; Chester Cooper, Lost Crusade (New York: Dodd, Mead, 1970), p. 291; and Senator Mike Mansfield, "Perspective on Asia: The New U.S. Doctrine and Southeast Asia," Report to the Committee on Foreign Relations, United States Senate, 1969.

2. Japanese Defense Agency, Defense of Japan, 1982, pp. 32-46.

3. Boston Globe, March 17, 1982; and Department of State, Chemical Warfare in Southeast Asia, March 22, 1982.

4. FBIS, Asia and Pacific, July 22 and 30, August 5, and November 1, 1982, and January 27, 1983.

5. In June 1983 Yuri Andropov appeared to favor a reform package with some decentralization and limited capitalist incentives; his emphasis on repression and punishment of alcoholism on the job tells the story.

6. Kipling, Naulahka.

8

Partnership with Japan, the Giant of Asia

The most important American ally in Asia, if not in the world, is Japan. Just as the Soviet Union constitutes the major threat to peaceful progress in Asia, Japan constitutes the major impetus for that progress. In 1982 Japan produced goods and services valued at some $1.2 trillion and that constituted 40 percent of the combined East Asian GNP. Its developmental assistance to other nations of the region, already exceeding that of the United States, is expected to increase still further, and its technology and capital transfers will continue to play a major role in furthering regional economic development. Moreover, the example of Japan is there for all to see. It boasts a democratic society and a free enterprise system, and gives every evidence of maintaining its competitive international position in the years ahead. U.S. relations with Japan are therefore critical to the success or failure of American policy throughout East Asia and the Western Pacific. They shape the future of both the world's two leading industrial democracies and the progress that our dynamic nations are capable of stimulating throughout East Asia.

Although a relationship as multifaceted as that between the United States and Japan involves many complexities and interests, none has been more important in recent years than mutual cooperation in international crises, bilateral trade, and defense. These three are likely to remain top priority items on the agenda of both nations in the years ahead, with all the special problems as well as benefits attending them. The first is part of a greater U.S. effort to secure allied support in an increasingly interdependent world in which U.S. action is effective only when allied support is forthcoming. It is well illustrated by the Japanese role in the crises in Iran, Afghanistan, and Poland.

In February 1981, American Embassy personnel, having been held prisoner for over a year in Tehran, returned home to a tumultuous welcome from a relieved nation. It was a happy ending to an agonizingly painful episode attending the rise of Khomeini and the disregard for diplomatic rights evinced by his regime. Little noticed amidst the joy of reunion was the resumption later that month of Iranian oil shipments to Japan of some 150,000 barrels per day. Although only a quarter of the 600,000 barrels per day Japan had been receiving from Iran prior to the seizure of the U.S. Embassy in November 1979, the oil shipments marked the final chapter of a drama that severely challenged not only the relationship between Japan and the United States, but also the overall foreign policies of the two economic superpowers.

Following seizure of the Embassy in Tehran, the U.S. government had embargoed normal commercial trade with Iran. The effectiveness of the embargo was contingent upon allied support, which America expected as both a symbol of solidarity and as a response to the violation of international law and custom that the seizure of an embassy represented. Frustrated by incapacity to resolve the crisis swiftly, the administration looked for allied support in an atmosphere of heightened emotional tension.

It was with shock and grave concern, therefore, that American officials heard of increased Japanese spot purchases of Iranian crude in the wake of the U.S. embargo. During the second week of December 1979 they lashed out at Japan for the purchases. Secretary of State Cyrus Vance, while visiting Paris, reportedly said Japan had acted with "unseemly haste" in buying the oil. High officials with the Secretary said Japan ranked lowest in foreign concern for U.S. efforts to resolve the hostage crisis. Senate Majority Leader Robert Byrd reiterated the oil complaint and accused Japanese bankers of helping Iran overcome a U.S. freeze on assets. Twelve other senators sponsored a resolution condemning the purchases and urging Tokyo to prevent Japanese firms from profiteering on Iranian oil. In the House, Speaker O'Neill reacted even more strongly, saying, "they had their 'day of infamy' many years ago," and charging Japan with "consorting with the enemy."[1]

The situation had all the makings of irreparably damaging Japanese-American relations. It flew in the face of three principles that have guided American diplomacy toward Japan in recent years:

1. Recognizing the importance of our bilateral relations
2. Treating Japan as an equal
3. Trusting Japan

On December 15, 1979, Ambassador Mike Mansfield met with Prime Minister Masayoshi Ohira to discuss the problem. Both men realized that the U.S. government had issued no policy and made no request for Japan to reduce Iranian oil purchases—indeed, some U.S. officials indicated Japan was not expected to cut back on oil purchases lest it place further strain on free-world supply. The preceding month, the Japanese Ministry of International Trade and Industry (MITI) had issued administrative guidance for companies to reduce their purchases of high-priced Iranian crude, but a few companies, adhering to the philosophy "that all is fair in love, war, and business," had gone ahead with additional spot purchases. After his meeting with Mansfield, Mr. Ohira announced that Japan would reduce imports of Iranian oil to the level that existed before the seizure of the U.S. Embassy in Tehran, a policy that was rigorously adhered to in the following months.

It took until April, however, until U.S. policy could be sorted out in conjunction with our allies regarding economic sanctions against Iran. At that time it was Japan that took the critical first step of joining the United States by refusing to pay a price increase levied by the National Iranian Oil Company. In so doing, Japan knowingly cut off its supply of Iranian crude, which constituted 12 percent of all Japanese oil purchases, as of April 21, 1980—a cutoff that remained in effect until after the hostage release some ten months later.

The Japanese decision was a watershed. It de facto detached Japan from its fledgling "omnidirectional" foreign policy by committing the nation politically in support of an ally whose interests conflicted with those of an important energy supplier. Dependent on imports for 99.7 percent of its oil supply, Japan at length received the recognition it deserved for its sacrifice. American spokesmen and the press across the nation warmly welcomed Tokyo's support in a manner succinctly summarized in this New York Times report: "Japan deserves this nation's gratitude. . . . Japan has provided the first dramatic allied support in the hostage crisis. It has emerged as the leader among allies in supporting Washington."2

Similar comments were soon echoed after the Soviet invasion of Afghanistan. Japan supported American sanctions fully. Despite strong sports-minded feeling throughout the country it joined the Olympic boycott. It supported the grain embargo. It delayed several industrial projects pending with the Soviet Union, and refused the Soviets new credits for major projects. In some cases this meant lost business; for example, Nippon Steel lost a $300 million project to construct a steel plant south of Moscow to the French firm Creusot Loire. Prime Minister Ohira succinctly summarized his government's position as follows:

> Japan stands ready to demonstrate solidarity with the
> United States. We must remain firm in meeting the
> challenge posed by this Soviet aggression and lend a
> helping hand to countries in the Middle East and
> Asia. . . . My government's position is that Japa-
> nese participation in the Moscow Olympics under
> present circumstances is not desirable.[3]

Finally, Japan acted as a responsible ally with respect to
Poland. In early 1981 national leaders enunciated a clear warning
of Japanese intentions. Chief Cabinet Secretary Miyazawa: "If
Soviet forces intervene in Poland, the GOJ will have no choice but
to take measures in consultation with other advanced democratic
nations."[4] Vice Foreign Minister Takashima: "If the Soviet forces
intervene in Poland, it will be far more serious than the Afghan
problem, and we will have to take stronger sanction measures."[5]
After taking office in 1980, Prime Minister Suzuki, otherwise not
known for strong statements, declared with respect to Poland that
his government would not adopt a "loose principled" policy of separating politics from economics."[6]

In concrete terms these statements reflect the determination
of Japanese authorities, in the face of considerable protest by the
companies involved, to forego economic advantage for the sake of
its alliance with the United States. In 1982 Japan, while continuing
to export pipelayers contracted before the U.S. export ban, curtailed its involvement in the six-year-old Russo-Japanese offshore
oil and gas project near Sakhalin, and moved to ban industrial robot
sales to Soviet-bloc countries. Together with its actions on Iran
and Afghanistan, this type of Japanese support is of inestimable
value to the United States. It comes at a time when the Soviets are
actively seeking technology and credits for major projects that are
crucial to their stagnating economy. Given the importance of these
projects, as well as the criticality of Western assistance to their
accomplishment, there is no telling what influence Japan may have
exerted on Soviet decisions regarding Poland.

These aspects of Japanese-American political relations are
significant for three reasons. Firstly, they show that the United
States has in Japan an ally whose support is vital to overall American policy worldwide. Too often American officials focus narrowly
on specific problems of our bilateral relationship, and neglect this
important dimension of friendship. Secondly, they illustrate again
the continuous need for mutual trust and understanding. By showing
confidence in Japan and exhibiting confidence in itself as an ally,
the United States can attain the maximum benefit from what may
well be its most important relationship for the rest of this century.

Finally, they shape the political context in which Japanese and American economic and security relations must move forward.

The Japanese-American economic relationship, and in particular bilateral trade, forms the second and perhaps most volatile area of policy requiring nearly constant attention. The United States posted trade deficits with Japan of $15.8 billion in 1981 and $16.8 billion in 1982. Recent and current problems include access to government procurement, tobacco, and autos. Some progress was made when American companies were permitted to bid on Nippon Telephone and Telegraph (NTT) annual procurement of $3 billion and total Japanese government purchases of over $7 billion, but in 1982 Americans sold NTT only $40 million in hardware.[7] After discussion with American representatives, Japan unilaterally reduced tariffs on tobacco and agreed in principle to expand distribution outlets for foreign tobacco. As a result, some additional American sales are expected. More significant was the voluntary agreement, subsequently extended, whereby American imports of Japanese vehicles were limited to 1.68 million units annually. In 1980 the total had reached 1.91 million units and was rapidly increasing. Without the agreement, therefore, Detroit would have been in grave difficulty. In June 1983 Japanese Trade and Industry Minister, Sosuke Uno, reportedly indicated his intention to seek complete removal of the import limits when they expire in 1984, but Ambassador Mike Mansfield was quick to state that this was not an official Japanese position and was probably a "misinterpretation." The agreement was later extended at 1.85 million units until 1985.

The problem is also being reduced by Japanese investment. Honda has begun construction on a plant in Ohio that will produce 10,000 cars a month and directly employ over 2,000 people. In 1982 Nissan broke ground on a plant in Tennessee that will produce 10,000 small trucks a month and employ some 2,200 people. Toyota's studies and its discussions with General Motors have led to similar decisions, with a major joint venture planned for Fremont, California.

Despite these measures, Japanese-American economic relations in the 1980s remain tense. In 1982 Secretary of Commerce Malcolm Baldrige charged Japan with tolerating a profound inequality in our access to the Japanese market, and maintaining cultural traditions that simply have to be changed. Later that year, presidential aspirant Walter Mondale strongly castigated the Japanese for what he considered unfair trade practices. He stated that if elected he would get tough with the Japanese and improve the trade balance. American plant closings in several basic industries, as well as agreements for wage increases well below cost-of-living increases have contributed significantly to three oft-repeated charges against Japan: unfair competition, dumping, and the erection of nontariff barriers.

The unfair competition charge centers on the idea of reciprocity—that the United States should treat Japanese imports in the same manner as they treat ours. However, this principle has not been the basis for the structure of American trade under the General Agreement on Tariff and Trade (GATT). The formula under which we and other GATT members, including Japan, operate is equal treatment for imported goods according to the legal system of each nation. Under this principle the United States would have no complaint, for example, if Japanese auto emission standards are more stringent than those of the United States, as long as U.S. auto exports to Japan are accorded the same treatment as that of third nation exports. The problem with this system is that it was formulated at a time when international trade was far less important to national economies and the United States enjoyed a sufficient lead in technology and production capacity not to worry about it. Now, in a different era, it is a problem that must be addressed on a multilateral basis.

Dumping, where Japanese are accused of selling goods on the U.S. market at prices below those in their own market, is another irritant in bilateral economic relations. One problem is that the lengthy and meticulous process required to prove dumping tends to delay effective legal countermeasures well beyond the damaging economic impact of the dumping itself. American television industry, for example, correctly claimed that Japanese dumping in the early 1970s contributed to ruining much of our domestic industry. A subsequent orderly marketing agreement by which Japanese-exported television sets were temporarily limited in the U.S. market came too late. Steel is another industry in which Japan has been accused of dumping, despite a clear Japanese competitive advantage in steel production. A "trigger price mechanism" was instituted in the late 1970s to resolve this problem, which was mainly with European manufacturers. The cost of Japanese production together with shipping insurance and other costs were factored in as a basis for "triggering" an assumption of dumping. Here the mechanism worked with varying degrees of satisfaction, but did not solve the basic dissatisfaction of U.S. industry.

Nontariff barriers form a third and most acrimonious series of problems. Why, for example, must a standard-sized U.S. automobile be treated as a luxury item in Japan and thereby be highly taxed, in addition to large inspection fees and distribution costs? Why have American cigarettes been restricted to a small percentage of Japanese outlets until quite recently, and priced well above their Japanese competition? Why has superior American telecommunications equipment been used by Japan's powerful Nippon Telephone and Telegraph system in such limited quantities? These and many other questions constitute a basis for complaints by U.S. business against Japanese trade practice and form a potentially explosive political backdrop against what is otherwise a healthy and generally harmonious U.S.-Japanese economic relationship.

While it is impossible in this short space to analyze and evaluate the complex set of factors involved in each of these major problem areas, it is important to keep in mind the following general observations. First, American trade relations with Japan contribute significantly to our national prosperity. Difficulties associated with certain bilateral problems too often obscure the immense benefits that both nations derive from economic interchange. In 1982 alone, two-way trade exceeded $60 billion, the largest overseas trade in world history. It is demand-led trade, typified by U.S. purchases of Hondas and video tape recorders, and Japanese purchases of coal and aircraft. Japanese manufacturers have an excellent reputation in this country. Many Americans prefer their products and are willing to pay the price for them, often because that price is below that of comparable U.S. goods. Treasury Secretary Donald Regan took note of the deflationary impact of Japanese goods when he warned in 1981 that action to limit automobile imports must be viewed with great caution. For its part Japan enjoys American imports in which we have a comparative advantage, and has been our largest foreign agricultural market in recent years, purchasing some $6 billion annually, including 60 percent of all American beef exports and 40 percent of all American citrus exports. Thus bilateral trade helps to maximize overall production in both countries while it dampens inflations by bringing quality products to market at prices more affordable than possible locally.

Second, the fact that the United States has registered a large trade deficit with Japan in recent years is less significant than the overall current account balance of both nations. This is true for two reasons. First the global account gives a better picture of international competitiveness than trade with any single nation, and second the current account considers the balance of services as well as goods, an area in which the United States had traditionally excelled. These services, such as repatriated earnings on U.S. overseas investment, financial services, insurance, tourism, engineering, and construction services and international transportation links are often referred to as invisibles. They constitute a major factor in our international trade, so much so that while our overall trade balance for the past four years was $111 billion in deficit, our overall current account was roughly in balance.

On the other hand Japan, despite a $42 billion surplus in merchandize trade, ran an $8 billion global current account deficit for the four years. Although the trend in the Japanese current account is toward a surplus, these facts demonstrate that the United States still equals Japan in overall international economic competitiveness and enjoys an immense lead in its exports of invisibles.[9]

Third, the basic imbalance in our bilateral trade structure is primarily a function of relative productivity levels. Japan built 14 large and medium-sized steel mills in the past 20 years. The United States built two. By the early 1980s Japan enjoyed a steel production cost advantage close to 30 percent. Its direct labor productivity was estimated 50 percent greater than that in the United States, while its raw materials costs were lower than those in our country.[10] A similar condition exists in the auto industry. Heavy investment in plant, automation, and robotics has made Japan the largest producer of vehicles in the world. Japanese gross fixed capital formation is 32 percent of GNP, compared to 7 percent for the United States. The ratio of savings to disposable income is 20 percent in Japan but only 5 percent in the United States.[11] The Japanese worker averages a 41-hour work week. The U.S. average is 37 hours. Japanese industry employs thousands of industrial robots to enhance efficiency. Even though Americans pioneered the idea, we still use very few. Japanese are busy worldwide learning and adapting new industrial techniques. We tend to rest on our laurels in too many cases, and restrict our business outlook to the domestic market.

The United States can learn a lot from Japan, just as Japan learned a lot from the United States. The long-term viability of U.S. basic industry may depend on it. In the absence of a major effort to increase productivity, the structural problem of a basic imbalance in U.S.-Japan trade will persist. It is in the American interest, therefore, to alleviate some of the problems naturally associated with its huge volume of bilateral trade, to recognize the mutual benefits derived from that trade, and to sustain efforts to enhance the benefits of this trade through unprecedented economic cooperation. This will not always be easy, particularly when a weakened yen is tending to increase Japanese export volume. Nevertheless, it is necessary if we are to continue to improve the livelihood of both our citizenry, and stimulate the economies of Asia and much of the rest of the world as well. Japan and the United States are the industrial giants of the modern era, and the way they address economic issues is critical to the well-being of the world in which our nations play a leading role.

Security constitutes the third vital element of Japanese-American relations. Since the Battle of Midway, the United States has been preeminent in its ability to project power in the Western Pacific. For several years that power went uncontested. Then, first in Korea and subsequently in Vietnam, the United States found itself engaged in conflicts in which the full force of its military strength could not be utilized. Both involved internal national struggle, with the use (Korea) or threatened use (Vietnam) of Chinese intervention delimiting U.S. objectives.

Despite such limitations, U.S. forces were considered more than adequate to maintain the balance of power necessary to prevent any one nation from achieving hegemony, either in Southeast or Northeast Asia. American naval and air power were unchallenged in Asia, and could be rapidly reinforced in an emergency. Memories of Japan's war machine remained strong throughout Asia, and at least four internal factors inhibited Japanese militarization. These included the legal constraints of Article 9 of the Constitution, the budgetary constraints of a devastated and then rebuilding economy, the psychological constraints of antimilitarism, and the opposition of nearly all political groups except a narrow band of right-wing extremists. Under these conditions it was considered neither important nor desirable for Japan to strengthen significantly its military capabilities.

During the 1970s, these conditions underwent considerable adjustment as Soviet military power in Asia increased and U.S. strength declined. The fact that the Soviet buildup was gradual and not confined to Asia alone, however, tended to dampen any fundamental military reassessment on the part of Japan. As part of the overall buildup following the Cuban missile crisis of 1962, Soviet force strengthening in Asia proceeded methodically and persistently, punctuated only by two important periods of rapid acceleration. The first was quantitative in nature and occurred in conjunction with the Sino-Soviet border crisis of the late 1960s. The second was qualitative, and proceeded as part of naval and air modernization of the late 1970s and early 1980s. The response of Japan to the former was subdued, owing to both strong U.S. forces in the region and the fact that the Soviet buildup was presumably directed against China. In addition, Japanese antimilitarism had been reinforced by the American involvement in Vietnam. The latter Soviet buildup, however, produced a defense debate unparalleled in postwar Japanese history.

As the debate proceeded and before a consensus could emerge on major issues, the American response to the Soviet buildup began to take form and exert a powerful influence on the debate itself. In 1975, Secretary of Defense Schlesinger called for increased Japanese defense capabilities. This was followed in 1976 by the Pacific Doctrine of President Ford, which placed greater expectations on the Japanese-American alliance as the cornerstone of U.S. policy for peace and security in the Pacific. Toned down in the early Carter years, U.S. requests for Japan to strengthen its defenses became pronounced after the President's call for allied burden sharing just prior to the Soviet invasion of Afghanistan. With that invasion, and with the dispatch of one of two carrier groups in the Western Pacific to the Indian Ocean, American spokesmen came to call upon Japan to make "steady and significant" increases in its defense posture. Secretary of Defense Harold Brown made a special appeal to this effect just prior to the Japanese cabinet decision on its fiscal year 1981 defense budget, and subsequently expressed disappointment when that budget increased 7.6 percent rather than the 12.2 percent for which he hoped.

The Reagan Administration took office committed to a roles and missions approach toward Japanese defense efforts. Aware of the constraints on the Japanese military and committed to private diplomacy rather than public criticism, the administration did not seek to pressure Japan on the issue. Nevertheless, the same conditions that prompted the Carter Administration to urge greater Japanese effort were building. The Reagan Administration took office inheriting a defense budget of $162 billion for FY 1981 and nearly $200 billion for FY 1982. It faced specific defense problems best reflected in a CIA estimate that the Soviet Union had outspent the United States on defense by 40 percent over the last decade. It faced serious threats to the strategic balance globally and in Western Europe, a real possibility of Soviet military intervention in Poland, a conventional imbalance in Southwest Asia and heightened Soviet activity in Vietnam and other parts of Asia.

It was in this context that the administration raised both defense spending and its expectations of allied defense burden sharing. When asked about NATO defense efforts, then Secretary of State Alexander Haig stated, "What we have to find is a way for everyone to do more—and I include Japan in that." As the administration moved to improve American defense capabilities and urged additional efforts by our NATO allies, it became clear that Haig's statement presaged a new round of diplomatic efforts to persuade Japan to do more on defense. President Reagan sought a rational division of labor in his May 1981 meeting with Prime Minister Suzuki, who said Japan would undertake to defend its sea lanes to a distance of 1,000 miles. By 1982 administration spokesmen had become increasingly critical of Japanese efforts. For example, Secretary of Defense Caspar Weinberger publicly chastised Japan for an inadequate defense posture, stating that "it can provide much more for its own defense."[12] Finally, in November 1983 President Reagan again raised the issue on his mission to Japan.

How these requests are received in Japan depends in no small measure on how well they are attuned to changes in the aforementioned military constraints. Externally, these constraints are at their lowest ebb since 1945. Opposition from China has changed to support for a strengthened Self Defense Force (SDF), while ASEAN nations perceive a strengthened SDF favorably as long as it does not project forces to their shores and is not accompanied by a U.S. drawdown in the Pacific. Internally, the situation is more complex.

The legislative constraint was challenged by then Justice Minister Okuno during the summer of 1980, when he claimed the Japanese Constitution did not prohibit nuclear weapons, and to a more limited extent by General Takeda in early 1981 when he stated Japanese Self-Defense Forces could respond to an attacker in self-defense without political approval. Despite these highly publicized events, support for the constitution in Japan remains strong, with 71 percent of the population against the revision to permit armed forces, 13-15 percent for revision to that end, and the remainder without opinion.[13] Upon taking office in late 1982, Prime Minister Nakasone said the question of constitutional revision should at least be studied, but he backed off from any initiatives for revision. Given the general public attitudes on the subject, as well as lack of political support for a change, the likelihood of constitutional revision seems remote indeed. There is, moreover, a significant body of opinion among the national leadership that holds that there is considerable room for Japanese military improvements within the constraints of the constitution. Both the 1976 National Defense Program Outline, which calls for Japan to "repel limited and small-scale aggression, in principle without external assistance," and the policy to defend sea-lanes to 1,000 miles, are objectives requiring considerable enhancement of Japanese defensive capabilities. This opinion maintains that Japan should build a first-class defensive force to cooperate closely with American forces, and that it is a waste of political capital to attempt to alter the constitution or the program outline under which the SDF now operate.

The budgetary constraint poses a more formidable obstacle to increased defense effort in Japan. During the past four years at least one-third of the government budget was deficit-financed by public bonds. The powerful Ministry of Finance succeeded in reducing bond issuance to finance the public debt by a trillion yen in 1980, two trillion yen in 1981, and had planned to reduce such bonds by additional increments of two trillion yen each in 1982 and 1983, leading to a balanced budget in 1984. The failure of the Suzuki Administration to meet these goals, or even to reduce the swelling fiscal deficit at all, led directly to the Prime Minister's resignation in October 1982. Barring a tax increase, therefore, the government of Japan budget will appear increasingly tight, with increases in defense expenditures running strong risk of being perceived as coming at the expense of vested interests in the domestic arena. Coming at a time of Finance Ministry guidelines for a 10 percent decrease for other governmental ministries, the 1983 6.9 percent increase in Japan's defense budget might appear to some Japanese as substantial, or even excessive. Yet when one considers that defense accounts for less than 1 percent of GNP, that high savings rates and low taxation enable Japan to afford higher defense costs, and that Japanese consumption and welfare costs rise more each year than the entire defense budget, this argument becomes less compelling. Nevertheless, in Japan as in the United States, perception is as important as reality for political decision makers, making American efforts to urge greater Japanese defense efforts a difficult, if necessary, diplomatic undertaking.

The psychological constraint appears to be less binding than ever before. Recent polls show only 5-10 percent of the population still oppose the Treaty of Cooperation and Mutual Security or the maintenance of the SDF. About 25 percent favor strengthening the SDF, with the remainder for maintaining them at present levels. These figures represent significant changes from the strong antimilitary sentiment of 10-20 years ago. Ironically, a major share of the shift in Japanese opinion is attributed to the heightened Soviet military activity intended to intimidate Japan. Pictures of Soviet aircraft and ships transiting the straits surrounding Japan are frequently featured by the media, often accompanied by commentary pointing out the Soviet military buildup in Asia. At the same time, public opinion polls show the Soviet Union reaching new lows in the esteem of the Japanese people. It would be a mistake, however, to represent movement in Japanese opinion as a compelling force for strong defense enhancement at this time. Rather, it has permitted a more moderate defense improvement and a more active defense cooperation with the United States with a level of controversy far reduced from what otherwise would have been the case.

Finally, the political constraint has lost much of its postwar intensity. The Democratic Socialist Party has become a solid supporter of both the Mutual Security Treaty and the SDF, and the Komeito Party has quietly moved to such a stance. The Japan Socialist Party, meanwhile, has not protested military programs and activities with zeal. Still the position of several Liberal Democratic Party leaders remains lukewarm on defense. While most party leaders support a moderately strong self-defense capability, there is considerable opposition from a very few antimilitary elements, a few Cabinet members jealous of defense increases greater than that of their own ministries, and several politicians who view U.S. pressure as interfering with the autonomy of Japanese policymaking.

Thus, legislative and psychological constraints have become relatively weaker in Japan, with the likelihood they will continue in that direction. Budgetary constraints remain strong in the near term, but could change with a resumption of rapid economic growth, or earlier if new taxes are introduced. Political constraints are less predictable; although unlikely, powerful underlying nationalistic feelings could upset past moderate defense growth either by a return to militarism or by a refusal to submit to U.S. pressure on defense in the name of autonomy, coupled with the idea that Japan can make unique contributions to world peace through the example of its relative pacifism. More likely with enlightened leadership, Japan could increase its defense expenditures steadily and significantly, so as to achieve its stated objectives more expeditiously. In so doing Japan would both build a more effective deterrent and greatly defuse American criticism, which is likely to escalate if Nakasone does follow with deeds his words on improving Japanese capabilities.

The future of Japanese-American security relations, therefore, depends to a large extent on how and what the United States asks Japan to do and how those requests are perceived in Japan. In this regard, and in view of this discussion, the following framework, adhered to in varying degrees by agents of the U.S. government, is recommended in approaching Japan.

First, the United States must reaffirm its commitment along with its requests—pointing out America's intention privately and occasionally publicly to remain a firm ally and a major military power in East Asia and the Pacific, and to support that policy statement with a credible force structure in the region. To do otherwise is to undermine the confidence necessary for an effective alliance. A 1978 poll indicated, for example, that 56 percent of Japanese citizens thought the United States would not assist Japan in an emergency. This feeling could be reinforced if the Japanese see U.S. requests for Japan to do more as an expression of U.S. weakness. We should point to our increasing defense capabilities and to the fact that we seek Japanese improvements as a complement to those capabilities in Northeast Asia, not as a substitute for our weakness. We should also point to increasing public support in the United States for the Japanese alliance. A 1980 Potomac Associates poll, for example, showed that fully 68 percent of Americans favor coming to the defense of Japan if it were attacked, as compared to 50 percent in 1978 and only 37 percent in 1974.

Second, U.S. requests should focus not on asking Japan to do more, but on deciding jointly what Japan will do and what the United States will do. This is a process already begun in our military planning, and may be expected to acquire increasing political importance in the future. Nebulous requests for Japan to increase its defense budget by a certain percentage, if they are not related to specific military programs we jointly agree are necessary, are bound to be perceived in Japan as meddling in an internal budgetary political process. Instead, U.S. requests should be relatable directly to international conditions and a joint plan for dealing with those conditions as they affect the security of Japan. Goals such as maintaining a regional balance of power must be translated into political-military objectives such as opening or closing sea lanes under various international conditions. A worthwhile and recent example of such cooperation is the plan for Japan to defend its sea lanes out to 1,000 miles from the home islands, beyond which the United States would assume responsibility. Such objectives are essential political prerequisites to the realization of joint military plans. Formulated jointly in the arena of political relations, they both justify and provide direction to the military programs being developed in other fora. In Japan both justification and political direction are especially sensitive, and therefore all the more necessary for effective implementation of plans and programs to defend Japan.

Third, the United States should adhere persistently to well-conceived doctrine and policies for Japanese security. The Nixon Doctrine of 1969, for example, contains reasonable elements for U.S. policy today. Its first two elements, that we will keep our treaty commitments and that we will provide a shield (umbrella in Japan) against nuclear threats, require no modification. The third element, that "the U.S. will furnish military and economic assistance when requested," but "look to the nation directly threatened to assume the primary responsibility for its own defense," is also reasonable but requires at least two important caveats. The first is that the statement be understood in the context of the external threat in Northeast Asia in the 1980s, not the internal threat in Southeast Asia in the 1960s. Secondly, it must be understood that the statement in no way implies a U.S. withdrawal from Asia, as the Nixon Doctrine became widely interpreted in the 1970s. Appropriately caveated, then, the Nixon Doctrine could provide an established overall policy framework within which to set goals and objectives for the security of Japan in the 1980s. In stating that Japan is primarily responsible for its own defense while at the same time reaffirming the U.S. commitment, the doctrine meshes nicely with the mutual increased efforts needed to maintain a healthy security environment in Northeast Asia in the years ahead.

The fourth and final recommendation regarding U.S. approaches is that they take cognizance, in their tone and in their substance, of the strategic value of Japan. As long as the United

States operates on the basis of a forward deployment strategy, Japan will remain the linchpin of the U.S. position throughout Northeast Asia. Its geographic position places it astride and across the sea lines of communication and egress of the majority of the Soviet Pacific Fleet. Its economy is the heart of a great system of international commerce, technology transfer, and investment that is pushing the free nations of Asia into a position of unquestioned preeminence over their socialist neighbors, with all the long-range political results that implies.

Under these conditions close political and military cooperation with Japan, coupled with frank private discussions at the highest levels of government, will be more important than ever. For our part that means keeping Japan informed of our views regarding the increasingly dangerous world in which we live. It means approaching Japan in a frank manner, recognizing that any decision Japan will make on defense is indeed a Japanese decision. As one Japanese official put it, "Don't tell us what to do; tell us your problem and we will decide what to do."

Japan is still a highly nationalistic country. In facing the common challenges of this decade and beyond it is vital that the United States and Japan consult closely and act with full regard for each others' interests. Japan should not and must not be taken for granted. Close cooperation, based on mutual trust, will be necessary to reaffirm the U.S. commitment to Japan, to maximize the benefits of defense cooperation, and to discuss realistically improvements in Japanese self-defense capability. Japan can and should do more for its own defense. Japan is willing to cooperate with the United States in doing more, but in the final analysis the defense of Japan is a mutual effort serving mutual Japanese-American interests.

NOTES

1. United Press International, December 11, 1979; and The Japan Times, December 13, 1979.

2. Editorial, New York Times, April 22, 1980.

3. Public statement by Prime Minister Ohira, May 3, 1980.

4. Press conference, December 5, 1980, as reported in Tokyo Shimbun, December 6, 1980.

5. The Japan Times, January 6, 1980.

6. Public statement by Prime Minister Suzuki, August 2, 1980.

7. Department of Commerce, FT-990, Highlights of U.S. Export-Import Trade, December 1982; exports f.a.s., imports custom value basis; and Business Week, July 18, 1983, p. 204.

8. _Christian Science Monitor_, July 14, 1983, p. 1; and _Nightly Business Review_, July 13, 1983 (Washington, D.C.: Public Broadcasting System); and _The Washington Post_, November 2, 1983.

9. U.S. Department of Commerce, _International Economic Indicators_, June 1983; for the period 1979-83.

10. Charles Bradford, Vice-President, Merrill Lynch Institutional Report, _Japanese Steel Industry, a Comparison with Its U.S. Counterpart_, and Don Stingle, former Director of the U.S. Export-Import Bank, "How U.S. Neglect Is Wrecking Exports, Increasing Deficits," _Government Executive_, April 1982.

11. U.S. Department of Commerce, op. cit.

12. Secretary of Defense Caspar Weinberger, as quoted in _The Wall Street Journal_, April 29, 1982.

13. These percentages resulted from independent polls taken by the _Asahi Shimbun_ in 1978 and the _Yomiuri Shimbun_ in 1981.

9

For or Against Us?
China Comes Out
of Hibernation

On January 1, 1979 the world's most populous nation joined hands with the world's most advanced nation in normalizing diplomatic relations. By this act the United States recognized the government in Beijing as the sole legitimate authority over all of China and acknowledged the Chinese position "that there is but one China and Taiwan is a part of China." During the years immediately following this event the skeletal outlines of normalization were given flesh, commencing with the exchange of ambassadors and the establishment of embassies two months later. By the early 1980s the United States and China had agreed to release assets frozen since the Korean War as repayment for the property claims of U.S. nationals, to promote cooperation in hydroelectric power and water resources management, to accredit resident journalists, to allow direct exchange of letters and post items, to negotiate U.S. involvement in Chinese offshore oil exploration, and to initiate settlement of civil aviation affairs. Protocols were also signed involving atmospheric, marine, and fisheries sciences, metrology and standards, the management of scientific and technological information, and cooperation in the science and technology of medicine and health, nuclear physics, transportation, aeronautics, and biomedicine. Cultural exchanges were initiated on a broad basis, most-favored-nation tariff treatment was mutually approved, and the U.S. Export-Import Bank was authorized to loan China up to $2 billion for trade purposes and to develop hydroelectric power. Overseas Private Investment Corporation programs were begun, providing political-risk insurance for U.S. companies doing business in China; a long-term grain agreement was signed; and the first U.S. commercial flights began regular landings in Beijing. Consultations also took place on a wide variety of bilateral matters, including drug abuse, technology transfer, sports, telecommunications, and mining. Strategic consultations were frequent and wide-ranging, highlighted by visits to China of virtually every high-ranking American official with foreign affairs responsibilities from the vice-president on down, and many without such responsibilities as well. Chinese visits to our country included those of Vice Premier Deng Xiaoping, Vice Premier Geng Biao, and Deputy Chief of Staff of the People's Liberation Army Liu Huaqing. In 1983 over 100,000 Americans visited China, while 10,000 Chinese students were studying at American educational institutions.[1] Sister-city and sister-state relationships were established between numerous American and Chinese localities, and China was permitted for the first time to receive exports of American goods on the Commodity and Munitions Control Lists.

This rapid development of the relationship over such a broad range of issues was quite remarkable, especially in light of the preceding 30 years of bitter bilateral hostility. America had fought the Chinese in direct combat in Korea, entered the war in Vietnam in part to contain perceived Chinese expansionism in Southeast Asia, and suffered thousands of casualties at the hands of Chinese weapons provided to Hanoi and the Viet Cong. When in 1982 the United States began providing certain arms to the very nation that had drawn American blood in two wars within a generation, it marked both the logical culmination of the strategic realignment of China described in Chapter 4 and a significant departure in strategic cooperation between erstwhile enemies. Nevertheless, Sino-American cooperation, prompted almost entirely by tensions emanating from the Sino-Soviet split, could and would be severely disrupted by the issue of Taiwan and by Soviet ploys to attract China. The relationship might survive the tempest, but would do so with assurance only if reinforced and expanded by the U.S. role in what has become most vital to the people and leadership of China—economic modernization. Thus as we enter the mid-1980s it can clearly be seen that tremendous progress has characterized recent Sino-American relations, but that the future shape of those relations is by no means certain. High on the agenda of both our nations and on our future relations are three fundamental but interrelated issues—(a) the degree of strategic cooperation possible and desirable, (b) Taiwan, and (c) Chinese modernization and the U.S. role therein.

STRATEGIC COOPERATION

The degree of Sino-American strategic cooperation depends to a large extent on the state of Sino-Soviet relations. With Moscow

building its military power to unprecedented levels and actively interfering in Third World areas, it is obvious that current ties with
China derive from the basic view that "the enemy of my enemy is
my friend." Richard Nixon succinctly stated this view upon returning from his late-1982 trip to China: "The key factor that brought
us together 10 years ago was our common concern with the Soviet
threat, and our recognition that we had a better chance of containing that threat if we replaced hostility with cooperation between
Peking and Washington. This overriding strategic concern dominated
our dialogue, and our relationship, during the first decade."[2]

Since it was strategic factors that brought us together in the
first instance, it would be well to consider whether strategic factors
can keep us together in the future and what level of strategic cooperation will maximize our interests. In 1979 Vice-President Walter
Mondale visited China and spoke of the "parallel strategic interests"
of our two nations. High officials of the Reagan Administration continued this terminology, saying our mutual policies toward Soviet
expansion and hegemonism "run on parallel tracks." Both the Carter
and Reagan administrations also emphasized that the United States
and China are friends, not allies, and that the level of U.S. military
cooperation was to be determined within that framework.

The first major breakthrough in the military relationship came
in January 1980, when Secretary of Defense Harold Brown met with
the top Chinese leadership in Beijing. The Secretary at that time
affirmed that "increased cooperation between China and the United
States is a needed element in the maintenance of global tranquility."
He then indicated three specific areas of strategic cooperation—liberalization of export controls on high technology civilian goods with
possible military application (dual-use items), authorization of certain nonlethal military support equipment, and plans for regular consultations on Southwest Asia and other international issues of mutual
concern. Iterated by the Secretary of Defense at the outset of the
1980s, these three remain the principal areas of strategic cooperation in this decade.

Liberalization of export controls on dual-use items was codi-
fied three months after the Brown visit when the Department of Commerce established a new and unique category, P, for China under
U.S. commodity control export regulations. The licensing policy
for this category permitted exports at significantly higher technical
levels than for most other communist countries. It called for consideration of each export application individually, and did not necessarily preclude approval of equipment or data in the design, development, or manufacture of tactical military items. It further stated:

> Approval is not likely when the potential military appli-
> cation is so significant that the export would present an

unacceptable risk regardless of the stated end-use. Of
particular concern are technologies that would make a
direct and significant contribution to nuclear weapons
and their delivery systems, electronic and anti-sub-
marine warfare, and intelligence gathering.[3]

Establishing a policy is one thing; implementing it is quite another. The difficult task of determining precisely which exports to
approve and which to reject was left to the foreign policy bureaucracy, whose interpretation of export regulations is likely to vary
widely by department and even by individual. In June 1981 Secretary of State Alexander Haig found it necessary to obtain White House
agreement to direct the bureaucracy to loosen up on the restrictions
they were imposing on China. Known as the "two times" rule by virtue of its original application to computer capacity, the directive
was broadly defined as "a predisposition for approval for products
with technical levels twice those previously approved for China."[4]
Still, the governmental debate to what does and what does not go
continued. Delayed decisions on license applications were common.
After two somewhat rather confusing years, both as to the meaning
of the policy and its implementation, and marked by increasingly
vocal Chinese criticism, the administration announced in June 1983
a new and clearer policy. China was to be moved from category P
to category V on the export commodity control list, the same as
other friendly countries such as India and Yugoslavia. Export license applications will continue to be reviewed under national security procedures, but a promise was made to expedite such licenses
under the clearer policy. In the wake of this policy declaration, an
immediate warming in the Chinese relationship became apparent.
    Policy articulations on the issue of direct military exports to
China also followed closely in the wake of the Brown visit. In March
1980 the Department of State issued Munitions Control Newsletter
No. 81 (MC 81), opening the People's Republic of China for the first
time to case-by-case consideration of items and technology on the
U.S. munitions list. Authorized for possible approval were a variety
of combat support categories, including trucks, recovery vehicles,
certain cargo/personnel-carrying aircraft and helicopters, some
training equipment, certain communications equipment, and aerial
cameras. In May, Deputy Chief of Staff of the People's Liberation
Army (PLA) and Chief of PLA research and development, General
Liu Huaqing, led a delegation to visit several American defense installations and industries, with the expressed intent on both sides
of modernizing PRC defenses. Vice Premier and Defense Minister
Geng Biao simultaneously held discussions with President Carter
and high-level U.S. officials on matters of mutual strategic interest.

In 1981 the Reagan Administration sought to maintain the momentum of defense cooperation by sending Secretary of State Haig to China. It was in conjunction with this visit that Haig announced a new policy that would make China eligible to purchase items on the munitions list on the same case-by-case bases as for other friendly, nonallied countries. During the visit Haig invited General Liu Huaqing to bring a delegation to the United States in August, to discuss Chinese interest in U.S. military items and technologies, a prospect that was not possible under MC 81, which was in effect during the Chinese general's May visit.

The Liu visit never materialized. The issue of U.S. arms sales to Taiwan, which had remained relatively dormant under the Carter administration, began to take on increasingly contentious overtones in 1981. It took six months before the policy announced by the Secretary of State in June found its way into U.S. export regulations. Those regulations, promulgated on December 14, 1981, removed China from the list of those nations for which it is U.S. policy to deny approval for munitions list exports. By this action the policy announced the previous June by Secretary Haig was institutionalized, and China became eligible to receive U.S. weapons and military equipment in accordance with standard case-by-case review procedures of the U.S. government. Still, as of 1983, there had been only one congressional notification on the sale of significant military equipment to the People's Republic of China. Some China observers note that the issue of Taiwan strongly impedes further development of Chinese-American relations, and that significant PRC military purchases are not likely as long as Taiwan continues to receive substantial American arms. Postponement of the Liu visit and the sometimes virulent Chinese criticism of U.S. arms transfers to Taiwan substantiate this view. Others, however, point to the poor foreign exchange position of the Middle Kingdom, saying that until the Chinese economy improves there simply are not enough funds available for military purchases. Another explanation is that the PLA has a limited capacity to rapidly absorb large amounts of sophisticated military technology. In addition, there is a strong and traditional desire for self-reliance which permeates the Chinese leadership and bureaucracy. Finally there is a view, not often heard, that Chinese purchases of American arms locks that country into a long-term military dependency for which Beijing is not quite prepared. Whatever the explanation, it is clear that large Chinese purchases of American arms are unlikely in the near future, and that it is technology, not arms, that the Chinese seek.

The various reasons that curtail Chinese arms purchases, however, certainly do not apply equally to the transfer of military technology. China takes the long view of history, and in that per-

spective the technological lead of the West is but a passing phenomenon. They continue to believe that the country that invented
gunpowder will reassert the genius of its people, now over a billion
strong, and that through concentrated efforts China will once again
be able to stand up to the military forces of outside powers, of whatever origin. In this regard China has at least three concerns. First,
it perceives the need to develop a nuclear force capable of deterring
a Soviet first-strike, thereby removing the implicit threat of such a
strike from the "correlation of forces" at the foundation of their relationship. Second, it seeks to modernize its conventional forces
to avoid humiliation at the hands of Vietnam or the Soviet Union, and
to refurbish PLA prestige in an era when surrounding nations have
far more military forces. Finally, and most importantly for China,
it must modernize its forces with the minimal expenditure possible,
for, as indicated in Chapter 6, China can only with extraordinary
difficulty afford the luxury of purchasing the highly sophisticated and
commensurately expensive weapons systems on international markets today.[5] Thus the Chinese turn to technology is a natural consequence of balancing a need to modernize with limited means to do
so. The result, as would be expected, is an intense effort to modernize through massive injections of technology over a relatively extended period, so as to achieve self-reliance as a modern military
power, if not in this generation, then perhaps in the next.

The Chinese task will not be easy. It is no secret that PLA
equipment and conventional war tactics are out of date, and that PLA
performance against the Smaller Dragon in 1979 was rather pathetic.
Moreover, except for its nuclear forces, which are estimated to receive some 3-4 percent of GNP, the PLA has recently declined both
in the size of its force and in budgetary allocations. In 1982 PLA
strength is estimated to have declined from 4.75 million to 4 million
men. When Secretary Brown visited the People's Republic in 1980
he stated that PLA weapons were at least ten years behind those of
the United States, while members of his party stated the gap was
more like 25 years. Experts on China have estimated the cost of
modernizing this force at over $40 billion for weapons alone. More
recently, U.S. intelligence specialists testified before Congress
that the Chinese also have major problems absorbing Western military technology. The CIA pointed to weaknesses in China's electronics industry that prevent wide-scale introduction of new radars,
sonars, and other electronic equipment, while the Defense Intelligence Agency (DIA) noted PLA inability to produce an engine for an
advanced fighter despite a ten-year effort to do so. Only in the
nuclear area has there been significant progress. In 1980 China
succeeded in launching an ICBM into the central Pacific Ocean some
6,000 miles down range, and on October 12, 1982 it launched an
IRBM carrier rocket from a nuclear submarine in the East China Sea.

    In view of this situation it is apparent that the United States
and China are not now and cannot now easily become military allies.
On the nuclear side, recent PRC activities give every evidence of
building a force that could destroy Soviet cities and major military
installations in Asia. While such a force may have certain benefits
for preventing conflict, it is not in the U.S. interest to support the
Chinese nuclear weapons program. It is a program we do not control either as to pace or direction of development. Should conflict
erupt in Asia involving China, the risk of nuclear use, albeit small,
is heightened. In addition, there is always a risk that China might
share its technical expertise, or indeed the weapons themselves,
with other countries such as Pakistan or North Korea, although this
danger will be greatly reduced by Chinese participation in the International Atomic Energy Agency. Moreover, Chinese-American cooperation on nuclear weapons would be perceived throughout Asia and
in the Soviet Union as upsetting the military balance and threatening
regional stability. Finally, of course, there is the fact that China
appears to be moving toward ICBM development capable of striking
as far as the United States. In the indeterminate realm of international affairs we should not look with favor upon this capability,
much less support it.

    On the conventional side the PLA is strictly a defensive force,
with little experience in or capability for power projection. Ground,
air, and naval weapons are estimated between 10 and 25 years behind those of the world's leading military powers, and with little
prospect of closing the gap without a considerable technological in-
fusion. In modern warfare, therefore, the PRC would be compelled
to defend its territory in depth, utilizing a strategy of people's war
to attrite and render untenable any advantages gained by invading
forces. It is prepared to render any Soviet territorial gains extremely expensive through the use of massive people's guerrilla war in
conjunction with the defensive capabilities of its 66 divisions oriented
against a Soviet attack. If the Kremlin's experience in Afghanistan
is any kind of barometer, it should be obvious that any Soviet incur-
sion would be most costly. Under these circumstances, the advantage of a U.S.-Chinese military relationship would tend to be not in
joint operations, but in prudent U.S. technological transfers that
would upgrade a relatively primitive defensive force. For the United
States to attempt more, such as seeking military alliance with China
bilaterally, or in conjunction with Japan multilaterally, is both un-
realistic and would do little to raise the cost of potential Soviet aggression in the Far East. By providing Beijing conventional defensive arms that threaten neither Taiwan nor the Soviet Union, on the
other hand, the United States can enhance the defensive capability on
which China depends without destabilizing the region through a

mythical encirclement of Russia or an offensive buildup threatening Asian nations.

Although arms and technology transfer form a core element of American-Chinese strategic cooperation, consultation on a wide range of bilateral and world problems is also indispensable. Secretary of State George Shultz, during his 1983 visit to Beijing, quoted President Reagan that "there is a great need for renewal in United States-China dialogue," an open admission of the difficulties of placing the new relationship on an even keel.

On a bilateral basis such consultations help alleviate the problems and misunderstandings naturally inherent in our developing strategic relationship. Whether the issue is Taiwan, limits or delays on U.S. arms and technology flow, or Chinese expectations of the American role in its modernization programs, close and continuous consultations are essential to minimizing the difficulties. The mutual sharing of information and perceptions on the Soviet Union is also extremely important. Soviet hegemonism was the impelling force that brought our two nations together in the first place, and it remains today a factor deserving continuous consultation. The Chinese are certainly interested in any START of INF negotiations with the Russians, while we are interested in the nature and extent of recent Sino-Soviet talks. On Third World issues both countries have tremendous need for consultations, as they can affect dramatically our entire foreign policies. For example, if the talks between China and India were to resolve outstanding disputes between those nations, the primary rationale for close Soviet-Indian military cooperation would evaporate, the momentum of the Soviet southward push to the Indian Ocean would suffer a severe setback, and the opportunity for improved American-Indian relations would be immense. China and America also share similar interests in Vietnamese withdrawal from Kampuchea and Russian withdrawal from Afghanistan. We both seek an end to Soviet exploitation of Third World nations and the peaceful development of those nations. While we do have differences of opinion on many international issues, such as Poland and the Middle East, the degree of commonality deriving from a desire to stem the tide of Soviet expansionism is an overriding common concern. The important thing is that we maintain a dialogue on our views of the world and on how to go about addressing world problems. The strategic dimension of that dialogue is vital to building and maintaining the mutual trust that allows other forms of cooperation to go forward. It is crucial in maintaining the strategic realignment of China and with it the correlation of forces necessary for peace in Asia.

TAIWAN

The second major issue of U.S.-Chinese relations is Taiwan. Despite the major strategic advantages to both China and the United States of a close and cooperative relationship, the issue of how to treat Taiwan remains a serious irritant, if not a potential obstacle, to normal bilateral relations. The U.S. breakthrough with China in 1972 led to the Shanghai Communiqué, by which the United States acknowledged "that all Chinese on either side of the Taiwan strait maintain there is but one China and that Taiwan is part of China."[6] In the same document, the United States affirmed "the ultimate objective of the withdrawal of all U.S. forces and military installations from Taiwan," an objective completed in 1978 in preparation for normalization of relations. As part of the price of normalization, the United States also severed diplomatic relations with Taipei, terminated the Mutual Defense Treaty with the Republic of China, recognized Beijing as the sole legal government of China, and promised not to conclude new agreements for the sale of arms to Taiwan during 1979, while retaining the right to sell arms on a selective basis at a later date. On this last point U.S. officials stated that both sides "agreed to disagree," and on January 1, 1979 diplomatic relations were established.

Still the issue of Taiwan tended to inhibit full development of Chinese-American ties. In November 1978, just prior to normalization, the United States agreed to the co-production in Taiwan of 48 additional F-5E air defense fighter-interceptors. The F-5E was chosen over more advanced aircraft such as the F-16 because of its shorter range and less sophisticated electronics. The Chinese protested at the time, but in view of the advantages of normalization and the U.S. promise to withhold military contracts for a year, did not allow the issue to prevent normalization. In 1980, U.S. military sales to Taiwan resumed, but did not include "big ticket" items such as a follow-on to the F-5E. Meanwhile, Congress passed the Taiwan Relations Act, which authorized a structure of commercial and cultural relations, and stated: "the United States will make available to Taiwan such defense articles and services in such quantity as may be necessary to enable Taiwan to maintain a sufficient self-defense capability."[7]

The Chinese protested the Act but again did not allow the issue to impede further development of political and economic relations. Warm exchanges of American and Chinese delegations proceeded in abundance and the pragmatic Deng Xiaoping continued to consolidate political control. The time was propitious to resolve the question of a follow-on aircraft for Taiwan, but the American side seemed to procrastinate in the knowledge that the 48 F-5Es authorized for co-production in 1978 would continue to be produced until 1983. Widely mentioned for Taiwan was the so-called FX, or export fighter, of which the Northrop F-5G (F-20) was the prime contender. The aircraft seemed ideal for Taiwan because of its added thrust and payload, while falling short of the highly advanced and longer range F-15 or F-16 aircraft then entering U.S. inventories. In 1980 the U.S. government authorized Northrop to discuss the F-5G with Taiwan, but continued to postpone a decision on actual sales or co-production. Without such a decision and with other aspects of the relationship developing rapidly the issue persisted in a manageable way into 1981.

Despite the appearance of normality, however, the issue of replacement aircraft for Taiwan remained a festering sore in relations with China. The longer the United States delayed in reaching a decision the more acrimonious the eventual decision was likely to be. By the second half of 1981 the issue had become an emotional bone of contention as aircraft sales were widely rumored to be under active consideration by the U.S. government. As 1982 began, the PRC lashed out at U.S. arms sales, pointing to the reasonableness of its offers made in September 1979 and September 1981, for peaceful reunification of Taiwan with the mainland. These offers included a promise of no change in Taiwan's social system, no lowering of Taiwan's standard of living, the maintenance of foreign investments in Taiwan, and the allowance of its existing armed forces.[8] In view of this position the Party newspaper, People's Daily, reflecting views expressed earlier by senior Chinese leaders, reported as follows: "Now we must state explicitly that if the United States desires to preserve and develop its relations with China, it must seek, on the basis of genuine respect for China's sovereignty, a solution to the issue of selling arms to Taiwan."[9]

In January 1982 Assistant Secretary of State John Holdridge visited Beijing to inform the Chinese of the U.S. decision to reject the more advanced F-5G (F-20) aircraft in favor of further extension of the F-5E co-production line in Taiwan.[10] Although this represented a considerable concession by the U.S. government and appeared to offer a reasonable solution to satisfying both Chinese and Taiwanese needs, the Chinese reacted with a scathing denunciation of the action. Deng Xiaoping stated flatly that our bilateral relations were not good, and that China could do without the United States if it had to. Chinese Foreign Ministry spokesmen stated that relations with the United States had reached a state of crisis.[11] Through the spring and summer of 1982, relations remained tense, necessitating a visit to China by Vice-President George Bush in an attempt to calm the situation. In April President Reagan went so far as to write Premier Zhao Jiyang that the United States expects "that in the context of progress toward a peaceful solution, there would naturally be a decrease in the need for arms by Taiwan."[12]

Intense negotiations continued through the summer as both sides sought to resolve the issue to their satisfaction. During this period the situation was so tense that Congress was not formally notified regarding either a previously announced $97 million aircraft spare parts package for Taiwan or the F-5E co-production arrangement. With a U.S. decision deadline for continuing aircraft production in Taiwan nearing, and with the Chinese Twelfth Party Congress ready to convene and finalize the direction of China's long-term domestic and foreign policy, both sides finally agreed on a mutually satisfactory joint communiqué on the question of U.S. arms sales to Taiwan. The communiqué, issued August 17, 1982, stated as follows:

> The Chinese Government reiterates that the question of Taiwan is China's internal affair. The Message to Compatriots in Taiwan issued by China on January 1, 1979, promulgated a fundamental policy of striving for peaceful reunification of the motherland.
>
> The nine-point proposal put forward by China on September 30, 1981, represented a further major effort under this fundamental policy to strive for a peaceful solution to the Taiwan question. (Article 4)
>
> The United States Government understands and appreciates the Chinese policy of striving for a peaceful resolution of the Taiwan question as indicated in China's Message to Compatriots in Taiwan issued on January 1, 1979, and the nine-point proposal put forward by China on September 30, 1981. . . . (Article 5)
>
> Having in mind the foregoing statements of both sides, the United States Government states that it does not seek to carry out a long-term policy of arms sales to Taiwan, that its arms sales to Taiwan will not exceed, either in qualitative or in quantitative terms, the level of those supplied in recent years since the establishment of diplomatic relations between the United States and China, and that it intends to reduce gradually its sales of arms to Taiwan, leading over a period of time to a final resolution. (Article 6)

The communiqué succeeded in averting a major crisis, but did not settle the Taiwan question. The Chinese could take some satisfaction in the U.S. commitment to reduce the quantity and quality of its arms sales as well as the stated U.S. intention to reduce

gradually those arms "over a period of time leading to a final resolution." The United States, on the other hand, could stress the importance of the Chinese statement regarding its "fundamental policy"
of striving for a peaceful resolution of the Taiwan question. [13] President Reagan subsequently pledged not to reduce arms sales to Taiwan
unless there was progress toward a peaceful solution. [14] The Chinese
vociferously objected to this interpretation, and relations once again
chilled. Thus it was obvious that the communiqué had not solved the
question of Taiwan, and that management of the arms sales issue
would require the utmost skill by American diplomats and successive administrations. It was also obvious that Chinese protests of
the U.S. decision to continue F-5E co-production were not so much
directed against that specific decision as against the sale of American arms to Taiwan in general. [15]

The Chinese leadership is worried that a continued American
supply of arms to Taiwan will undercut the Taiwanese incentive to
negotiate based on fear of eventual Chinese military action. They
fear that the current generation of leadership on the island—nearly
all of whom are Kuomintang Chinese who fled China in 1949—will be
supplanted by indigenous Taiwanese whose historic ethnic links to
China might be compared to those between the Scots and the Irish—
old and long forgotten. The spectacle of indigenous Taiwanese leadership, bright and confident, and supported militarily by U.S. and
third nation arms transfers, flies in the face of long-proclaimed
Chinese aspirations and may be one reason the Chinese appear to
have a sense of urgency regarding Taiwan.

American policy, on the other hand, seeks to balance the aspirations of the people of Taiwan for democracy and free enterprise
with its own aspirations for good relations with China. The United
States agrees that Taiwan is part of China but insists that both political entities work out their modus vivendi in a peaceful manner. As
far as the United States is concerned, the arms that Taiwan may receive are explicitly for the purpose of self-defense. If no threat to
Taiwan eventuates, then the basis for U.S. arms evaporates. Thus
there is room for maneuver by all sides. On the other hand, given
the vacillations of Chinese domestic and foreign policy over the past
25 years, the uncertainties surrounding future Chinese attitudes toward the forceful "liberation" or subjugation of Taiwan are considerable. Thus it is difficult for our nation to set a time limit on arms
sales to Taiwan. In 1983 it was reported the United States would
supply Taiwan nearly $800 million in arms, and that a ceiling had
been set on such arms that would decrease over time. [16] An optimistic outcome would have peaceful conditions in the Taiwan Strait combine with less hysteria in China to allow the arms transfer problem
to dissipate, thereby giving Taiwan a double incentive (Chinese good

will and U.S. arms policy) to negotiate an acceptable state of autonomy within the Chinese nation. Such an outcome would remove both a long-term difficulty in bilateral relations and a long-term target for Soviet exploitation. A less optimistic solution would have the People's Republic choose a time when U.S. confrontation with the USSR is at a high point to resurrect its demands on Taiwan, highlight them, and seek to extract the maximum concession from the United States. Such action, as in the FX case, would demonstrate the fragility of the new relationship, which from the time of normalization, has been developing its own momentum and appears to blend so well with American strategic interests worldwide.

MODERNIZATION

The American role in the modernization of China is the third major issue on our bilateral agenda. In view of the uncertainties with regard to both Taiwan and the future direction of China in world affairs, as well as the difficulties in maintaining the momentum of Sino-American relations, it is imperative that new trans-Pacific links with China be established so as to strengthen and extend the common bond of opposition to Soviet expansionism that drew our two nations together in the first place. The key to developing such a new relationship is Chinese modernization. As described in Chapter 6, the People's Republic of China is today a most backward society by nearly every barometer of economic progress. The present leaders of China know this all too well and, contrary to the practice of pre-Deng politicians, are determined not to bury their heads in the ideological sand of Maoism, but to address the fundamental problems of the Chinese economy with realistic developmental programs. Under its new and pragmatic leadership China announced, in the late 1970s, its plan for revamping the economy by virtue of the Four Modernizations in the fields of agriculture, industry, science and technology, and defense. Deng had supported these Four Modernizations for some time, and proclaimed them as top priority objectives at the Third Plenary Session of the Central Committee in December 1978. They were reiterated by then Chairman Hua Guofeng in February 1979 and have ever since been upheld as China's primary national goals.

Top priority among the Modernizations is agriculture. [17] The effort required simply to feed over a billion people is tremendous. Over 80 percent of the population now lives or works in rural areas. With a population increase of over 15 million annually, China today must devote increasing resources to food production simply to stave off the specter of mass starvation. This effort necessarily draws resources from other economic sectors. During the latter half of the 1970s China imported $5.5 billion of foodstuffs, much from the United States.[18] Still the per capita food supply remained quite low. The imports adversely affected China's foreign exchange reserves, which in 1980 were less than $1.4 billion, forcing China to cut back on imports of machinery and other commodities crucial to balanced growth.

Beginning in 1980, therefore, China placed renewed emphasis upon food production, and initiated reforms to stress the centrality of the individual family, rather than the commune or brigade, as the basic unit of production. Known as the "agricultural responsibility system," the reforms include premiums for above quota production and have resulted in substantial productivity gains in the 1980s. As a result of these policies, by the time the Chinese Communist Party Twelfth Congress confirmed agriculture as the most urgent of the "four modernizations" in late 1982, China had already substantially reduced its food imports. In 1983 the grain crop reached 360 million tons, the highest in Chinese history to that date.[19]

The role of the United States in this process is twofold. First, the American system of individual farms and free enterprise stands as a model for productivity and future planning. The fact that only 4 percent of Americans can farm enough to feed not only the entire nation, but export over $40 billion of food products annually, is not lost on the Chinese leadership. Seeking to quadruple food production by the year 2000, China cannot emulate a more successful system. Second, the United States has a long lead over any nation in the technology needed for efficient farm production. While capital-intensive mechanized agriculture is not directly applicable, high yields in poultry, dairy products, livestock, and grains are characteristics of American farming that are in large part the result of a scientific approach that could also be utilized in China. In short, the world's leading food producer can do much to assist the world's leading food consumer.

Industrial modernization is also of vital importance to the future of the Chinese people. Investment in heavy industry has been curtailed in recent years as a result of both its high energy requirements and Chinese inability to absorb rapidly foreign technology. Petroleum output peaked in 1979 at just over 2 million barrels per day. Declining output from the major onshore fields, Daqing and Shengli, have not been compensated for by the small gains in the Bohai Gulf. Exploration in the East China Sea has not yet yielded dividends, and the appreciable oil in Sinkiang is difficult to extract and transport economically to production centers in Manchuria and along the coast. Only the South China Sea appears to offer hope for a long-term increase in oil production. In 1982 some 33 companies, half of which were American, submitted bids on 31 concession blocks. In May 1983 the first five contracts for joint exploration and development were signed with companies from Britain, Australia, Brazil, and Canada. The conspicuous absence of American firms was attributed to the cooling bilateral relationship at the time, including difficulties over U.S. textile imports, U.S. asylum to Chinese tennis star Hu Na, and continuing difficulties over technology transfer and Taiwan. Nevertheless, the more recent warming trend in the relationship, coupled with American expertise and Chinese entrepreneurship, should soon favor American contracts, and if all goes well many of them should be pumping oil in commercial quantities by 1987. In the meantime, Chinese oil production is expected to continue to decline, and with it the output of heavy industry across the board.

The second factor impeding heavy industry is technological. In 1978 Japan and China signed a long-term trade agreement whereby Japan, in exchange for raw materials such as coal and oil, was to help finance and build a wide array of industrial plants, including enough steel production to enable China to achieve a target of 60 million tons by 1985. Prominent in this effort was the Baoshan steel mill near Shanghai, a modern integrated plant under contract to Nippon Steel at a cost of $1 billion. This ambitious project was scaled back dramatically in 1980 when it became apparent that, in addition to a shortage of foreign exchange, technological problems plagued the Chinese effort. Similar setbacks have characterized a wide range of Japanese projects, to the point where knowledgeable Japanese officials see Chinese progress taking place only after a long gestation period of technological and management training, coupled with material incentives and financial backing. A dramatic illustration of Chinese problems occurred in 1980, when Chinese engineers lost control of a large offshore rig being towed toward Hainan Island, resulting in its loss and the loss of all personnel aboard.

While China has come to recognize the difficulties of heavy industrialization and has turned to light industry to partially offset those difficulties, Chinese leaders also recognize that long-term economic development will be facilitated by balanced industrial growth. In seeking alternatives to the old Soviet technology China has turned largely to Japan. It is in the American interest that both these nations succeed in their joint endeavors. Baoshan was the first non-Soviet steel mill to be constructed in China since the 1930s, and represents a potential "wave of the future."

At the same time the United States has the opportunity to exploit its own commercial advantages in building an economic relationship with China. China desperately needs offshore oil, and the United States is the best and largest producer of offshore rigs in the world. China needs to develop its coal resources, and U.S. mining capability is still among the best in the world. Such enterprises need not necessarily be in competition with the Japanese, as was illustrated by a 1982 proposal whereby Occidental Oil of the United States is to produce in China some 15 million tons of coal annually, one-third of which will be exported to Japan. The United States also enjoys a considerable comparative advantage in computers and communications equipment. In these and other high technology areas the United States must, on a case-by-case basis, carefully weigh the economic and political advantages of cooperation against potentially adverse strategic consequences. In this regard it cannot be assumed, as in Soviet-bloc countries, that the technology transferred will be retransferred to the Soviet Union. It is also important to note that by "buying American" in these and other areas, China is strengthening the bonds of shared mutual interests. By being as forthcoming as possible the United States can not only better appreciate what is happening in China but also expand its ability to influence developments therein.

The third modernization effort focuses on science and technology. In 1978 a delegation of American scientific advisers visited China to assess the problems and prospects for an American role in helping the Chinese scientific community. The Americans were appalled at what they saw. Libraries were devoid of scientific literature for a period of 13 years dating from the beginning of the Cultural Revolution in the mid-1960s. Scientific institutes theoretically staffed with top Chinese specialists were in fact education centers with but a small percentage of truly qualified scientists, typically elderly men. A decade of closed universities and political upheaval had bred a certain cynicism, even among the most professional. Knowledge of scientific advances in the West and elsewhere was minimal. In a word, the scientific bases for self-reliant technological progress being sought by the nation's leadership was woefully inadequate. Since that time China has made strenuous efforts to rebuild its scientific infrastructure. Chinese students both abroad and at home may be the cutting edge of this effort, but it will take years merely to reach the level of achievement that existed in 1965. In other words, China is at least a generation behind the United States in scientific achievement and, by its own efforts alone, is not likely to close that gap anytime soon. Given Chinese attitudes, however, these facts, even if fully understood, are not likely to deter their making a concerted and sustained effort for scientific advancement.

As with the other Modernizations, the U.S. role in this area can contribute significantly to the direction and pace of Chinese progress. The world's most scientifically advanced nation certainly has the ability to assist China in overcoming the many obstacles it faces, not the least of which is the psychological impediment of indoctrination. The range of nonstrategic cooperation is very broad, with immense potential to improve Chinese education, transportation, agriculture, industry, and energy production.

Adding to the difficulties attending any of the Four Modernizations is the sluggishness of the international economy today. At the very time that China is looking outward for trade, investment, and assistance, world economic growth is generally sluggish. Consequently as China seeks to expand its exports it faces protectionism in many areas. Most nations are already resisting the free flow of Chinese textiles and, as Chinese manufacturers improve in quantity and quality, that resistance is bound to increase. Unlike Japan or the United States, which began decades ago, China faces the need to develop its industrial and transportation infrastructure at a time of high energy costs. China is also trying to enter the foreign trade market at a time of considerably greater competition than was the case 10 or 20 years ago.

Despite these and other problems China is looking outward in a way unparalleled in recent history. Trade with the United States has increased fifteenfold in the last five years, to some $6 billion in 1982. Annual trade with Japan is nearly $10 billion, and commerce with Hong Kong is well known as a point of reexport to and from other areas of Asia, such as Taiwan and South Korea, and gives some indication of Chinese participation in East-Asian trading patterns. Figure 7 depicts recent trends and also highlights the relative importance of Soviet commercial relations.

In China today, modernization is the name of the game. It is clearly in the American interest not only that China succeed in its modernization, but that American support and assistance play a role in that success. There are risks involved in an American role but there are even greater risks without one, as China will attempt to modernize with or without U.S. help. First, a Chinese failure to progress economically could undermine not only the stability of the regime but of the entire country. Soviet exploitation of the confusion could be expected, and a new leadership, perhaps reverting to a brand of Maoism or even alliance with the USSR is a possibility. If a monolithic Sino-Soviet threat ever emerged it would upset the entire strategic balance in addition to destabilizing Asia as a whole. Second, it can be expected that failure on the mainland would result in selection of scapegoats, with both the United States and Taiwan as convenient targets for deflecting criticism of the regime. On the other hand, successful Chinese modernization done in cooperation with the United States gives China greater incentive to seek a

peaceful solution to the issue of Taiwan. Third, Chinese modernization with American support creates mutual economic interests
that neither nation would seek to upset. These interests eventually
would link China to the United States through long-term trade, investment, technology transfer, and developmental assistance.

FIGURE 7

Chinese Two-Way Trade

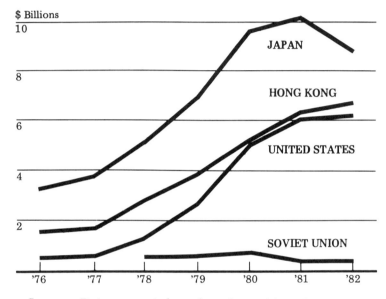

Source: Data presented are based on tables of the IMF, Direction of Trade Yearbook, 1983.

Unlike its economic links with the Soviet Union, American ties
to China are not likely to feed a hostile military force by enabling
the regime to concentrate less on internal economic development.
The need for Chinese modernization is too urgent, its armed forces
too backward, and its need for Western assistance too great. Finally, without a strong American role there is every likelihood that economic adjustments incorporating individual incentives will go the
way of the Lieberman reforms in Russia.[20] On the contrary, American participation in Chinese modernization should facilitate Chinese
integration into the dynamic Pacific Basin economic system, and
even could encourage further free enterprise in China itself.

In any case China cannot be taken for granted. The tremendous strategic advantages the United States derives from the new relationship are not axiomatic. They were made possible by the threat of Soviet expansionism, but Sino-Soviet differences alone are insufficient to underpin Chinese-American relations into the twenty-first century. Strategic cooperation, keeping Taiwan in perspective, and modernization are essential to a new and durable Chinese-American relationship, and U.S. strategy in Asia and the world hinges upon cementing the bonds of that relationship. The future of both our peoples deserves no less.

NOTES

1. Paul Wolfowitz, Assistant Secretary of State for East Asian and Pacific Affairs, Statement before the Subcommittee on East Asian and Pacific Affairs of the House Foreign Affairs Committee, February 28, 1983.

2. Richard Nixon, as quoted in the New York Times, October 11, 1982.

3. Paragraph 385.3, U.S. Export Administration Regulations, October 1, 1982. The categorization took effect April 25, 1980.

4. Federal Register, Vol. 46, No. 249, December 29, 1981, p. 62836.

5. During the 1970s China imported annually an average of less than $120 million in arms. The U.S. Arms Control and Disarmament Agency, World Military Expenditures and Arms Transfers, 1971-1980, 1983.

6. Text of Joint Communiqué, issued at Shanghai, February 27, 1972.

7. U.S. Congress, "Taiwan Relations Act," Public Law 96-8, April 10, 1979.

8. These principles were announced by Vice Premier Wang Zhin on September 28, 1979, and have been reiterated many times since. In September 1981 they were expanded to a nine-point peace proposal. Asian Security, 1980, op. cit., p. 105. In July 1983, Deng Xiaoping reportedly stated Taiwan could fly its own flag and retain complete autonomy in internal matters. The Washington Post, July 30, 1983, p. A-20.

9. As quoted in The Washington Post, January 1, 1982, p. A-18.

10. When the F-5G sale fell through, prospects for sales of the aircraft elsewhere dimmed. It was redesignated the F-20 in late 1982, at which time there was only one aircraft in operation.

11. The New York Times, February 28, 1982.

12. Bureau of Public Affairs, Department of State, May 1982. The letter was dated April 5, 1982.

13. See, for example, Don Oberdorfer in The Washington Post, "China Sees Diplomatic Victory in Pact," August 18, 1982; and Ronald Reagan, "Presidential Statement on Issuance of Communiqué," August 17, 1982. U.S. arms sales to Taiwan were reportedly valued at $835 million in 1980 (The Washington Times, August 27, 1982).

14. President Ronald Reagan, in Human Events, February 26, 1983, p. 19.

15. China has also emphasized that cultural and economic dealings with Taiwan are internal matters to be handled through Beijing. See The New York Times, August 18, 1982.

16. The Washington Post, July 16, 1983, p. A-15.

17. The Far Eastern Economic Review (FEER), October 1, 1982, pp. 49-50.

18. Research Institute for Peace and Security, op. cit., p. 75.

19. FEER, op. cit., and "China Reports Record Harvests," The Washington Post, November 12, 1983, p. D-1.

20. The Lieberman reforms allowed the Soviet farmer to increase his private plot, provided material incentives to the worker, and introduced a limited profit incentive for producers. Introduced in 1965, they did increase Soviet production, but not enough to overcome the opponents of "capitalist decadence," and were terminated in the late 1960s, only recently to be resurrected in a more limited way.

10

Let Freedom Ring:
The Great Revolution in
East Asia and the World

The Colonel leaned forward with an intense air of meditation as he gazed across a Southeast Asian ricefield. He had served in Her Majesty's service for 35 years, all of it in Asia. He had fought the Japanese attack into Southeast Asia and the Communist terrorist movement in Malaya. He had served throughout East and South Asia and had witnessed the dynamic force of revolutionary communism arise with the promise of a better tomorrow and spread with the discipline of militant true believers. China, Tibet, and North Vietnam were symbolic of the trend. Nepal was vulnerable, India was flirting with communist government in its Kerela and West Bengal states, and with Moscow in New Delhi. Soviet-supported cadres were aggrandizing political power in Afghanistan, and Pakistan appeared about to fall apart. South Vietnam, Laos, and Cambodia had just succumbed to the force of communist arms. It was 1975.

"This is just the beginning," he said. "Thailand will fall like a broken reed, Burma will have no choice, and India will not resist. The power of Communism will overwhelm any opposition all the way from Indochina to the Middle East. It is only a matter of time." He predicted a dismal and difficult future for freedom in our time, not unlike the precarious condition of 1941 when the lights had gone out across Europe and only Britain and America remained as beacons of liberty for a threatened world. We had come through then, by the skin of our teeth, and were now entering an even more dangerous period for Western civilization and for all mankind. Such was the prognosis of one very seasoned British veteran of East Asian affairs.

A short time later presidential candidate Jimmy Carter was sounding a different tune. "The spirit of liberty is on the rise," he said, and the United States should recognize this reality and avoid becoming embroiled in every international problem that comes along. Mr. Carter discerned some of the positive trends in Asia and the world and, despite the recent communist victory in Vietnam, Laos, and Cambodia, believed that the human thirst for liberty was the dominant underlying force in world affairs. In his view it was of prime importance for America to identify with positive human aspirations, and to engage the Soviet Union, as well as other nations, in a moral struggle in which the American commitment to human rights, especially freedom, would prevail. He blamed our defeat in Vietnam upon failure to live up to this task, stating that as it relates to Vietnam, "our foreign policy has not exemplified our commitment to moral principles."[1]

A few years later, with some experience in that most responsible of offices under his belt, the president would sound a bit differently. While retaining his commitment to high moral principles and human liberty, he came to recognize that in the rough and tumble of international politics just sitting on the sidelines and rooting for freedom is not enough. He rescinded his orders for defense cuts, announced a 5 percent real annual growth in American military spending over an extended period, expressed surprise and dismay at the Soviet invasion of Afghanistan, announced a doctrine to defend the Persian Gulf region against further Soviet encroachments, and agreed to retain the American ground troops in Korea that he had previously vowed to pull out. But in 1975, that was all in the future, and Vietnam was still on his mind.

President Reagan entered office with a different view of Vietnam and its significance in U.S. foreign policy. With considerable supporting evidence, he pointed out that conflicts within the Third World are being aided and abetted, and in some cases, instigated by the Soviet Union and its proxies, such as Cuba and Libya. His response was to strengthen the armed forces of the United States even more than had his predecessor, in order to implement, on a selective basis, a policy of global containment. In view of the fact that the Soviets had leaped the boundaries of nations contiguous with Mother Russia to promote Marxist rule internationally, the president felt it necessary that the United States be able to move to defend threatened regions in the Middle East, Africa, and Latin America. For two years, the president was blessed with the absence of crisis situations demanding implementation of this policy. By 1982, however, the cauldron in Central America was heating up, and by 1983 seemed ready to boil over. The government of El Salvador was threatened by rebel forces with links to Nicaragua, and the regime in Nicaragua was creating a military force far larger than that of its neighbors. Soviet and Cuban arms and advisors were playing a crucial role in the struggle. The Reagan response, to dispatch a carrier battle group, to increase economic and military assistance, and to request funds for these and other programs, met with considerable legislative and media opposition. "No more Vietnams!" was the repeated refrain of critics in Congress and across the country. In April 1983 the president addressed the issue before a Joint Session of Congress. In a statement that drew a sustained and standing ovation from both sides of the aisle, he declared: "Let me say to those who invoke the memory of Vietnam, there is no thought of sending American combat troops to Central America; they are not needed—indeed, they have not been requested there." The president concluded, however, by emphasizing that the United States has a "vital interest" in Central America, where "the national security of all the Americas is at stake." Clearly, then, the president would be prepared to send American troops if he felt the action necessary. The analogy with Vietnam is obvious. Troops were not deemed necessary until 1965, when it was decided the threat to American "vital interests" in Asia could no longer be contained by economic and military assistance. The United States was prepared to up the ante in the belief that the other side could not or would not match our national will. We were wrong. The power of revolutionary communism, cloaked in the nationalist mantle, was still in the ascendancy.

There have been many "lessons" postulated from the American experience in Vietnam, but looking at the scene from the advantage of hindsight it appears none is more undeniable than the fact that Hanoi wanted South Vietnam more than did either Saigon or Washington; and it was prepared to pay the price to get it. That the view of American foreign policy in Vietnam as morally corrupt should permeate to embrace national leaders such as Jimmy Carter highlights the fact that it was American hearts and minds, not Vietnamese, that were blinded by the storm, weakened in resolve, and finally defeated in the pursuit of "a free and independent South Vietnam." Just as President Carter underestimated Soviet covetousness in Southwest Asia in the 1970s, so President Johnson had underestimated North Vietnamese covetousness in Southeast Asia in the 1960s. The perception that Vietnam would be a relatively easy war, that all the United States had to do was scare everyone by introducing American units and airpower, that U.S. technology would overcome any military difficulties, and that by preaching the blessings of liberty we could inspire South Vietnam to match the storm, all begged the question of whether American willingness to sacrifice over the long term would match that of our opponent.

Ho Chi Minh wanted South Vietnam more than Truman, Eisenhower, Kennedy, Johnson, Nixon, and Ford—and he got it.

There is a myth that the fall of South Vietnam proved the correctness of communist doctrine in meeting the legitimate needs of Third World nations. It is claimed that Vietnamese society was corrupt beyond repair and that the cleansing fire of communist revolution was necessary to purge the decadent society and replace colonial and neocolonial dictatorship with a government dedicated to egalitarianism and righteousness. It is further asserted that similar revolutions will sweep the developing nations and should be viewed not as power grabs by a communist minority but as grassroots nationalistic and libertarian movements independent of the Soviet Union and espousing communist doctrine only as a vehicle to achieve government of, by, and for the people. The communist victory in Vietnam is often seen as a vindication of this hypothesis, and the implications are seen as no less real for Angola, Nicaragua, and El Salvador.

Yet the perception of America as morally bankrupt and communist revolution as the wave of the future is inconsistent with the reality of Vietnam and the rest of Asia today. Ho "wanted the gold and he got it," but in the words of the poet, "somehow the gold isn't all."[2] Instead, what he created is a dictatorship of the proletariat far from the dream of those who supported those magic words doc lap (independence). Joan Baez, long a supporter of a free and independent Vietnam, who had visited Hanoi in the 1960s in support of the antiwar movement, wrote this open letter, signed by over 80 former antiwar activists, to the new masters of Vietnam:

> The jails are overflowing with thousands upon thousands of detainees. People disappear and never return. People are shipped to reeducation centers, fed a starvation diet of stale rice, forced to squat bound wrist to ankle, to suffocate in small boxes. People are used as human mine detectors, clearing live mine fields with their hands and feet. . . . Torture is rampant, life in general is hell, and death is prayed for.[3]

Later Baez would say:

> All this horror in Vietnam makes it difficult for some people who would like to ignore it. The left wing doesn't want to think about it and the right wing is not human rights oriented and lots of people have just really had it with the word Vietnam.[4]

In 1976 the name "democratic" was properly removed from the title of the Democratic Republic of Vietnam and was replaced by the word "socialist." Premier Pham Van Dong himself is said to have expressed concern over the lack of democratic processes in the new Vietnam. Nevertheless, the failure of this and other communist governments to live up to the ideals proclaimed during their revolutionary phase should come as no surprise. "Power corrupts and absolute power corrupts absolutely," Lord Acton has told us, and there is no more absolute power on earth than that of a communist dictatorship.

Still, the haunting question we must address is why two nations, the United States and France, whose traditions of liberty are symbolized by the revolutions of 1776 and 1789, failed in their bid to assure the blessings of liberty in Vietnam. Besides underestimating the tenacity of the foe, it is now apparent that both our great nations lost confidence in the cause for which we fought. Frenchmen came to see their struggle as a hopeless colonial war while Americans came to doubt its Vietnamese ally and itself as the struggle proved longer, more difficult, more costly, and more bloody than we had been led to believe. Slowly but surely we questioned, then doubted, the rightness of our commitment. We took little notice of the quiet but greater revolution throughout the rest of East Asia, wherein the lure of communist promises fell on hardened soil that had witnessed firsthand the bloody methods of communist terrorism in action. Of those who did notice the political and economic progress taking place in free Asia, fewer still asked why the great transformation was taking place and what adverse impact it would have on the spread of communism in Asia. Instead, like the British veteran, we worried about the defeat we had suffered in an area in which we had already sacrificed so much. Indeed, we reacted with introversion and disassociation, abandoning Vietnam and withdrawing from much of the rest of East Asia. In the belief that our cause must have been wrong we lost, temporarily, the will to carry on the struggle despite the difficulties. Together with our Vietnamese allies we had already won the guerrilla war against the Viet Cong, and with China increasingly fed up with Soviet intransigence, were on the verge of isolating and containing North Vietnam. By that time, however, we had lost confidence in ourselves and were unable to pursue "the right as God had given us to see the right."

As we look at East Asia today, we behold an entirely different picture from that of 20 or more years ago. The dramatic and progressive change in the free nations of Asia stands in sharp relief to the dull and uninspiring monotony of communist decadence. The conflicts in East Asia today are not to be found in the free nations of Asia, but in and between the communist powers. The amazing economic growth of free Asia is still a gleam in the eye of communist leaders whose very vision of successful development is impaired by the antiquated and distorted prism of Marxism-Leninism. Finally the political maturity of free East Asian governments, willing to chance in varying degrees the unfamiliar structure of democratic institutions, provides the greatest contrast to the centrally controlled communist systems whose trust of the people has declined each day following the revolutionary phase of their struggle to power. The picture in Asia today is not one of communism on the march, but of communism in decline. The tide of history has definitely shifted, much of it due to American blood, sweat, and tears in war, economic and military assistance in peace, and political encouragement and inspiration throughout. Though the ratio of the latter may have been only 1 percent of our total effort, as Edison described in another day, that small hope for a better life, free from fear, hunger, poverty, disease, and arbitrary government, is a seed that found fertile ground.

As we enter the final decades of this century of strife, therefore, we can look with pride to the results of confident and responsible American assertion of human rights and liberty in Asia. At the same time we can see that liberty in itself is not enough. Freedom abused is freedom lost, and the U.S. frustration in Vietnam may have been caused by, more than anything else, the abuses of liberty in an earlier day when colonial France, as well as certain Americans, tended to run the show and take care of things for their little Asian brothers. That a new day has come for the rest of Asia is partly attributable to a parallel and more pronounced characteristic in American international behavior, that of dealing with the nations of the world on the basis of equality and mutual respect. American willingness to shed blood in battle, to administer aid programs when they are needed, to give political support to democratic forces, to help in education and in missions, to engage in free and fair trade, to share appropriate technology, to invest in worthwhile projects, and to help secure peace in the region is part of a pattern of concern for the needs of others, which in the long run has served American interests as well. Together with considerable and concerted indigenous effort they have helped stimulate the very favorable long-range socioeconomic and political developments now permeating this most populous region of the world.

Nevertheless, the continuation of this favorable trend is not guaranteed. The possibility of regression is very real, made more so by an American tendency to withdraw from and neglect the region in the absence of a crisis. The assassination of Benigno Aquino, for example, has come to symbolize the serious problem of American-supported democracy in the Philippines, where political violence has become increasingly common. Peaceful progress throughout East Asia was not and is not automatic, and constructive American advice and support for democratic processes continue to be needed. Although the economic aid element of American policy is no longer as necessary as it once was, and although there is much the United States can never change, concerted and continuous attention to the problems of the region are still required.

The favorable political, economic, and strategic changes in the region today are, in part, a result of past American interest and involvement. By helping the nations of Asia transit the difficult path between tradition and modernity, the United States did stand as a beacon in the night, and did help the people of Asia progress to a point where their record of achievement speaks for itself. America has a right to be proud of its involvement in Asia and can derive from that experience lessons critical not only to Asia today, but to successful policy toward other nations now entering, or already in, the tumultuous transition to a more modern society.

Many of those nations, particularly in Africa and Latin America, are in a position analogous to that of most East-Asian countries in the postwar era. Their per capita income is very low. Disparities of wealth and opportunity are great. People have become aware, through increased education and communication, of the possibilities for change, and indigenous organizations have formed to direct their efforts. Unlike the nations of East Asia, however, their prospects for constructive change are dimmed by the will and ability of the USSR to provide arms and other support, either directly or through surrogates, to Marxist revolutionaries committed to violent replacement of existing governments. The capture in Grenada of over 10,000 Soviet-bloc weapons and 5.6 million rounds of ammunition well illustrates this fact. Unlike the nations of East Asia, which benefited from an assertive and generally constructive American role during a critical phase of their development, many of the nations of Africa and Latin America today are faced with ruthless drives for power by outside-supported guerrillas and terrorists, while America eschews involvement under the rubric, "No more Vietnams."

Vietnam taught many lessons of caution regarding foreign involvement. However, as American success in the rest of East Asia illustrates, it did not and should not be construed as vindicating a policy of noninvolvement. On the contrary, the American experience in Vietnam and East Asia provides, besides the all-important element of national will discussed earlier, several guidelines for assessing and addressing the problems in El Salvador and elsewhere. First, it teaches that the difficulties in newly developing nations are not a passing phenomenon. Rather, they are at the core of a long-term struggle for the political allegiance of the people, and as such require long-term solutions. Second, the problem of political instability has two root causes—existing societal injustices themselves, and the exploitation of those injustices by groups with communist support. While the former is normally the principal threat to long-term stability and development, the latter is seen by the Reagan Administration as immediately threatening American security. Both problems must be addressed. Third, the Marxist promise of freedom and independence for the masses will not be fulfilled, but it does capture the imagination of many nationalists. After the Marxists seize power it will be too late for the disillusioned. Fourth, the coup or revolution will likely be rendered "irreversible" by alliance with Moscow. "Liberated areas" do not have a track record of "counterrevolution." Fifth, the Western response to this situation tends to be just that—a response and a reaction to communist initiative. When the United States does respond it is typically with too little strength to reverse the situation, but enough to heighten nationalist fervor in the revolutionary phase, or drive the new regime into greater dependence on the Soviet Union during the consolidation phase. Sixth, only through positive and constructive initiatives can America help reverse this tragedy.

As in East Asia, the elements of a positive American approach must be economic, political, and military. It was pointed out earlier that during the postwar period (1946-52), U.S. economic assistance alone to East Asia totaled $20 billion in present value. This was the price paid by American citizens at a time when our economic strength paled in comparison to what it is today. As a matter of fact, the Federal Reserve reported that the real net worth of the nation has quadrupled since 1945. During those same postwar years economic aid to Africa and Latin America combined was only 4 percent of that to East Asia. While the situation today is considerably reversed, with East Asia a mere 14 percent of the combined African and Latin American figure, the fact is that the reversal is due more to the dramatic reduction in the necessity for aid to East Asia than from munificence toward the other regions.[5] An effective aid program, however, need not and should not be the responsibility of the United States alone. American friends and allies, many in part as a result of earlier American aid, are now in a position to assist the poorer nations more than they do at present. Together, we can make a major difference in the future development of much of the Third World.

Given the dangers facing these regions, it is also possible that the United States will be called upon to become involved militarily. Vietnam offers many comparisons and contrasts for decision makers, but based on the analysis of Chapter 2, perhaps none is more important than establishing clearly defined military objectives. American commanders and combat troops must know their mission in order to be able to perform it, and Congress and the American people must know it in order to properly support their armed forces. Vietnam taught the importance of the rules of engagement. If a hostile force is granted sanctuaries that render its destruction impossible and allow it to seize and retain the strategic initiative, as was the case in Vietnam, then American casualties are certain to mount along with American frustration. The nuclear age appears to have forced a return to limited conventional war, and if there is to be such war, every effort should be made to end it swiftly, and with decisiveness. If, on the other hand, American participation is to be defined more narrowly, then a clear statement of the military objective, such as to prevent outside support from reaching indigenous guerrillas, is required. In any case no effort should be spared to avoid American military involvement, but if war does come, then clear military objectives must be established, and the resources to attain them must be allocated.

The political factor in any American involvement—economic, military, or diplomatic—is of paramount importance. American involvement in East Asia has taught the extreme importance of respecting nationalist goals and aspirations. To struggle against the grain of nationalism is a recipe for failure. On the other hand, by taking a genuine interest in the long-term development of nations and peoples, the United States can play a tremendous role in helping them overcome the many obstacles to national independence, freedom, and well-being. Cooperation with friends and allies, whether in collective security arrangements or multilateral economic development programs, can and should be of assistance in this regard, but the key to success is American interest in the country itself.

The United States was thrust onto the world stage as a major actor in a military role in World War II. The postwar period called for an economic role, and the country responded with the Marshall Plan and a host of other programs designed to foster a healthy international economic climate. Somewhat hesitantly at first, but as time passed with increasing assertiveness, we became heavily engaged in the great realm of international politics. As far as major involvement in the Third World is concerned it can be well argued that we "cut our teeth" in East Asia. We had some notable failures but they are overshadowed by a far greater number of splendid achievements.

It is from this perspective that the United States can look forward to a great future in Asia, and, if appropriate action is taken, in the rest of the Third World. We should not and must not permit a national obsession with failure in Vietnam to impair our vision or determination to play a constructive role in Asia, Latin America, Africa, or the Middle East. The perception of some of these regions as remote, far away, unimportant, without strategic significance, likely to lead to another Vietnam and impervious to American influence are simply inconsistent with the facts. Certainly there will be difficulties associated with American involvement, but just as certainly those difficulties would be magnified immensely without our involvement. This does not mean we should become the policeman of the world; on the contrary, Vietnam taught us that Americanization of internal conflicts is a sure road to disaster. On the other hand, it does mean that we should deal with the problems of an Angola or an El Salvador with confidence in ourselves and the values of our nation. We should not hesitate to make maximum judicious use of available economic, political, or military means to sustain the freedom and independence of such states from outside coercion and, if deemed necessary, from inside terrorism. To do this we will have to pay a price, but withdrawing to fortress America and pretending they do not need us and we do not need them will lead to a far greater price for our children in the years to come.

The future will continue to challenge American ingenuity and will. The global Soviet socialist steamroller has momentum and is intent upon reversing favorable winds of freedom and then declaring the result irreversible. In some ways it seems like a no-win situation. Czechoslovakia held an election in 1948 and voted in a communist leadership. It has not held another democratic election since.

Soviet leaders continue to seek opportunities for the exploitation of turmoil throughout the world. Whether Europe in the 1940s and 1950s, Indochina in the 1960s and 1970s, or Africa and Central America today, the chance to support a Marxist dictatorship with the force of Soviet arms has an intoxicating appeal in the Kremlin. It conforms to the ideology on which Soviet leaders were raised, and to the Soviet idea of matching the West in implementing a global foreign policy. It is also reinforced by the increasing importance of the military at the highest levels of Soviet decision making, and by the traditional esteem accorded the military in Russian society. The Soviet perception is that they are merely expediting a predetermined world movement toward socialism and then communism, and that the underlying advantages of military air and port access, economic interchange, and potential destabilization of neighboring areas by proxy just happen to coincide nicely with the glorious ideals of world revolution.

The myth that Soviet military power would unilaterally confine itself to defending the Eurasian glacis of its heartland no longer holds much currency in the United States, but the necessity for a coherent and comprehensive policy to deal with this situation has yet to gestate sufficiently in the American psyche. Instead we worry about fears of another Vietnam; we doubt our ability to influence distant lands and peoples; and in some cases have even begun to doubt the blessings of liberty upon which our nation was founded.

We are in troubled times, it is true, but it is also true that we have several advantages of immense consequence in the struggle in which we are now engaged. First, we have trustworthy and formidable allies. In Europe, in Asia, and in much of the rest of the world, we share a common necessity for a common defense of a way of life that, though varying from culture to culture, respects the human being as an individual and a member of society. While not always agreeing on the means of securing our destiny, we do share the goal, and in this age of unparalleled danger our allies, unlike those of the USSR, can be trusted to bear some share of the burden of common defense. Second, we can see that the nations of the world, even communist nations, do not take easily to the Soviet dictat. In East Asia the Soviet imperium does not control the destiny of China, or, though this could change, the destinies of North Korea and Vietnam. To the degree to which these and other communist states remain independent of the Kremlin, they may in time be influenced by the momentum of truly democratic movements throughout the world. Finally, we in the United States enjoy the advantage that free political and economic systems are alive and well, and succeeding in meeting genuine human needs far beyond the performance of communist systems. What has transpired in East Asia in the past 25 years demonstrates beyond a doubt that the promise of communism is an illusion. The real revolution in East Asia today is not one of rising expectations, but of rising political, economic, and social performance, and the real winners in that regard are not the communists—they are the peoples of free Asia.

In Tokyo, Japan, there is an American Ambassador who never tires in telling his visitors of the great importance of East Asia to America. He usually ends his analysis of the situation by stating as follows, "This is where it's at, this is what it is all about, this is the future." Mike Mansfield first visited Japan and China as a young Marine over 50 years ago. During his lifetime he has seen Americans push westward in his native Montana, and on to the Pacific coast and beyond. He maintains that while the cultural pull of America is eastward, its dynamic push has been westward, and that includes American presence in Asia and the Western Pacific. Certainly the considerations presented in this writing confirm this thesis. They also point to the fact that a better life for all people lies in the path of freedom, and that the

American role in helping to promote the great revolution sweeping most of East Asia today demonstrates the power and indivisibility of freedom. It is in witness of this phenomenon that this book was written, and in the hope that the word will continue to spread in furtherance of the dream of that great American who, on a hot August day in 1963, raised his indomitable voice under the shadow of Lincoln with the impassioned cry:

> Let freedom ring
> from the prodigious hilltop
> from the mighty mountains
> from every hill and molehill
> from every mountainside
> from every town and hamlet
> from every state and every city
> let freedom ring.[6]

Martin Luther King was speaking about different sections of America at a crucial time in our nation's history, and his words went out to millions to inspire greater freedom in the United States. They are equally applicable for the rest of the world today, and the example of the free nations of Asia bears them out. Therefore, as we approach the final years of this tumultuous century, let us ring the bell of freedom loud and clear. Let us, in Lincoln's words, "strive to finish the work we are in," that this nation and this world, "under God, shall have a new birth of freedom—and that government of the people, by the people and for the people shall not perish from the earth."

NOTES

1. Jimmy Carter, Why Not the Best (Nashville: Broadman Press, 1975), pp. 123 ff.

2. Robert W. Service, "The Spell of the Yukon," in The Complete Works of Robert Service (New York: Dodd, Mead, 1944), p. 3.

3. Joan Baez, Open Letter to the Government of Vietnam, as quoted in National Review, June 8, 1979.

4. Joan Baez, U.S. News and World Report, October 1, 1979. As of this writing the continued exodus of over 4,000 Indochinese refugees per month bears witness to Ms. Baez's statements.

5. U.S. Agency for International Development, U.S. Overseas Loans and Grants (Washington, D.C.: U.S. Government Printing Office, 1983), pp. 33, 65, and 85; and The Washington Post, November 13, 1983, p. G1.

6. Martin Luther King, address at the Lincoln Memorial, August 28, 1963, as quoted by Coretta Scott King, <u>My Life with Martin Luther King</u>, p. 240.

Bibliography

Acheson, Dean. Present at the Creation: My Years in the State Department. New York: W. W. Norton, 1969.

Barnett, A. Doak. China's Economy in Global Perspective. Washington, D.C.: Brookings Institution, 1981.

_____. Uncertain Passage: China's Transition to the Post-Mao Era. Washington, D.C.: Brookings Institution, 1974.

_____. U.S. Arms Sales: The China-Taiwan Tangle. Washington, D.C.: Brookings Institution, 1982.

BDM Corporation. A Study of Strategic Lessons Learned in Vietnam. McLean, Va.: BDM Corporation, 1981. A study accomplished under the auspices of the U.S. Army War College. Vol. I, The Enemy; vol. II, South Vietnam; vol. III, U.S. Foreign Policy 1945-1975; vol. V, Planning the War; and vol. VI, Bk. 1, Conduct of the War.

Bergamini, David. Japan's Imperial Conspiracy. New York: Pocket Books, 1972. Originally published by William Morrow, 1971.

Bonds, Ray, ed. The Vietnam War. New York: Crown, 1979.

Braestrup, Peter. The Big Story: How the American Press and Television Reported and Interpreted the Crisis of Tet-1968 in Vietnam and Washington. 2 vols. New York: Westview Press, 1977.

Brown, Harold. Thinking about National Security: Defense and Foreign Policy in a Dangerous World. Boulder, Colo.: Westview Press; New York distributor: Hearst Books, 1983.

While there exists considerable literature on many of the themes presented in this book, this list presents some of the publications suggested for further reading.

Bull, Hedley. Asia and the Western Pacific. Melbourne: T. Nelson, 1975.

Bunge, Frederica M., et al., eds. China: A Country Study. Foreign Area Studies, American University, Washington, D.C.: Department of the Army, 1981.

Buttinger, Joseph. The Smaller Dragon. New York: Praeger, 1958.

_____. Vietnam: A Dragon Embattled. 2 vols. New York: Praeger, 1967.

_____. Vietnam: A Political History. New York: Praeger, 1968.

Cady, John. Postwar Southeast Asia. Englewood Cliffs, N.J.: Prentice-Hall, 1969.

_____. Southeast Asia: Its Historical Development. New York: McGraw-Hill, 1964.

Caves, Richard, and Masu Uekusa. Industrial Organization in Japan. Washington, D.C.: Brookings Institution, 1976.

Center for International Affairs, Harvard University. U.S.-Japan Relations in the 1980s: Towards Burden Sharing. Annual Report 1981-1982 of the Program on U.S.-Japan Relations. Cambridge, Mass.: Harvard University Press, 1982.

Clubb, O. Edmund. Twentieth Century China. New York: Columbia University Press, 1964. Second paperback printing, 1966.

Colbert, Evelyn. Southeast Asia in International Politics, 1941-1956. Ithaca, N.Y.: Cornell University Press, 1977.

Colby, William. Honorable Men: My Life in the CIA. New York: Simon and Schuster, 1978.

Committee on Armed Services. U.S. Senate. United States-Japan Security Relationship—The Key to East Asian Security and Stability. Washington, D.C.: U.S. Government Printing Office, 1969.

Cooper, Chester. The Lost Crusade: America in Vietnam. New York: Dodd, Mead, 1970.

Council on Foreign Relations. The China Factor. New York: American Assembly, Columbia University, 1981.

Dawson, Alan. Fifty-Five Days: The Fall of Vietnam. New York: Prentice-Hall, 1977.

Destler, I. M., et al. Managing an Alliance, the Politics of U.S.-Japanese Relations. Washington, D.C.: Brookings Institution, 1976.

Devillers, Philippe, and Jean Lacouture. End of a War: Indochina, 1954. New York: Praeger, 1969.

Directorate of Intelligence. Handbook of Economic Statistics, 1982. Washington, D.C., 1982.

Dommen, Arthur J. Conflict in Laos: The Politics of Neutraliza-tion. New York: Praeger, 1974.

Donovan, Robert J. Tumultuous Years: The Presidency of Harry S. Truman, 1949-53. New York: W. W. Norton, 1982.

Eckstein, Alexander. China's Economic Revolution. New York: Cambridge University Press, 1977.

Eisenhower, Dwight D. The White House Years: Mandate for Change, 1953-1956. Garden City, N.Y.: Doubleday, 1963.

Ellsberg, Daniel. Papers on the War. New York: Simon and Schuster, 1972.

Emmerson, Donald K. Indonesia's Elite: Political Culture and Cultural Politics. Ithaca, N.Y.: Cornell University Press, 1976.

Enthoven, Alain, and K. Wayne Smith. How Much Is Enough? Shaping the Defense Program, 1961-1969. New York: Harper & Row, 1971.

Fairbank, John K. The United States and China. 4th rev. ed. Cambridge, Mass.: Harvard University Press, 1979.

Fall, Bernard B. The Two Vietnams: A Political and Military Analysis. Rev. ed. New York: Praeger, 1967.

_____. The Street Without Joy: Indochina at War. Harrisburg, Pa.: Stackpole, 1964.

_____. Vietnam Witness, 1953-1966. New York: Praeger, 1966.

_____. Last Reflections on a War. Garden City, N.Y.: Doubleday, 1967.

Fifield, Russell H. Southeast Asia in United States Policy. New York: Praeger, 1963.

_____. Americans in Southeast Asia: The Roots of Commitment. New York: Crowell, 1973.

Gibney, Frank. Japan: The Fragile Superpower. New York: W. W. Norton, 1975.

Girling, J. L. S. People's War: Conditions and Consequences in China and Southeast Asia. New York: Praeger, 1969.

Gorshkov, Sergei G. Red Star Rising at Sea. Trans. by T. A. Neely. Annapolis, Md.: U.S. Naval Institute, 1974.

Graebner, Norman. Nationalism and Communism in Asia: The American Response. Lexington, Mass.: D. C. Heath, 1977.

Greene, Fred. United States Policy and the Security of Asia. New York: McGraw-Hill, 1968.

Gurtov, Melvin. The First Vietnam Crisis, 1967. Problems and Prospects of United States Policy in Southeast Asia, 1969.

Halberstam, David. The Making of a Quagmire. New York: Random House, 1965.

_____. The Best and the Brightest. New York: Random House, 1972.

Hall, D. G. E. The History of Southeast Asia. 3rd ed. New York: St. Martin's Press, 1970.

Halle, Louis J. The Cold War as History. New York: Harper & Row, 1967.

Hammer, Ellen. The Struggle for Indochina, 1940-1955. Stanford, Calif.: Stanford University Press, 1954.

Harrison, James Pickney. The Long March to Power: A History of the Chinese Communist Party, 1921-1972. New York: Praeger, 1972.

Hauser, William L. America's Army in Crisis. Baltimore: Johns Hopkins University Press, 1973.

Henderson, Gregory. Korea: The Politics of the Vortex. Cambridge, Mass.: Harvard University Press, 1968.

Herr, Michael. Dispatches. New York: Knopf, 1977.

Herrick, Robert W. Soviet Naval Strategy. Annapolis, Md.: U.S. Naval Institute, 1968.

Hersh, Seymour M. My Lai 4. New York: Random House, 1970.

_____. The Price of Power: Kissinger in the Nixon White House. New York: Summit Books, 1983.

Hickey, Gerald C. Village in Vietnam. New Haven, Conn.: Yale University Press, 1964.

Hilsman, Roger. To Move a Nation: The Politics of Foreign Policy in the Administration of John F. Kennedy. Garden City, N.Y.: Doubleday, 1967.

Ho Chi Minh. On Revolution: Selected Writings, 1920-1966. New York: Praeger, 1966.

Honey, P. J. Genesis of a Tragedy: The Historical Background to the Vietnam War, 1968.

Honey, P. J., ed. North Vietnam Today: Profile of a Communist Satellite. New York: Praeger, 1962.

Hoopes, Townsend. The Limits of Intervention: An Inside Account of How the Johnson Policy of Escalation Was Reversed. New York: David McKay, 1969.

Hough, Richard. The Fleet That Had to Die. New York: Ballantine, 1960.

Houn, Franklin W. A Short History of Chinese Communism. Englewood Cliffs, N.J.: Prentice-Hall, 1967.

Hubbell, John, et al. P.O.W. New York: Reader's Digest Press, 1976.

Huntington, Samuel P. The Common Defense: Strategic Programs in National Politics. New York: Columbia University Press, 1961.

_____. Political Order in Changing Societies. New Haven, Conn.: Yale University Press, 1968.

Janos, Radvani. Delusion and Reality. South Bend, Ind.: Gateway Press, 1978.

Japan-United States Economic Relations Group (Wise Men's Group). Report of the Japan-United States Economic Relations Group. Tokyo: 1981.

Japanese Defense Agency. Defense of Japan. Tokyo: The Japan Times, 1976-1983.

Johnson, Lyndon Baines. The Vantage Point: Perspectives of the Presidency, 1963-1969. New York: Holt, Rinehart and Winston, 1971.

Jordan, Amos A., Jr. Foreign Aid and the Defense of Southeast Asia, 1962.

Just, Ward S. To What End: Report from Vietnam. Boston: Houghton Mifflin, 1968.

Kalb, Marvin, and Elie Abel. The Roots of Involvement: The U.S. in Asia, 1784-1971. New York: W. W. Norton, 1971.

Karnow, Stanley. Vietnam—A History. New York: Viking Press, 1983.

Kattenburg, Paul M. The Vietnam Trauma in American Foreign Policy, 1945-1975. New Brunswick, N.J.: Transaction Books, 1980.

Kenny, Henry J. "The Changing Importance of Vietnam in United States Policy: 1949-1969." Ph.D. dissertation, American University, 1974.

Khrushchev, Nikita. Khrushchev Remembers. Boston: Little, Brown, 1970.

Kinnard, Douglas. The War Managers. Hanover, Conn.: University Press of New England, 1977.

Kirby, Stuart. Towards the Pacific Century: Economic Development in the Pacific Basin. London: Economist Intelligence Unit, 1983.

Kissinger, Henry. White House Years. Boston: Little, Brown, 1979.

Komer, Robert. Bureaucracy Does Its Thing: Institutional Constraints on U.S.-GVN Performance in Vietnam. Santa Monica, Calif.: Rand, 1972.

Krause, Lawrence B. U.S. Economic Policy Toward the Association of Southeast Asian Nations: Meeting the Japanese Challenge. Washington, D.C.: Brookings Institution, 1982.

Kwak, Te-Hwan, et al. U.S.-Korean Relations, 1882-1982. Seoul: Kyungnam University Press, 1982.

LaCouture, Jean. Ho Chi Minh: A Political Biography. New York: Vintage, 1968.

_____. Vietnam: Between Two Truces. New York: Random House, 1966.

Lansdale, Edward G. In the Midst of Wars. New York: Harper & Row, 1972.

Leifer, Michael. Indonesia's Foreign Policy. Winchester: Allen and Unwin, 1983.

Lewy, Guenter. America in Vietnam. New York: Oxford University Press, 1978.

Marshall, S. L. A. Ambush. New York: Cowles, 1969.

_____. Battles in the Monsoon. New York: Morrow, 1967.

_____. West to Cambodia. New York: Cowles, 1971.

McAlister, John T., Jr., and Paul Mus. The Vietnamese and Their Revolution. New York: Harper & Row, 1970.

McNamara, Robert S. The Essence of Security: Reflection in Office, 1968.

Morgenthau, Hans J. A New Foreign Policy for the United States, 1969. Vietnam and the United States, 1965.

Morrison, Charles E., ed. Threats to Security in East Asia-Pacific. Lexington, Mass.: Lexington Books, 1983.

Muqiao, Xue, ed. Almanac of China's Economy 1981: With Economic Statistics 1949-1980. Hong Kong: Modern Cultural Company, 1982.

Nguyen Cao Ky. Twenty Years and Twenty Days. New York: Stein and Day, 1976.

O'Ballance, Edgar. The Indo-China War, 1945-1954: A Study of Guerilla Warfare. London: Faber and Faber, 1964.

Oberdorfer, Don. Tet! Garden City, N.Y.: Doubleday, 1971.

Office of the Chief of Naval Operations. Understanding Soviet Naval Developments. Washington, D.C.: U.S. Government Printing Office, 1981.

Oksenberg, Michael, ed. China's Developmental Experience. New York: Praeger, 1973.

Oksenberg, Michael, and Robert B. Oxnam, eds. Dragon and Eagle: United States-China Relations, Past and Future. New York: Basic Books, 1978.

Osborne, Milton E. The French Presence in Cochinchina and Cambodia. Ithaca, N.Y.: Cornell University Press, 1969.

Osgood, Robert E. The Weary and the Wary, U.S. and Japanese Security Policies in Transition. Baltimore: Johns Hopkins University Press, 1972.

Osgood, Robert, et al. America and the World: From the Truman Doctrine to Vietnam, 1970. Limited War, 1957.

Patrick, Hugh, and Henry Rosovsky. Asia's New Giant: How the Japanese Economy Works. Washington, D.C.: Brookings Institution, 1976.

The Pentagon Papers: The Defense Department History of United States Decisionmaking on Vietnam. Senator Gravel, ed. Boston: Beacon Press, 1971.

The Pentagon Papers as Published by the New York Times. Chicago: Quadrangle, 1971.

The Pentagon Papers, U.S.-Vietnam Relations, 1945-1967. Washington, D.C.: U.S. Government Printing Office, 1971.

Perkins, Dwight H., ed. China's Modern Economy in Historical Perspective. Stanford, Calif.: Stanford University Press, 1975.

Pike, Douglas. The Viet Cong. Cambridge, Mass.: MIT Press, 1966.

_____. War, Peace, and the Viet Cong. Cambridge, Mass.: MIT Press, 1969.

Prange, Gordon W. At Dawn We Slept: The Untold Story of Pearl Harbor. New York: McGraw-Hill, 1981.

Race, Jeffrey. War Comes to Long An. Berkeley: University of California Press, 1972.

Reischauer, Edwin O. Beyond Vietnam. New York: Knopf, 1967.

_____. The Japanese. Cambridge, Mass.: Belknap Press, 1977.

Reischauer, Edwin O., and John K. Fairbank. The Great Tradition, I: A History of East Asian Civilization. Boston: Houghton Mifflin, 1960.

Research Institute for Peace and Security. Asian Security, 1979, 1980, 1981, 1982. Tokyo: 1979-1982.

Ridgeway, Matthew B. Soldier. New York: Harper & Row, 1956.

Rostow, Walt W. The Diffusion of Power, 1957-1972. New York: Macmillan, 1972.

Sainteny, Jean. Histoire d'une Paix Manquée. Paris: Librairie Fayard, 1967.

Samuels, Marwyn S. Contest for the South China Sea. New York: Methuen, 1982.

Sansom, George. Japan, A Short Cultural History. New York: Appleton-Century, 1943.

Sansom, Robert L. The Economics of Insurgency in the Mekong Delta. Cambridge, Mass.: MIT Press, 1970.

Scalapino, Robert A., ed. The Foreign Policy of Modern Japan. Berkeley: U.C.L.A. Press, 1977.

Scalapino, Robert A., and J. Wanadi. Economic, Political, and Security Issues in Southeast Asia in the 1980s. Berkeley: Institute of East Asian Studies, UCLA, 1982.

Schemmer, Benjamin. The Raid. New York: Harper & Row, 1976.

Schilling, Warner, et al. Strategy, Politics, and Defense Budgets. New York: Columbia University Press, 1962.

Schlesinger, Arthur M., Jr. The Bitter Heritage: Vietnam and American Democracy, 1941-66. Boston: Houghton Mifflin, 1968.

_____. A Thousand Days: John F. Kennedy in the White House. Boston: Houghton Mifflin, 1965.

Shaplen, Robert. The Road from War: Vietnam, 1965-1970. New York: Harper & Row, 1970.

_____. The Lost Revolution: The United States in Vietnam, 1946-1966. New York: Harper & Row, 1966. Time Out of Hand: Revolution and Reaction in Southeast Asia, 1969.

Sigur, Gaston J., and Y. C. Kim. Japanese and U.S. Policy in Asia. New York: Praeger, 1982.

Singapore: Economic Prospects to 1986. London: Economist Intelligence Unit, 1982.

Smith, Hedrick, and William Beecher. "The Vietnam Policy Reversal of 1968," The New York Times, March 6 and 7, 1969.

Snepp, Frank. Decent Interval. New York: Random House, 1977.

Sorenson, Theodore. Kennedy. New York: Harper & Row, 1965.

Strausz-Hupe, et al. Protracted Conflict. New York: Harper, 1959.

Summers, Harry G., Jr. On Strategy: The Vietnam War in Context. Washington, D.C.: U.S. Government Printing Office, 1981.

Taylor, Maxwell D. Swords and Plowshares. New York: W. W. Norton, 1972.

Terrill, Ross. "China in the 1980s." Foreign Affairs 58, no. 4 (Spring 1980):920-35.

Terrill, Ross, ed. The China Difference. New York: Harper & Row, 1979.

Thompson, Sir Robert. Defeating Communist Insurgency: Lessons of Malaya and Vietnam. New York: Praeger, 1966.

Trager, Frank, ed. Marxism in Southeast Asia. Stanford, Calif.: Stanford University Press, 1959.

Truman, Harry S. Memoirs: Year of Decisions, 1945. Garden City, N.Y.: Doubleday, 1955.

_____. Memoirs: Years of Trial and Hope, 1946-1952. Garden City, N.Y.: Doubleday, 1956.

Truong Chinh. Primer for Revolt. 1963.

Tuchman, Barbara W. Stilwell and the American Experience in China, 1911-45. New York: Macmillan, 1970.

Tucker, Robert W. Nation or Empire? The Debate Over American Foreign Policy. Baltimore: Johns Hopkins University Press, 1968.

U.S. Agency for International Development. U.S. Overseas Loans and Grants and Assistance from International Organizations. Washington, D.C., 1982.

U.S. Army Center for Military History. Communist Atrocities at Hue, a briefing prepared for the vice president, December 5, 1969, by the Deputy Chief of Staff for Operations, U.S. Army. Washington, D.C., 1969.

U.S. Department of State. Aggression from the North: The Record of North Vietnam's Campaign to Conquer South Vietnam, 1965; American Foreign Policy, 1950-1955 Basic Documents, 1957; A Threat to the Peace: North Vietnam's Effort to Conquer South Vietnam, 1961; The Legality of U.S. Participation in the Defense of Vietnam, 1966.

U.S. Mission in Vietnam. Documents and Research Notes #1-108. 1966-1973. Saigon: American Embassy, 1963-1973.

United States-Vietnam Relations, 1945-1967. Study prepared by the Department of Defense for the House Committee on Armed Services, 92nd Cong., 1st sess. Washington, D.C.: U.S. Government Printing Office, 1971.

Van Tien Dung. Our Great Spring Victory: An Account of the Liberation of South Vietnam. New York: Monthly Review Press, 1977.

Vance, Cyrus. Hard Choices: Critical Years in America's Foreign Policy. New York: Simon and Schuster, 1983.

Vien, Cao Van. The Final Collapse. Washington, D.C.: U.S. Government Printing Office, 1983.

Vietnam and Southeast Asia. Report by Senator Mike Mansfield, et al. 88th Cong., 1st sess. Washington, D.C.: U.S. Government Printing Office, 1963.

Vo Nguyen Giap. People's War, People's Army. New York: Praeger, 1962.

Vogel, Ezra. Japan as Number One. Cambridge, Mass.: Harvard University Press, 1979.

Walt, Lewis W. Strange War, Strange Strategy: A General's Report on Vietnam. New York: Funk and Wagnalls, 1970.

Warner, Denis. Certain Victory: How Hanoi Won the War. Kansas City: Sheed Andrews and McMeel, 1977.

_____. The Last Confucian. New York: Macmillan, 1963.

Webb, James. Fields of Fire. Englewood Cliffs, N.J.: Prentice-Hall, 1978.

Weinstein, Franklin B. Indonesian Foreign Policy and the Dilemma of Dependence: From Sukarno to Soeharto. Ithaca, N.Y.: Cornell University Press, 1976.

Westmoreland, William. A Soldier Reports. Garden City, N.Y.: Doubleday, 1976.

Westmoreland, William, and U. S. G. Sharp. Report on the War in Vietnam. Washington, D.C.: U.S. Government Printing Office, 1969.

Wheeler, J. W., et al. Japanese Industrial Development Policies in the 1980s. Croton-on-Hudson, N.Y.: Hudson Institute, 1982.

Whiting, Allen S., and Robert F. Dernberger. China's Future: Foreign Policy and Economic Development in the Post-Mao Era. 1980s Project, Council on Foreign Relations. New York: McGraw-Hill, 1977.

Wolf, Charles, Jr. Foreign Aid: Theory and Practice in Southeast Asia. Princeton, N.J.: Princeton University Press, 1960.

_____. United States Policy and the Third World. Boston.

Zagoria, Donald S. Vietnam Triangle. New York: Pegasus, 1967.

Zagoria, Donald S., ed. Soviet Policy in East Asia. New Haven, Conn.: Yale University Press, 1982.

Zasloff, Joseph, Jr. The Role of the Sanctuary in Insurgency: Communist China's Support to the Vietminh, 1945-1954. Santa Monica, Calif.: Rand, 1967.

Zasloff, Joseph J., and Macalister Brown. Communism in Indochina. Lexington, Mass.: D. C. Heath, 1975.

Index

About the Author

Dr. Kenny is a senior foreign affairs officer for Asia with the U.S. Arms Control and Disarmament Agency. A native of Chicago, he graduated from West Point in 1961 and served two tours of duty in Vietnam. He was wounded during the Tet offensive of 1968 and, while recovering at Walter Reed hospital in Washington, D.C., attended American University where he earned a Ph.D. in International Relations. Dr. Kenny has a Masters in Business Administration from Marymount College of Virginia, and has served as an international trade specialist with the Department of Commerce. He has also served with the Department of Social Science at West Point, where he taught international relations, comparative politics, and problems of developing nations.

Dr. Kenny, who is fluent in the Vietnamese language, directed area studies for U.S. Special Forces personnel on orders to Vietnam in the mid-1960s. He subsequently built a Special Forces Camp in War Zone D, advised a province chief, and commanded an infantry company in Vietnam. In 1975 he was appointed deputy staff director of the House Select Committee on Missing Persons in Southeast Asia, in which capacity he visited Vientiane and Hanoi in pursuit of an accounting for missing Americans. In 1977 he returned to Hanoi with a Presidential Commission on the same subject.

From 1977 to 1981 Dr. Kenny was Special Assistant to Ambassador Mike Mansfield in Tokyo, where he provided advice on political, economic, and military matters. He joined the U.S. Arms Control and Disarmament Agency in November 1981.